LETTERS FROM INDIA

LADY WILSON was born Anne Campbell MacLeod in 1855 and grew up in Glasgow. In 1888 she married a Scottish civil servant whom she accompanied on his return to India in 1889.

Far removed from the usual image of the British in India, Lady Wilson was an intelligent woman of humble grace and charm and she conceived a great love for the real and native India. First published in 1911, these are the collected letters which she wrote to those at home during her twenty-year stay. They form a unique and lively eye-witness account of how British women actually lived their lives in India.

Lady Wilson's book is a forgotten classic among India writings, at last in print again. It is introduced in this edition by Pat Barr, the author of numerous non-fiction books on the Orient including *The Memsahibs*, and best-selling author of *Jade*, an epic novel set in China. Pat Barr has lived in Japan and travelled extensively: to Hong Kong, Singapore, Malaysia and India.

LETTERS FROM INDIA

LADY WILSON

Introduction by Pat Barr

CENTURY PUBLISHING
LONDON

LESTER & ORPEN DENNYS DENEAU
MARKETING SERVICES LTD
TORONTO

Introduction © copyright Pat Barr 1984

All rights reserved

First published in Great Britain in 1911
by William Blackwood and Sons

This edition published in 1984 by
Century Publishing Co. Ltd,
Portland House, 12–13 Greek Street, London W1V 5LE

ISBN 0 7126 0455 3

Published in Canada by
Lester & Orpen Dennys Deneau Marketing Services Ltd
78 Sullivan Street, Ontario, Canada

The cover shows a detail of 'The Benares'
by William Daniell

Reprinted in Great Britain by
Richard Clay (The Chaucer Press) Ltd, Bungay, Suffolk

INTRODUCTION

THE STEREOTYPE of the memsahib as created by past chroniclers of the British in India – most memorably, if cruelly, by Rudyard Kipling – is of an essentially small-minded, snobbish, selfish, helpless, racially arrogant woman whose increasing presence on the Imperial Scenario distracted the male Empire builders from their tasks and widened the gulfs between rulers and ruled. Recently this cliché is falling into well-deserved disrepute as historians examine the actualities of what British women really did in India, and more of their own writings are re-discovered and re-appraised.

On this count alone Lady Wilson's letters are well worth reprinting and they provide also a candid, entertaining account of many years of varied Indian experience – the freedoms of camp-life, problems of housekeeping and child-rearing, the onerous responsibilities as well as the pleasurable rewards of being among the ruling elite. Lady Wilson's Scottish husband, James, was one of these – a 'Covenanted' civil servant who first went to India in 1875 and worked his way up the administrative hierarchy, mainly in the Punjab with spells of desk-bound duty in Calcutta as a Secretary to the Government.　Like many of his kind, James's heart remained in the district where he'd first worked as a young settlement officer at heat-and-dust level; he wrote definitively about its language and tribal customs, and returned voluntarily to the Punjab as Financial Commissioner in 1909.

The woman he married in 1888 was born Anne Campbell MacLeod in 1855, third of the nine children of Catherine Anne Mackintosh and Norman MacLeod.　MacLeod was a Scottish divine, well-known in his day as a church-leader, orator, theologian, author, editor of *Good Words* magazine and personal friend of Queen Victoria.　He was a dynamic man of wide sympathies who preached the gospels of moder-ation and toleration within the Church and who obvi-ously inspired his daughter with a similarly devout faith that was outward-looking and humanitarian, rather than dogmatic and narrowly pious.

Anne grew up in a secure, Christian, middle-class home in Glasgow with her several brothers and sisters; she received a good education for a girl by the stan-dards of the day; she later travelled briefly in Europe.　Her first recorded venture into print was in 1882 – a small biography of Girolano Savonarola, the fifteenth-century monk and martyr; five years later she edited a collection of her late father's writings entitled,

'Love and the Fulfilment of the Law'. She first went
to India in 1889 with her husband who already had
many years' experience of the country which she
found so astonishing and exhilarating, and the letters
describing her early adventures in a remote district of
the Punjab are among the liveliest of this
collection. They first appeared in her 'After Five
Years in India' (1895) and she wrote two other books
while living in the country: 'An Account of Hindu
Music' (evidence of a rather unusual interest at that
time) and 'Hints for the First Years of Residence in
India' (1904). The latter is a charming period piece
that instructs new arrivals on such matters as camp-
life necessities (dress-shirts, cheese plates, cotton bags
for meat and dusters); training servants (don't let the
cook smoke his hookah in the kitchen); and how to
keep ponies healthy on bran-mash.

Lady Wilson's main work however is this little-
known collection of letters that covers the whole of her
stay in India from 1889 to 1909. It is difficult to say
exactly why they have been so long neglected considering their undoubted merit, but it may well be
because the period she describes was something of a
peaceful plateau, especially for British women in
India. It was the era of the High Raj. Viceroys
and vicereines, maharajahs, colonels and their ladies
came and went through the dignified portals of
Government House feeling present and future
secure. The earlier rigours of travel, the discomforts
and isolation of 'up-country' life had been consider-

ably ameliorated by the railways and the ever-increasing numbers of British residents.

India was no longer a frightening, savage *terra incognita* that took three months to reach by dangerous sailing-ship. It was a tamed Empire, easily accessible by P & O, mapped, surveyed, disciplined by the tight administrative network that Lady Wilson describes with such admiration, made congenial by familiar faces and long-established rules of social behaviour. Moreover, hundreds of females born into Anglo-Indian families (as the British living there were then known) had spent at least part of their lives there – as girls, wives, mothers – they had survived, knew the ropes, passed on the hints, as did Lady Wilson.

Past generations of memsahibs had lived in the long-looming shadow of the Indian Mutiny of 1857–8 that had left a bitter legacy of distrust, ill-feeling and fear, and, in consequence, they had lived almost as if in purdah, eschewing practically all social contacts with Indians, particularly men. By Lady Wilson's time however the fear had receded, taboos were relaxing and considerable trust existed between the two races. Prejudice was still rife of course, but some British women of intelligence and determination mixed socially with Indians of the aristocratic and professional classes and began to interest themselves in the welfare of the poor – a new spirit of philanthropic concern that had received official sanction from Lady Dufferin, a vicereine of the '80s who started a fund for medical aid to Indian women.

This trend towards a more humanitarian outlook, more energetic participation in India's social problems by the wives of British officials developed further during the early twentieth century; but Lady Wilson herself, though she made a point of mixing with some Indians, was neither pioneer philanthropist nor social innovator. Nor was she anything of a feminist, for she uncomplainingly accepted the conventional memsahib's role of supportive wife, fond mother, careful housekeeper, diligent hostess and pleads not for any extension of it, but that its disadvantages should be better understood, its worth more highly valued.

Her own life within that role was varied but not specially exceptional for the time and place. Many women of similar rank moved about in the wake of their peripatetic husbands to far-flung outposts; many felt the pangs of prolonged separations from children sent Home to school like 'Dear Jack'; many others enjoyed (even while they gently mocked) the gossip and games of hill-station life that was at its most hectic and flamboyant in Simla of the '90s, where those in the upper echelons like the Wilsons disported themselves in the hot seasons (it wasn't called 'Mount Olympus' for nothing!).

Lady Wilson describes these and other quintessential episodes of Anglo-India life with zest, colour and occasional humour. Endowed with an inquiring mind, she interests herself in several aspects of Indian culture and, in a manner typical of her age, meditates rather conventionally on the mysteries of the human

and the divine. Equally characteristic are her lapses
into sentimentality, her comments about servants,
Eurasians and social inferiors which, though 'meant
well' sound distinctly patronising, and her generally un-
critical endorsements of British rule. (Not until 1907
does she mention the concept of Home Rule for
Indians for example, though it was a matter for political debate long before that.)

However, these defects, which would scarcely be re-
garded as such by her contemporaries, are not ob-
trusive enough in any case to mar the various
pleasures of this book. Chief of which, in my view, is
the vivid immediacy and actuality of much of the
writing that conveys in unmistakable tones the
original voice of the person-on-the-spot. The 'spots'
themselves are graphically conjured up for us – the
interior of an 'up-country' tent; mud-brown villages
on the plains at sunset; the isolation of a fortified dak
bungalow on the Northern Frontier; the ghats at
Benares; the Pass of Kohat; a Simla villa – and so are
the people Lady Wilson meets on her various sojourns:
the swashbuckling Captain Speedy, the 'conscientious
little treasure', Miss M. . .; the chief of the Tiwanas
with his tales of ancient glories.

These and many others are essentially Victorian
characters and though the good Queen died while the
Wilsons were in India ('She was worshipped by Her
people', Lady Wilson wrote when she heard the
news), British India remained more or less Victorian
in its framework and outlook for another twenty

years.   Indeed, those, who, like the Wilsons, left it forever at the end of their working lives for the very different climate of Edwardian England must sometimes have felt rather lost at 'Home'.   Perhaps it was when this sense of loss most assailed them that they rounded up their 'Indian letters' from relatives, sorted through trunks for old journals and 'Notes on Various Indian Subjects' with a view to possible publication.   Certainly we should be grateful that they did, for it is the invaluable, vivid voice-on-the-spot that keeps the history of lost Empires alive.

PAT BARR

PREFACE

A FEW words are necessary to explain how these
letters found their way into print. About fifteen
years ago I published a book, called 'After Five
Years in India,' which gave an account of the
administration of our Eastern Empire, and had
its brief day of success.

In that book a few letters written from camp
to one's friends were embodied, and several kind
readers asked me why I did not publish more of
the same informally personal type. This suggestion
was recalled to my mind when, just before leaving
India, many bundles of old correspondence were
returned to me by my family.

It occurred to me then that some of these letters,
amplified where necessary by my own recollections,
might possibly interest a larger circle of readers,
both as giving them a certain idea of the daily
lives and interests of their countrymen in different
parts of the Indian Empire, and also because it

was our good fortune to come into contact with various sides of Indian life, a life so full of mystery that even a faint light cast on it may not be unwelcome.

I have only to add that the original three camp letters, on which the others were built, have been included in this volume by the kind permission of Messrs Blackie & Sons: and that the sketch I have given of Indian Music and Poetry was largely incorporated in my 'Short Account of the Hindu System of Music,' which was published some years ago.

A. C. WILSON.

59 CADOGAN SQUARE, LONDON,
April 1911.

LETTERS FROM INDIA.

DEAR J.,—Farewell to the four walls of a house and all hail to a nomad existence in the wilds, under canvas ! The string of 28 camels left an hour ago, with chairs, tables, and rolled-up tents roped on their backs, boxes filled with house-linen, dishes, silver, glass, pots and pans, clothes and books, fitting into huge paniers; and such an assortment as you never saw of hen-coops, baths, and every kind of incongruous extras piled on to their humps. Men followed walking, with beds on their heads. I watched the start, and was much amused.

The live stock left this morning, including three dogs, one cat, and two cows with their calves, a dozen sheep, and two extra horses for Jim to ride, the whole accompanied by the grooms, milkman, and sweeper. We make up to them in the evening. Jim rides, as he has to inspect the fields as he goes along. I shall drive

in a tonga, which we have hired for the winter.
It is a cart, like an old - fashioned English
waggon, with a seat in the centre and a covering hood, a pair of lanky and boisterous horses,
and an Afghan as a driver.   He is a splendid
old man, with a turban and coat of many colours,
and a horn to blow to clear the way as we go,
or to announce, perhaps, that we are coming.
He sits beside me, and my ayah and his stable-
boy sit behind.   We are going to be in camp for
some months.   It is the nearest approach to
living the life of a gipsy which, I suppose, I
shall ever enjoy, and I am looking forward to it
immensely.   In the meantime I have a day of
blessed idleness before me, and I am going to
employ part of it in writing to you.

Five weeks have passed since we landed, and
they have seemed like five years.   So many novel
experiences have been crowded into the time.
First of all, there was the journey from Bombay,
which occupied four days,—think of it, you who
consider twelve hours in the train to London an
undertaking!   It must be granted that the trial
is mitigated as far as may be ; the seats are
arranged, for instance, like a waggonette, so that no
one sits with his back to the engine.   The compart-
ments are broad and comfortable, and only four
people occupy them at night, upper berths being

let down to complete the four beds. Each carriage has a dressing-room, and the windows have outer wooden venetian shutters to keep out dust and sun if possible. Still, the four days and four nights, never hasting, never resting, were to me interminable.

The immensity of everything struck one like the statistics that might be given by an American fond of 'tall' stories. One saw miles upon miles of flat land, and knew that thousands of miles lay behind them, and such masses of people swarmed everywhere. Every station platform was densely crowded by them, and it seemed to me that the later it grew, the livelier and younger the people became! In the small hours of the night women rushed about, with babies in their arms and crying children at their heels; men ran helter-skelter, as you never see able-bodied men running, from sheer excitement and the love of screaming to their friends, at a railway station, at any rate in Scotland! And water - carriers and sweetmeat - vendors shouted above the pitch of their voices, as if there were no such thing as night and sleep in their programme. From which you may judge that there was practically very little sleep in mine. Once, about four o'clock in the morning, Jim roused me to 'look at a glorious sunrise.' I explained to him very quietly that I hoped it was the last, as it was the

first, I had seen in India, and I do not think
this will occur on a railway journey again!

I honestly confess that the overwhelming crowds
of people frightened me. It was a very foolish
feeling, as I have since been told; still there it was.
What were we in the land, I thought, but a handful of Europeans at the best, and what was there
to prevent these myriads from falling upon and
obliterating us, as if we had never existed ? There
are many things to prevent it, independently of
their being, as everybody tells me, the most law-
abiding and loyal people in the world. But even
yet my scepticism and fears get the better of my
reason or my faith.

If anything could have reassured one, it would
have been the reception Jim received on his return
after six months' absence. At the first station we
reached on the outskirts of his district were a
crowd of Indian officials and notables, who travelled
along with us, their ranks swelling at each succeed-
ing station. Finally, when we reached Khushab
and looked out of the carriage window, behold the
moon shining down on the dusky faces and white
robes of several hundreds, waiting to welcome us!
Triumphal arches had been raised in our honour,
and as we walked through the crowd bowing in
answer to their salaams, it was naturally 'one
of the proudest moments of my life.' I felt as if

I were the Princess of Wales at least, without any of the responsibility. After an excellent champagne dinner, which good Mr O'D. had ready for us in the rest-house, we sat out of doors and enjoyed the fireworks and illuminations displayed in our honour.

Next day about fifty of the Indian 'squires' rode behind us as we drove to our home. At one point in the road an old veteran, in military gear and covered with medals, was drawn up with his retainers to fire a salute as we passed. He and his men had fought on our side in the Mutiny, and like the rest of the Punjaub, had been true to us throughout. Jim assures me that just such a kindly welcome as we have received would be given by the people of every district in the Punjaub, to any Civilian they had known before.

To return, however, to my own particular history. More than four weeks have gone since then, and I may tell you that it is with a great sense of relief I find myself at the end of my first experience of Anglo-Indian housekeeping. I have been busy from morning till night, and the impression left on my mind is one of baffled impotence. Firstly, because I was unable to make myself understood. Sometimes I had the trusty old bearer Akbar, the head butler, the ayah and the tailor all round me, trying to make out what I wanted to tell them,

but shaking their heads with respectful hopelessness. If I wished to give orders about the fire,
about the flowers, about the arrangement of the
dinner-table, about purchases, about breakfast,
lunch or dinner, not one Hindustani word could
I say that they could comprehend! Jim did what
he could for me; he translated my list of wants
at breakfast every day, interviewed the cook, went
through every room with me, accompanied by
Akbar, and ordered the contents to be moved, removed or destroyed. But he could not 'give up
to a party what was meant for mankind,' and act
interpreter the whole day long, which alone would
have solved my difficulties.

Then, even with a knowledge of the language,
Anglo-Indian housekeeping must be bewildering
at first. The aspect of everything is so different
from what it is at home. You see, individually we
are but birds of passage in India, and have to
build our nests of what material we can find. The
result is simply wonderful, considering the absence
of home appliances or skilled labour. The houses
are adapted to the climate, and there are a dozen
reasons why the arrangements should and must be
as they are. I daresay, like other Anglo-Indian
ladies, I shall get accustomed to the little differences, attached to them from use and wont, and
even in the end prefer them in some ways. Still,

at first you must just allow me to be as insular and as conservative as I please, and let me tell you of some of the domestic peculiarities while they are new to me, and before I forget to notice them.

Picture to yourself then, a square one-storied, flat-roofed house with a pillared verandah at each side; indoors nine rooms, three in a row, without an entrance-hall or any passage, each room opening into the other as rooms do in an *étage* abroad, each room having one or two door-windows into the bargain; and then count how many doors or windows there must be—a blessing no doubt in the hot weather, but not ornamental in the cold. I find myself parodying,

'Here rooms have a thousand doors, and at home but one.'

I have seen already how pretty they may be made to look, notwithstanding the doors, with pictures, curtains, draperies and feminine knick-knacks and devices. It is only the bare skeleton that seems so gaunt, and certainly it is not 'when unadorned, adorned the most.'

Every room looks as high as a country church, the ceilings are of unplastered rafters, the doors are folding-doors, bolted in the middle. If you wish them shut, you must bolt them. If you wish to keep them open, you have to fix a wooden

block in behind the hinges. At present a white
cotton-sheet-like curtain hangs from a wooden rod
before each. The fireplaces, in which only wood
is burnt, are low brick slabs innocent of grating.
Every bedroom has a bathroom attached, with a
low wall in one corner surrounding the place
where the big bath is. The bath is emptied on
to the floor when one has done with it, the water
running off though a hole in the wall.

There is no home-like pantry, with dresser and
endless shelves, press, and hot and cold water
arrangement. There is no kitchen with plate-
rack, scullery and larder. The kitchen is a little
dark room, with a board on the mud floor to hold
the meat, two tumble-down brick 'ranges' in one
corner, a stone receptacle in another into which
the water is thrown, to run out through its hole
in the wall into a sunk tub. There are two.shelves
on which are an array of pots, a hatchet, drainer,
one or two tin spoons, and some pudding and pâté
shapes. Jim says a brick floor can be laid while
we are in camp, a sink made, the range rebuilt,
and tables, presses, or anything I choose to order
be put into the place ; so my spirits have risen
since I saw it first.

Our servants live in a group of small detached
houses. When I wish one to come an orderly, who
sits in the verandah, goes to bring him, for there

is, of course, not a bell in the house ; or he stops half-way and calls out the man's name, when he comes with an answering shout.

Needless to say, there is not an English shop within a radius of a hundred miles, and I have yet to find out what the native bazaar can supply, and how I am to procure what it does not contain. Meat is ridiculously cheap — three halfpence the pound, chickens threepence each, and eggs threepence the dozen. By the way, some red cotton and white reels of thread were brought to me by the native shopkeepers the other day, and on them were stamped the names of Glasgow and Paisley manufacturers.

We have thirteen servants, including groom, waterman, sweeper, milkman and house-servants ; but on questioning my neighbours as to the exact amount of work that should be performed by each without infringing on their caste distinctions, the conviction is distinctly borne in upon me that if one wants a thing done one must do it one's self, or at least superintend its being done ; that one must look after the filter, see to the milk, the feeding of the cows, sheep and poultry, the making of butter, bread, cakes, to the careful trimming of the lamps, to the dusting of books, pictures, furniture, to the tinning of pots and pans, to the way the cook uses his dishes or his dusters. 'Your only hope is to see your servant at work at these things,' say my neighbours. 'Never expect them to do anything rightly two days running.' So I have at present visions of attaining professional skill as head-housemaid, dairymaid and shepherd!

I rather enjoy the idea, however, of learning to do old duties in a new way. It will be in a new way; for it is one thing to order your glazier to come and clean the windows, and your housemaid to polish up the brass and furniture, and another to stand on your own resources, and determine how paint and putty should be removed from glass by an unskilled Mahomedan, and furniture polished without the aid of paste!

An experienced Anglo-Indian housekeeper would tell you, no doubt, that she finds housekeeping easier here than at home, that servants are more amenable and obedient; that you would not find a laundrymaid in England, for example, who would do up any particular bit of her work in a day's time without a grumble, if you needed it, or a tailor who would work beside you for a month, mending old things or making new, on a pound's wages. I expect I shall appreciate these advantages in time. I am only giving you just now my first and ignorant impressions.

Servants differ greatly in different parts of the country, and their employers' opinions of them as a class vary as widely, ranging from enthusiasm to despair. Take them as a whole, I think I find them as yet distinctly trying, not so much from what they do, as from what they leave undone, and I constantly recall the advice of the old Scotch lady I met when I landed, who, in answer to my question as to how I could help missions in India, said : 'The best way you can do that, my dear, is to keep your temper with your servants, and stick to your husband in the heat!'

It amuses me to notice the way the Indians reverse the order in which we do things. For instance, at home men take off their hats when they come into a house; Indians keep on their turbans, but take off their shoes. We beckon with the palms of our hands turned inwards; they beckon with them turned out. My ayah lays my slippers in a row with the toes pointing towards me. The cook begins to read his Hindustani book of recipes from the last page backwards, and writes his accounts from right to left. When the carpenter uses native screws, he screws them in from right to left, and saws *inwards*, which makes one nervous! And when they play cards, they deal from the undermost card in the pack, and send them round by their right. They think it rude to laugh, but they never hesitate to yawn!

You ask about our neighbours. You know we

are in the wilds.   There are three households
besides our own, and nothing could exceed their
kindness.   We meet daily in the evening for tennis
or golf, and dine with each other about once a
week, besides exchanging notes constantly that
come and go with books, home newspapers, flowers,
fruit and game.   Jim tells me I shall always find
a good Samaritan in every neighbour, and that in
times of sickness or sorrow an acquaintance acts
as if he were a near relation; while on ordinary
occasions, in isolated stations, people never hesitate
to borrow daily necessaries from each other, such
as stores or soda-water, if their own should have
run short before the arrival of their fresh supplies.
So we shall find no place without the possibility
of receiving and enjoying loving kindness, and
what more do we need to make us happy!   With
which moral I shall end my lengthy letter and
get ready to drive to our first halting-place in
camp.

DEAREST M.,—Anything cosier than our tent looks at this moment you could not imagine. We are sitting in our deck-chairs before the stove, with our feet on a wooden fender; the lamp behind us is hooked on to the central pole of the tent. Jim is reading the papers, while I am writing to you. A bowlful of Gloire de Dijon roses on the table beside me is a delight to my eyes; beyond is a little bookcase filled with our favourite books, and on the top of it is the guitar, the poor ill-used guitar! We have pictures on our walls, comfortable chairs, tables and rugs, and in short, are as snug as snug can be. You did not think that was what people's tents are like in camp, did you? But I forgot, you cannot imagine what our tents are like in the least; so I must try to be as circumstantial as possible, and tell you.

We have three tents—two for living in, and one for Jim's office-work. While we are using one, the other goes ahead, and is pitched at our next halting-place. We generally move on every second

13

or third day ; but this is not so unsettling as you
might think, for the next tent is a duplicate of the
one we have left, with everything in its place, our
baggage having gone on before us.　So the evening
drive is only a little longer than usual, covering a
distance of ten or twelve miles, and the daily
routine is not interrupted.　The servants occupy
a row of low tents like a gipsy encampment, and
the Indian officials who work under Jim have their
own small colony a little bit off.　Guess how many
we number altogether, of course including these
officials ?　Fifty !　You may well wonder how we
are fed, for we are out in the desert, remember,
in the barest and most thinly-populated part of
the district, and about sixty miles from head-
quarters.

Well, to begin with ourselves.　We carry with us
our own groceries, which come out from England
—or rather, as far as we are concerned, from the
Army and Navy Stores at Bombay—packed in tins.
We have also our filter, and our supply of soda-
water and wine with us.　We kill our own sheep
and chickens, have our own cows, and make our
own bread and butter.　We get our vegetables,
cabbages, cauliflowers, turnips and peas, from the
public gardens—the nearest is thirty miles from
our present halt—and that is where the sweet-
peas and roses come from also.

The servants feed themselves. For neither Mahomedan nor Hindu would taste what a European had touched or handled, although their prejudices apparently do not extend to our milk or butter, sugar or jam! The village grain-merchant brings a supply of flour, sugar, melted butter and tobacco from the nearest village, and squats with his goods and his balance underneath a tree, and there the servants surround him and make their purchases. He brings us grain for the horses and cattle, and labourers fetch our supply of grass and wood. So there you have the history of the whole commissariat.

I have not yet ceased to be pleasantly surprised by the clock-work regularity with which everything is done. A wizened old genius of the tents and Akbar, the bearer, are responsible for everything, and there is never a hitch. As for the cook, all that he seems to need is two bricks or a hole in the ground. He takes the pots out of the panier —they are big, copper, bowl-like pots, by the way, that need re-tinning every fortnight — lights his fire of wood or charcoal, and gives us a dinner as good as he ever prepared in his kitchen at home.

All this time I have never told you what our tent is like. Well, each tent is about twenty feet square. There are two tents, one inside of the other. A passage runs round between them, one central pole being enough for both. Our boxes are stored in this passage; the sideboard stands in it too, as well as the stove, which is right opposite one of the inner doors, and the table on which the milk for butter is kept in flat tin dishes. J.'s dressing-room is curtained off in another corner.

The inner tent has six doors which roll up, corresponding to six in the wall of the outer tent, with, outside of them, an arrangement called a chick, which is like a blind of split bamboos, meant to keep out flies while letting in air and light. The inner tent is also divided into two by a curtain, on either side of which are the bedroom and sitting-room. I have told you what the furniture of the sitting-room is. Besides the bed and toilet-table in the other room is a brass basin on a wooden stand, and we fix half-a-dozen brass hooks over the top rim of the figured-canvas wall, to act as wardrobe and towel-rack. The ground is first strewn with straw, then covered with dark-blue striped cotton carpets. You can't think how compact we are, everything fitting into the somewhat limited space, and having its own place and corner.

We are on high-lying ground where, at this time of year, the air is fresh and keen. The hard clay soil is barely irrigated by widely separated wells, no trees manage to live, and only two kinds of bush in a stunted fashion. One is not unlike mistletoe, the other is a straggling mass of leafless twigs. The cultivated lands round the village look like new patches on a faded dress.

We come across strange creatures, that are as much in keeping with the spirit of the scene as the jungle-cats and jackals; only these poor things have not so much life or aggressive power as the animals. They remind one more of the pariah dogs that slink about villages, half-starved, with their tails between their legs, ready to pounce on any food, if their watchful eyes let them hope for a moment that they can escape from sticks and stones. Like them, these people are outcasts; they are aborigines, and I question if they have always as good a time as the dogs.

Jim, knowing my interest in strange, out-of-the-way characters, often has them sent to the door of the tent. Some of them are wolf-catchers. Three short, wiry men, and an old wizened hag, clothed in sackcloth and ashes, brought four dead wolves and two living ones to the office-tent to-day, to claim the Government reward of seven shillings for each. The dead ones looked so very dead, although the men said they had only just been killed, that Jim is making inquiries to see if they have not been paid for them elsewhere and omitted the ceremony of having the ears cut off.

The living wolves were very much alive, and were muzzled by a cord and tied with a rope, by which they were dragged. The wolves are caught in a trap with two rows of sharp iron teeth, which snap together when the trap is stepped upon. Kid's flesh is placed in the centre of the trap to act as a lure.

Another set of people we once met on our evening walk were lizard-catchers. The only reward they work for is a good dinner, for they eat what they find, occasionally selling surplus supplies at a farthing apiece. Their mode of hunting is curious. One of the men we saw had a hoe, another a mallet, a third a spear, the fourth a brush of long grass. The lizard burrows under ground, and leaves a small mound on the surface, which betrays his home. It soon becomes a monument, however, raised above his last resting - place, for it is a welcome sign to the hunters of the lizard's whereabouts; and they delve and follow the tunnel made by the lizard, till at last they find him deep under ground, when the mallet ends the hunt. Sometimes the lizard closes the hole and hibernates near the surface of the mound. On these occasions the lizard-catchers come up warily, and pounce on him with the mallet, breaking his back; then they dance in a ring and sing a song of triumph. A good bag may be as many as forty. Boiled in water, salt and pepper, and allowed to simmer for two hours, a dish 'tenderer than kid' repays their labours. They declare that in summer they have only to rustle their bunch of dried grass at the entrance of the hole, and the lizard, believing it to be a serpent, comes out to have a look at him, and their work is done.

You remember C. M.'s story of the Highland gillie who capped one of his veritable *bonâ-fide* tales of personal sporting experience with—after a thoughtful pause — 'Speaking o' *lies* — Donald Cameron once told me, &c.' I am sometimes tempted to quote the gillie's comment to some of these people! But possibly they are telling the truth. When they are so nearly akin themselves to the beasts that perish, they ought to know their ways.

A dear old sportsman with twinkling face and small, piercing eye like a bird's, holds to it that he merely stands behind his target-umbrella, which is provided with two eyelet holes for his own observation, and imitates the cries of partridges, when he can walk a covey into a snare constructed of arches of cane and netting, with a door made to close when they are safe within, and that the birds flock to him placidly and are caught!

By far the most remarkable example of a keen sense for the ways of man and beast, we found in a cow-tracker. These men possess the eyes of a Red Indian, and are largely employed by natives in cases of cattle-theft. To test this man's capabilities we had our cow led out of camp and brought back by a circuitous path. While she was away we told the cow-tracker that we had lost all trace of her, and that he must find her, while we followed to watch his mode of operation. It was extraordinarily interesting to hear him unfold the history of everything that had happened. With bent head, half-closed eyes and unhesitating certainty, he traced faint marks in the sand, that we could barely distinguish. He described the shape of the cow's feet; then he told us that the man wore shoes that were patched in two places; that he had taken them off at this point; that he had a long big-toe and a flat foot; that he must be an old man; that he belonged to a certain caste accustomed to carry burdens; that going through this field of grain the cow had wished to eat, had been dragged after the man, and been tied to a tree. 'Now,' he chuckled to himself, after a quarter of an hour's work, 'I could follow that cow to Lahore, and know her among a hundred.' He was amusingly puzzled when it dawned on him that he had only to follow her back to her home in our camp, where she stood with her calf and her keeper to verify every deduction he had made.

Yesterday we went to see leech - gatherers in their tents, which were a collection of tattered rags stretched over bamboo frames. Their dress was a further sample of tatters. They sleep on straw, and their only property is one or two pariah dogs and donkeys, as lean and tottering on their legs as their naked children. They sell the leeches in mud jars for a penny, along with a doggerel charm to complete the cure, which they repeated to us. I could not help contrasting them with the old leech - gatherer whom Wordsworth met on the moors of Westmoreland. And yet the same world holds them both !

An Indian squire arranged to have tent-pegging for our benefit the other evening. It is a national sport in the Punjaub. His retainers, dressed in a uniform of red-cloth coats, yellow cotton leggings, white turbans, and armed with spears, rode at a hard gallop and picked up, as they passed, pegs of wood stuck into the ground. As they came they bent forward, making a whirring sound and shouting their war - cry of ' Aili, Aili,' and kept their spears on a level with the ground; whirling the peg with a shout above their heads, on the spear's point, if they were successful.

The news of the proposed *tamasha*, as they call their great oocasions, had spread like wildfire, and hundreds of men bordered the road as spectators. Some strolling performers were also present, men with bears, monkeys, goats, wrestlers and acrobats, who seem to have learnt the secret of the fourth dimension, and to have acquired the power of living in space in a condition of perpetual somersaulting. The performer who interested me most was a small boy who sang a song. He was a slight, graceful child of about fifteen, with a scarlet sash and turban. He climbed to the top of a pole, and then a burly giant poised one end of the pole on his chin, with the child on the top. The man had a brass ring round his right ankle, with bells attached. As he jingled these and the drummer beat on his tom-tom, the boy stretched out his arms, and sang his song with upturned face.

Indian music, to my ears, as a rule, is only another name for discord. But this song had a haunting beauty of its own. It reminded me of the song I heard the Spanish gipsy sing in Granada. It was the voice of the spirit of loneliness, like the sound of the wind,

'Wandering o'er the wastes of earth,
Sighing to the lonely stars of heaven.'

A song from the homeless hearts of outcasts. It was indescribably eerie, and gave me a lump in my throat. How strange these people are! What would I not give to be inside of their heads for an hour, to look out at life with their eyes! What do they think about, what do they love, what do they hate, what pains them or gives them pleasure? Are we really like each other fundamentally, or have we not a thought or a feeling in common? Oh the pathos and the loneliness of separate existence!

> ' In mystery the soul abides.'

And yet how horrible it would be if every mystery were dispelled, and everything were transparently intelligible! Have you ever thanked Heaven for unsatisfied curiosity? It is at the heart of life: to be a week without it is to be the prey of listless apathy. Curiosity is supposed to be a feminine attribute, and perhaps too many of us confine our curiosity to the limitations of the old lady who said of her daughter, ' There's Mary Jane, she takes an interest in the history of the Greeks and Romans; but, for my part, I'm satisfied to find out what I can about my next-door neighbour.'

It is all a question of degree. Animals are curious. Just look at birds with their inquisitive eyes, hopping on their little journeys of investigation; or dogs, with their cocked ears and tail erect! But they are only curious about what concerns their own interests. Without curiosity, on the other hand, Galileo would never have discovered that the round earth rolls through space, nor astronomers have learnt the laws of the most distant planets. While there is one thing left unknown to us on earth we can never weep, like Alexander, because there is not a kingdom left to conquer. Not till we have solved the last great mystery of all need it be said of any of us, 'There is no speculation in that eye,' and even then, who knows what surprises may await the wider vision?

This is wandering far from the account of the acrobats, but the boy's song is responsible for it. You must not imagine, however, that we spend our days interviewing jungle races. Jim's work begins at six in the morning, when he goes with a following of a score of horsemen to inspect the land. After his return he sits in his tent and carries on the business of the district, just as if he were in his office at headquarters.

As for me, if you saw our clothes and house-linen when they are returned by the washerman after being beaten with a stick on a board and then dried on thorny bushes, you would recognise that there was work to be done, not to speak of curtains, blinds, and sixteen dozen dusters to be hemmed before we return to the station; letters that wait to be answered, books and newspapers to be read.

Thanks to my Hindustani grammar, I can make myself understood now by the cook and bearer. I take Akbar's accounts about twice a-week, for he keeps the purse and is major-domo, local caterer, middleman between us and the villagers. The rest of our shopping has to be done by correspondence, and is associated in my mind with interminable receipts, which have to be signed by the sender and receiver, as well as by railway and post-office clerks. It is the method used by Government for checking and supervising the work of its agents, the said post-office and railway clerks. There is an excellent institution, called the value-payable post, according to the rules of which you must pay your debt to the shop through the post-office, before you can open the registered letter which tells you your purchase has been despatched, and encloses the railway receipt. It bristles with forms to be signed, but when one has fairly grasped who is the 'addressee' and who the 'payee,' further trouble is at an end.

The days are only too short for the work that has to be done. Sometimes I could wish that the Indians were less busy in the night-time! A certain number of them from the nearest village

volunteer to guard our tents and, seated around
the watch-fire, they while away the time by
shouting; for it seems a physical impossibility for
them to moderate their tones. Then the wells
are worked all night, and their voices become
audible as the village gossip ends. Sometimes
the creaking of the unoiled wheels, as the buffaloes
turn them round, has a high and low note that
are at war with one another, and sometimes two
or three wells 'talk much,' as the natives say,
in different keys. But at delightful intervals the
drone of the well is an old woman's croon, hushing
tired humanity to sleep, beginning with the poor
labourer on his plank beside his buffaloes, and
gently closing the eyes of weary workers, far
and near. And there is only a strip of canvas
between one and

'The huge and thoughtful night,
The night in silence under many a star.'

DEAR N., — 'The wind is up and the weather broken,' and now I expect I have had a sample of every vicissitude of climate presented by the Punjaub, excepting the hot weather. We had a beginning even of that, enough to generate a plague of flies—common house-flies—which buzzed by the hundred, and had to be killed with a fly-flapper of bamboo and leather, with great possibilities of execution in it, and the satisfaction attending on revenge!

Inanimate nature here is always still. The branches of the trees never stir, the leaves, grass, and corn are never turned over by the wind, and made to show what their other side is like, in the enchanting way with which one is familiar in the restless north. Everything has an air of being arrested, and makes me think of the stationary figures in the palace of the Sleeping Beauty, before the arrival of the Prince. Nature was peculiarly still a week ago, before the arrival of our Prince, in the shape of a dust-storm, upheaving, whirling, and carrying everything before it. Jim and I were riding the day's march, cantering fast, for we saw the dust-clouds on the horizon, and the air had become warningly cold. In spite of our pace we were overtaken by the storm; darkness that could be felt enveloped us; straw, dust and leaves whizzed past us, thunder rolled, hail beat on our faces. Bessie began to plunge. Jim dismounted to quiet her, whereupon his horse galloped off into the darkness. The dust-storm swept over us, but the rain was not ended. When we reached the tents we noticed they had been pitched on high ground. The servants' quarters had been placed as close to us as possible, straw had been laid down in the passages, and mounds of·earth heaped up against the outer wall of the tent. Every preparation had been made for 'the winter rains.'

The signs of the times had been anxiously studied for the last week by the peasantry, for unless the rains come in season and plentifully water their crops, the spring harvest will be poor. On the rains, therefore, the harvest depends. But their taxation for the next twenty years is being calculated by Jim at present, on the basis of the average value of their crops, and according as the harvests are likely to be good or bad, will the sum to be paid by the peasant be fixed. So whatever

his private hopes may be of plentiful rains and a
plentiful harvest, he warily only expresses his fear.
'The clouds are small,' he says; 'they are blowing over the district. There will be little rain,
and such as it is, it will do us no good.'

The clouds nevertheless have burst, and at night
it is as if a gigantic shower-bath were pouring
down on the canvas roof of the tent. In the
morning we were surrounded by a lake, as the day
went on we feared we might find ourselves in it.
So we started engineering operations, and shouted
out orders from the tent doors for the formation of
miniature canals to carry off the water; the old
tent-pitcher and his subordinate, covered with
blankets and barefooted, waded about in the
water, hewing out channels with their spades
through which the water could escape. Pools of
water, however, stood in the verandah in spite of
these precautions. Steadily the rain poured down
for four days, when it stopped as suddenly as it
began. Next day there was sunshine. Every
piece of furniture was turned out of the tent to
be dried; the damp straw was carried away,
carpets were hung upon ropes, everybody buzzed
and chattered and dried themselves in the sun,
and rubbed up and polished everything they could
lay their hands on. The trees looked ten years
younger in their fresh greenness. After a day or

two the wells, which had been out-rivalled and
stilled by the heavens, were noisier than ever, and
the birds sang as if they at least would confess
their gladness that they would enjoy a plentiful
crop.

But although the floods had abated, it was no
easy matter to get away from the scene of them.
There lay the pool of water still, and there was
the tonga on the other side. But how was I to
reach it? I refused to be carried, I would not
wade, and no bridge could be made. At last a
substitute for one was hit upon. A succession of
Indian beds was laid on the ground, and along
these I was able to make my tottering way.

I wished you could have been with us the
following evening, when five Indian musicians were
brought to our verandah. I think you would have
smiled, as I did, at the irony of the experience.
To think that this was music, music the divine,
music, the one embodiment in art of what would
otherwise be incommunicable!

Two of the instruments were like violins, the
third was much longer and thinner and its tone
was like a zither. The men sat on the ground.
They explained that their music is divided into
modes and that each mode has many daughters and
grand-daughters belonging to it. The exact meaning of this I do not know, not do I know if there

was insanity in the particular branch of the family to which we were introduced; all I can vouch for is, that there was a tendency in it to produce madness, and that as far as we were concerned it was a mode of torture.

Conceive three distinct strains of discord twanged on the violins with unrelenting vigour and insistence, and at interminable, unaccented length; three distorted faces uttering individual yells, starting afresh at odd moments, regardless of the violins or each other, two drummers beating a rapid accompaniment, and then imagine being told at the conclusion that this pandemonium was an oriental love-song!

Isn't it odd that the sense of colour seems to be the only feeling for beauty that very different races have in common? The Jap, Chinaman, Hindu, European by no means admire the same type of beauty in the human form. The music, poetry, architecture of one race may not appeal to another; but they all unite in enthusiasm over combinations of colour which appeal to each. One would have hazarded the theory that dancing was an elemental, universal language of the body until one had learnt, by seeing it, how unintelligible joy or triumph may remain to a foreigner when expressed through this medium.

Dancing certainly has a more cosmopolitan ele-

ment in it than music. We looked on lately at
a sweepers' dance, after dining with an Indian
squire, and one could quite follow the rhythm as
they kept time to their clapping hands with a
fascinating step like a waltz and reel-step combined. This sweepers' dance ended a very pleasant
entertainment, our first dinner with one of the
Indian gentry. Jim was not quite sure that I
should enjoy it, but we finally resolved to go, and
are glad we did, as it was all very pleasant.

The Malik, a great dandy, came to our tent to
conduct us himself to the English bungalow he
has built beside his house. We strolled through
the gardens first, to admire the illuminations which
marked out the edge of the pathways. They made
the garden so like a place that would be described
in one's ideal (!) of an Oriental love - song, when
Zuleika meets the young Hussain by moonlight,
while the nightingales sing and the scent of the
roses is wafted along! An old Mahomedan priest
met us at the entrance of the gardens, dressed
in scarlet turban and coat and white trousers.
He brought a bunch of sweet-smelling roses as a
present. He said he belonged to the sect of
Sufi, like Saadi, the Persian poet, and was
pleased when we answered that we knew Saadi
was also a lover of roses.

The Malik has built his bungalow English-fashion. On the floors of the drawing-room and dining-room cotton floor-cloths were laid, with a dark-red ground and dead-gold pattern on them, and a beautiful border. There was an ottoman in the middle of the room, an English fireplace and mantelpiece, chairs with net- and silk-embroidered antimacassars, and a table on which were placed a looking-glass, glass butter-dishes and salt-cellars, by way of ornament. Round the halls were hung framed Arabic texts, with English wooden cloth-pegs hanging evenly between them—also by way of ornament.

The table was set with our own things. So the Malik had arranged it with our servants, who waited on us. Our own food was also served, the Malik's being brought in towards the end, when we helped ourselves to several different dishes of meat and sweetmeats served on one plate. After dinner the baby was carried into the drawing-room by its uncle, to play with its father for half an hour and be shown to us. Then the Malik exhibited some of his wife's beautifully embroidered fancy-work, after which it was time to see the sweepers' dance and go home.

You must understand that some Europeans of the old school would not allow a lady to accept an Indian gentleman's proffered hospitality. They would not permit her to drive through an Indian town, be a spectator of tent-pegging, or receive an Indian as visitor, far less dine with him. They would, in short, prefer her to be as wholly absent from every kind of Indian society as are the inmates of zenanas. Their argument is that until an Indian gentleman will allow them to meet his wife, they will not allow him to meet an English lady.

A large section of the European community have different opinions. They hold, on the contrary, that there is such a thing as being too proud to be fearful of one's dignity, or to acknowledge that it could possibly be affected by the attitude of others. They think that where the convictions on either side are so diametrically opposed, the line of conduct cannot be the same. Social customs are not matters of religion with us. We don't think it a religious duty to conceal our mothers and sisters, we change none of our hereditary habits by allowing a lady to meet whom she pleases. So it does not seem to them to be just to demand a great sacrifice in exchange for none, and they believe that if it is desirable that Indian ways should be transformed, the best beginning is to show them a different state of things.

I am glad that Jim entirely sympathises with this view of the question. He likes me to go into the villages, visit the headmen's houses, see their wives making butter, grinding corn, and baking bread; watch the blacksmith work his bagpipe-bellows, the goldsmith with his blowpipe make gold and silver ornaments, or the weaver ply his loom. I have made the acquaintance of most of the ladies of the neighbourhood—beautifully dressed and bejewelled beings — and the squires bring their boys to read English to me, or show me their little English essays.

Jim takes me with him when he visits the dispensaries in the towns, or examines the boys in the schools. Our great ambition is to establish a school for girls, as well as an Indian woman doctor in each of the four towns before we leave the district. Whether we can accomplish this is doubtful, for these movements here, as elsewhere, cannot live unless the impetus is given from within. While we are trying to cherish the feeble, flickering beginning of a school we have helped to start in a large town, where it is not much appreciated, we hear that a girls' school, started by the people themselves, has sprung up and is flourishing in a central village of our range of hills. Large schools already exist in two of the towns, supervised by public - spirited citizens, and a dispensary for women has been opened in a third by the ladies of the American Mission. There they work day after day with an untiring devotion one cannot sufficiently admire, visiting the women in their homes, and trying to minister to the needs of their souls as well as of their bodies.

But now I must end this *olla podrida* of letter. Dear delightful camp life is at an end for this cold weather. We return in two days to the station, and if we leave it again before flitting to our summer quarters on the hills, we shall live in some of the gaunt, barely-furnished bungalows, or rest-houses as they are called, which are dotted over the district, to shelter wanderers like ourselves.

Sodhi, 1889.

Dear L., — Congratulate us on having accomplished the worst half of our journey up to Sakesar, Sakesar being a hill - station attached to the district, for which we have to thank our energetic predecessor, Sir William Davies, who, in his hours of leisure, engineered the road which winds up the steep hill to the station. He had four bungalows built at various points of the journey, which covers forty-five miles, and finally established a group of buildings on a peak of the Salt Range, to which tired workers can sometimes escape from the heat.

We are in his second bungalow, where I arrived last week in a doolie, and I should like to have borrowed a favourite custom from our Aryan brother, and to have erected a cairn as a token of gratitude that that bit of our ascent was accomplished. The doolie is the direct descendant of the palanquin, in which, fifty years ago, our countrymen had to agonise over so - called

37

roads, in the days when all over India only a narrow track of firm earth rose above dust or quagmire.

The palanquin, however, made a better show, with its painted poles, than its degenerate successor, my poor doolie, which is like a small four-poster bed, with cotton curtains and feet only four inches high. The palanquin too was carried by trained runners, with their pattering feet keeping step to a jingling rhyme of 'Tovie, tovie, ugham, ugham,' while I was at the mercy of untrained coolies, whose best endeavours only resulted in a swing from side to side succeeded by up and down jogs — as disturbing as the bob of a small boat on a stormy sea — alternating with bumps on the stony ground, once by a thud, as I was quite naturally and very hurriedly dropped when a snake wriggled over the foot of one of the coolies on its way to the grass! The journey uphill was, in short, 'a merry time of desolation'; but here we are at last in our Garden of Eden, with never a serpent to darken our peace.

We spend most of our day in the garden, which is shaded by willows and by apricot trees, laden with fruit, while the air is heavy with the scent of roses, verbena, mignonette and sweet-peas, displaying a mass of colour to which the glow of oleanders is added, and the drooping heads of poppies and passion-flowers.

In these romantic surroundings Jim sits at an office - table disposing of 'files.' That is the insignificant name bestowed on gigantic folios, sometimes printed, sometimes containing in manuscript the opinions written by different officials on some subject, which a new development has again brought under discussion, and which demands widespread advice. Jim hopes with good luck to tackle and finish three of these files to-day, one on the distribution of Government loans to peasants to help them to improve their lands, another on village banks as an alternative to the snares of money-lenders, and a third on primary education and on the form it should take.

I had once the temerity to read a long file. It reminded me dreadfully of a man I once met, who was so accustomed to writing historical leaders for a well-known newspaper, that if you made a trivial remark about the last outrage in Ireland, he instantly harked back to the death of Abel, and traced outrages through every successive century, till he reached the occasion of Pat hitting his landlord on the head, and announced his opinion of how he should deal with the fact !

The analogy lies in the necessity that over-worked officials seem to feel laid on their conscience, to recapitulate in a file, every one of them on the heels of the other, the history of the whole development of the circumstances under discussion, 'for reference,' as they call it. But surely they all know, for instance, what taxes are already imposed in India, and need hardly enumerate every one of them and their genesis, before stating which of them might be reduced in view of a bumper harvest!

I feel it is dreadfully disrespectful and preposterous of me to presume to criticise a civilian's handling of files, when I know so little about them. Only, when I see those poor, serious, overstrained workers rounding their backs and lengthening their foreheads over them, I do wish they would shorten their pages.

Meantime, while Jim is writing files, I am writing Hindustani exercises, and cover far less ground than he does by the time my task is accomplished. I find the mere construction of Hindustani sentences difficult. It is so different from that of any Western language. There is no definite or indefinite article, no neuter gender, everything is masculine or feminine, prepositions follow nouns, and verbs come at the end of the sentence.

To take an Ollendorfian sentence as an example
—'Why did the apothecary's wife put her child
on the table?' would have its words arranged in
Hindustani in this sequence—'Apothecary's wife
by table on her child why put was?' Quite as
hard for an ignoramus to make out and remember
as one of our modern puzzles.

Then the words themselves, which are in daily
use, are legacies left by every race that has ever
invaded or settled in India — Aryans, Moghuls,
Persians, Turks, Arabs, Pathans, Portuguese,
Anglo-Saxons, Jews, French, Dutch. So you can
imagine how much one has to memorise, with
very scant aid offered by any resemblance to an
old friend.

I wonder, by the way, if a language is richer
or poorer than others if it possesses a hundred
names for one thing, each name accentuating a
slight difference in the object? There are dozens
of names for a cow in Hindustani; one meaning a
cow with its right horn crooked, another a cow
with its right horn straight, a third a cow with
a small eye, a fourth a cow with a big one, a fifth
a cow with a brown tail, a sixth a cow with a grey,
and so on *ad infinitum*.

Jim says the differentiations are characteristic
of a pastoral people, who must be able to identify
their cattle, especially where rievers abound. Per-

sonally, it gives me the impression of an eternity of leisure to be employed as best may, just as sick folk, in their long hours of convalescence, take to counting the repetitions in the pattern of the wall-paper, to definitely settle how many times the bits like human faces appear in each stripe. Quite harmless employment, but not to be lightly begun on a busy day.

From all this you may gather that I don't find Hindustani by any means easy. But when one remembers how marvellously educated Indians have mastered our complicated language, with its arbitrary differences in the pronunciation of words spelt in the same way, and its many idioms, so entirely unlike their own, one is ashamed of one's own stupidity, and renews the attempt to learn their language for the pleasure of being able to talk to them in their own tongue.

My teacher is such a quaint little man, by name Hukum Chand. He is a doctor, and comes dressed in khaki trousers and a lilac cotton surtout, with a turban three times the size of his head. Like many people speaking a foreign language, he fancies he must shout to me, and becomes hoarse in five minutes.

I say, ' I am afraid you have a cold—pray don't hurt your throat by talking loud.' ' Not at all,

Madam,' he answers, 'it is of no consequence, thank you very kindly.' Then he begins to shout again, till he shouts himself hoarse and chokes. 'Pardon me, Madam, I must go,' he then whispers, retiring to the verandah, where, with his back turned to me, he still practices English. 'I do not know, Madam' (choke). 'Pardon me, Madam' (choke), 'Madam' (choke), 'your Highness' (choke). 'I must speet,' which he does dramatically, returning to shout again, to give me a nervous headache and bring on a fresh attack of choking, which results in his shortening the hour's lesson by twenty-five minutes. Are you surprised to hear that I always fall in with this daily suggestion?

We are getting on a little better now, and I can vaguely follow his Hindustani tales about the stars and his history of the Pleiades, whereof the chief star is really a perfect son and brother who, having died in a forest in the pursuit of his father's commands, shines now in the firmament surrounded by brothers, who must do him obeisance through time and eternity. But although I can guess what he means, as far as talking myself is concerned, I fancy I am not a bit further advanced than a young Hindu, whom I met in my evening walk yesterday, is in his English.

There is a beautiful glen in the hills which looks

down on our bungalow. Through the glen runs a burn, overshadowed by boulders like sphinxes, adorned by deep-red rhododendrons and tuftéd lichen and ferns. Here we sometimes amuse ourselves fishing. I had gone ahead to enjoy the sunset, while Jim added a tale to his file, when I was joined by a Hindu youth, who was lying in wait for Jim, and began his appeal to me, when we had the following conversation :—

'Good evening.'

'Good evening.　So you can speak English ?'

'Perhaps.'

'Where did you study it ?'

'Middle School examination.'

'Have you passed the Middle School examination ?'

'No sir, I am of the Bhera old family best. I beg you tell sahib, Mussulmans kill my brothers here. I beg sahib send me speaking English Lahore. I am lazy here.'

'You must speak to the sahib yourself.　It is against orders to make any request through me. How old are you ?'

'Seventy.'

'What does your father do ?'

'My father is eating his pay.'

At this point Jim came up with us and con-

cluded an interview which left me pondering on
the marvellous manners of Indians, who never
betray by a shade that one has probably tampered
as much with their language as the scion of the
'Bhera old family best' did with ours.

DEAR E.,—Blessings on the man who dreamt of Sakesar and made it an English home. I am delighted with our new quarters. You can't imagine the kind of material pleasure one has in material things that simply look English. The roof of this house enchants me, merely because it slants instead of being flat : the ceilings, because they are very much lower than those at Shahpur and are plastered, so that the beams are concealed. The woodwork is actually varnished : the bow-windows are really windows, not doors : the fireplaces are all in the right place ; and now that our books, pictures, piano and general household goods have arrived, we are as cosy as cosy could be, and feel as if we had been established for centuries, instead of five weeks.

We look down from our heights on valleys and mountains, the whole vista sometimes concealed by mists, perching us high above the whole world ! Sometimes the wind rises at night, and sweeps the mist before it with melancholy howls. When

it has said its say and whirled onwards, hundreds
of crickets chirp in unison from the branches of
olives, just beyond the verandah, the monotonous
yet cheery sound of little wakeful families.

Our hill-top is sparsely covered with olives and
wild figs, acacias and a few stunted fir - trees,
and has a narrow footpath running round it, giving
us a two-mile walk in the evening, with tennis on
the one little public tennis-court as an alternative
form of exercise.

Dotted along the northern side of the hill are
four bungalows, one called the Bannu Bungalow,
another the Deputy Commissioner's, a third the
Mission Bungalow, and the last the Policeman's.
Add to these a little house by itself on a down-
ward slope, in which an old gentleman lives with
his Indian wife and two children; a row which
houses the Indian subordinate officials, with an
Indian shop supplying their needs, and a temple,
where an old Fakir spends his life meditating
beside a small spring, and you can picture the
extent and contents of our little hill-station.

Our neighbours are an officer of the Indian
Army, who is here on short leave with his wife,
and hopes to carry away with him some good heads
of urial; a missionary couple on a short holiday;
two ladies and their families sharing a bungalow,
whose husbands are respectively a policeman and

a post-office inspector; while one or two solitary menkind come and go, perching their tents on any flat piece of ground they can find.

We had our first dinner-party last week and a children's party one afternoon, old and young dancing, and playing at 'musical chairs,' which every one seemed to enjoy.

Apropos of dinner - parties, I think I deserve some pity for being an inaccurate Celt, without any bump for officialdom or ability to remember any one's official position or title, far less their 'grades' and 'steps,' which is often a dreadful handicap. I don't even possess a copy of the Indian bible of precedence, which I suppose I ought to study, as it tells us all where our proper place, socially or otherwise, is in the official hier-archy. I expect I shall learn all about that however, sooner or later, as everybody apparently knows everybody else's post and pay, and frank allusions are made to both upon all occasions; rather a novelty, as so many people at home have the same kind of scruple about summing up your income for you as they would have about decrying your pedigree.

I heard a comforting story the other day, show-ing that at least one other person in India is as ignorant as I am about the laws of precedence. The tale goes that an irate Colonel, who had just heard where his place was to be at the dinner-table, said to his charming hostess that 'of course it was a matter of no importance, but he thought in his Position he ought to tell her he was a full Colonel.' She only said 'Are you really? Well, I hope that when dinner is over you will be still fuller!' A light answer, which it is to be hoped in this instance turned away wrath!

I am advancing at least in one branch of my new education, as I am learning by rapid strides the full inner meaning of 'chits' — these being scraps of paper with messages from neighbours, to which you are expected to add your answers at once.

One chithi asks 'if it would be convenient to kill a sheep to-morrow?' A second, 'What arrangements should be made about vegetables?' 'How bread could be got and, if our cook could make it, who would supply it when we were away?' 'Who could mend the roof of a house, and whitewash walls?' 'Might Mrs X. see to-day's papers, and could I oblige her by sending some tape, thread and buttons?' Another poor lady's groceries, soda-water and charcoal are always arriving, but never arrive. So the notes and queries multiply, till I sometimes should like to offer a prize for the best solution of some of the puzzles sent!

Life in a small hill-station is rather like being on a long voyage on a ship, with little news from the outer world, except what arrives in mail letters or newspapers, with their gossip about nations, or what can be absorbed from a nourishing book.

My own opinion is that if you want to love your neighbours you should not see them too often, not from any misanthropic fad, but simply because of the limitations of human nature. Even Arctic explorers, with all the adventures and hazards attending such enterprises, have found how necessary it was to isolate each member of the party in turn, if they were to retain their sense of proportion, and not end by applying the microscope to one another instead of the telescope.

A story is told of two couples, once the sole occupants of this very hill-top, who ended by cutting each other when they met on their evening walks on the narrow circular road, because there had been some misunderstanding about the daily supply of milk ! I cannot imagine any such tragi-comedy being played by our genial little company ; still, we all welcome any little change in our daily routine and any fresh air we can mentally get.

Captain and Mrs W.'s music is a great delight ; and our Missionary neighbour gave us two lectures, the first one in our verandah, on the Baluchis and Baluchistan, describing their customs and telling us stories about their shrewdness, humour and imagination. It was quite informal, with running comments and questions contributed by his audience. We all loved it, and he has promised to give us another next Saturday, in his own garden, on Egyptian history.

I am so sorry for one of our neighbours, with whom I sometimes read Molière, and whose children now and then come to play when they are 'too much joy' for their mother. She is such a pretty creature, dainty and *petite*, very pale, with delicately cut features, dark-blue eyes, and a mass of soft brown hair fastened in a low coil on her neck, a most attractive voice and a pathetic smile.

She wakens my deepest pity. She seems as if she had been born to be a butterfly, and I could picture her so well at garden-parties or at a dance, prettily dressed and saying airy nothings to a crowd of admirers. But to her life has been dealt in another measure. Nature has not given her much power to tackle difficulties. Her children are too much for her, her servants too much, life too much, and her means too little. There is something else too much for her, which is at the bottom of her hidden sadness, and which I can guess, but never hear. All I can do is to help her to keep on the surface of things.

I have been amusing myself making a bassinette for her. It was like playing at doll's house again, and it whiled away many an idle hour. It looked very sweet when it was all finished, and I put a tiny white shawl under the pillow for my little dolly.

Mrs D. came to say good-bye to me this afternoon, as we are going down to Shahpur to-morrow for a fortnight, and I handed over the bassinette to her, as a great surprise. Poor thing, she asked if she might give me a kiss, and threw her arms round my neck in torrents of tears. Mrs F., who had come with her, took her in her arms and soothed her, as if she too was a baby! 'Alas, the gratitude of man has oftener left me mourning.' When people can be *warmed* so easily, why don't we do it a hundred times oftener? Simply, I am certain, because we have not enough courage.

SODHI.

I HAVE kept this letter till to-day to add my best bit of news as a postscript, like the traditional woman. Who do you think arrived on Saturday to escort us back to Khushab? Who but our dear F. S., allured from his routine of work in Calcutta by the bait we threw out of ducks and the wily urial. The beaters have unfortunately brought us no 'khabar' so far of urial, but he and Jim went after some duck this morning near Sodhi, where we now are, and have replenished the larder.

We spend many an hour, he and I, talking of Fife and the old happy days at B., and the balls and friends we enjoyed together in Edinburgh. Then we drift from his home to mine, and I am conscious of a shadowy figure behind me, and have a vague suspicion that one is playing a pleasant part in what we used to call a 'double entendre friendship,' and that I represent some one, with whom I am linked in his mind!

I wish you could see him just now, seated

53

beneath a wide-spreading plane-tree, surrounded by Indian farmers, who, squatting on the ground and clasping their knees, ask him one question after another; while F. explains in his best Eton manner that he does not understand Punjaubi, and must refer them to Wilson Sahib for the information which they require.

The contrast of past and present makes it all seem like a dream.

DEAREST M.,—We have been overwhelmed by
visitors. A vigorous onslaught occurring last
week upon mail-day swept away every hope of
letting you even know we had survived the
attack.

I sometimes smile when I think of certain
austere friends in icy regions of Britain, who seem
habitually to study a new acquaintance through
their lorgnettes, as if they wished to analyse the
misty ghosts of his possible great-grandfathers
behind him, or the pedigree of his tailor, before
they could regulate their attitude to him. I
wonder what they would do if they found themselves planted, by some hideous practical joke, in
a lonely district in India with all the social
obligations this entails. For there is hardly an
official in any one of the two hundred rural
districts of India who does not hold himself
responsible for the comfort of every stranger,
official or non-official, who enters it. Who they
are and what they are is a matter of quite

secondary importance : they must be looked after in any case.

Some one descends out of space one morning, dines with us at night and disappears from our ken the following morning. As far as one knows, he might be Melchizedec, without antecedents or entail. All that one probably grasps of his immediate present is his official pedigree. He is perhaps a policeman, and we are given the history of the capture of a notable band of dacoits, who have kept the country in terror for months. Or he is a young soldier who has joined the Political Department, having just returned from Russia, where he has mastered the language and picked up some knowledge of the country and people. His home will soon be in some lonely Pass on the Frontier, or in some independent Native State. He must first, however, learn something of the Revenue system of India, and he is going to study this in a corner of the district.

Perhaps we may only know the latest arrival by note. The Doctor tells us that some one has put up in the Dak Bungalow, who is struck down by fever. The Dak Bungalow cooking is distinctly inadequate, so jellies and soup had better be supplied by us in the meantime, till a wan creature appears to express his thanks in person, before disappearing too in pursuit of his duty.

Don't you remember the stories dear Grannie so loved to tell us of her early life in the Highlands, and of how her mother used to study the latest arrivals from the occasional steam-boat through a telescope, and, if the travellers of those old days happened to exceed the number of rooms in the little Inn, how black Sambo was always sent to find out their names before she or her husband called to offer them a refuge under their sheltering roof? Our Dak Bungalow overflows sometimes too, and gives us an opportunity to receive many a welcome guest.

You may well ask what brings these stray visitors here? It is all the result of a huge system of inspection in every section of the vast machinery of Government, to ensure that every worker, whether English or Indian, is doing his work satisfactorily, so that the colossal administration may run smoothly. To me it is the greatest marvel that two races, who are more different than Celt from Saxon, should work so well together and accomplish so much, especially when you remember that 98 per cent of the workers are of the non-Saxon race, and that the area governed is as large as Europe with Russia left out.

It is an important moment when an inspector appears on the horizon, with blessings or curses on

his wings, for on the result of his inspection and
approval or disapproval of the work accomplished
hangs censure or promotion. The Deputy Inspector - General of Police appears, and the men
turn out for the inspection of their arms, uniform
and accoutrements, and of their proficiency in drill.
The Civil Surgeon arrives in an outlying Dispensary and sees that the instruments are clean,
that the supply of medicine is sufficient, that
poisons are safely under lock and key, that pre-
scriptions have been suitably chosen for the
different cases, and that the patients in hospital
are well cared for and comfortable. The Executive
Engineer satisfies himself that the roads, bridges,
and public buildings have been properly repaired;
the Canal Engineer examines the condition of
the channels and masonry-work required for the
precious water which fertilises the miles of fields.
Finally, the Deputy Commissioner and his superior,
the Commissioner of the Division, separately inspect
again everything which has already been inspected,
listen to any complaints, and do their best to
rectify all grievances.

So they flit across the stage and disappear,
Railway Inspectors, School Inspectors, Land
Revenue, Jail, Forest, Geological, Mineralogical,
and every other logical Inspector, all links in the
mighty chain which connects the watchman of the

smallest village with the Secretary of State for India, and an Empress with Her greatest dependency. Every head of all the districts that form the squares upon this mighty chess-board meets the other pieces in the great game, benefits from their expert advice, and does what he can to speed them on their way.

You must not imagine that such descents of visitors from the outer world are continual occurrences. Weeks pass in camp without our seeing a white face, just as weeks pass in our little station when even our small group of neighbours only appear and disappear at intervals from their tours through the district. I am only writing of things as they sometimes happen, to let you have a general idea of our life.

Jim is distinctly 'given to hospitality,' and has a special aptitude for discovering the maimed, the halt, and the blind, and inviting them to a feast. He even suffers bores gladly. What originals we have sometimes met in odd corners of the district, some of them passing through it on quests of their own, others without any apparent reason! We have had two quaint visitors in the last fortnight. The first was a little man who was rattling along the dusty road on a diminutive wooden cart, covered by a hood. When he saw our camp and learnt who the occupants of it were from his Indian driver, he immediately jumped out to call on Jim in his office-tent and remained until evening. He was the strangest little figure, dressed in a tight suit of brown, with a Tyrolese hat on his grey head adorned by a brown quill, and reminded me of those gnomes one used to see long ago, under initial letters in ' Punch.'

I don't know what he was in pursuit of,—if it is Truth, I fear ' he's a weary way to ride.' He told us some of the most marvellous tales I have ever heard outside of ' The Boys of England.' The numerous apparitions he had seen, the hairbreadth escapes from death or glory he had suffered, his adventures upon sea and land, would have filled volumes. I began to wonder if his occupation might be to tell these tales as he wandered from place to place, and half expected the Tyrolese hat to be sent round when they ended.

Do you remember when E. once told her best ghost-story to Dr Jowett, and asked at the conclusion ' What do you think of that, Master ? ' how the disconcerting answer in his high-pitched voice was ' It's a lie ! '

I recalled that episode more than once during Mr M.'s visit. However, I tried to see him in the light of a minstrel of the Scottish borders

brought up to date, minus a harp — or perhaps
an English bard, and tried not to be too severe
as a Scotch reviewer. As for Jim, he enjoyed
it all and said it was quite as exciting as listening to dreams. And when the poor little man
finally told us where his work lay and why he
had just left it, and Jim identified him and his
impecunious history, I believe that he positively
regretted the empty old Tyrolese hat.

He was one of those waifs and strays of
humanity who leave one sad, for I always think
of their mothers and how little they dreamt, when
they first held them in their arms, of what their
old age would be. I am sure, however, that old
Mr Z.'s mother is very proud of her John. I
can imagine I hear her discourse to her cronies
on 'John's by-ordinar brains, and abune a', his
by-ordinar powers when he gets upon animals.'
My only regret about John is that nothing
can induce him, once on, to get for a moment
off them. It is a hobby he rides till one
drops !

I must now, however, introduce you to John.
We might never have had the opportunity of
meeting him had it not been for a trifling little
episode in the Salt Range. Last summer the
peasants in these regions were full of tales about
a strange animal they declared they had seen

upon several occasions, which J. thought from their description must be a sort of Armadillo, a four - footed creature covered with scales. One evening, when he was in their company, he saw something that might be an Armadillo come out of a sand-hill. He tried to bring it down with his rifle but failed, and the beast disappeared.

That was all that happened. The result, however, was the advent only a week ago of a zoologist, Mr Z., with his factotum servant in a one-roomed rest-house, near which our camp was standing. The rumour of J.'s unsuccessful shoot had reached him as rumours do, when carried by village gossip, and he was bound for the Salt Range to visit the Armadillo in his lair, in spite of our assurances that he would find it a wild-goose chase.

'Oh, what a man was there, my countrymen!' John was not only Scotch but Scotchy, and there is as great a difference between the two as between good and 'goody.' He had more than the proverbial pertinacity of the race, and less than nothing of their proverbial taciturnity. What an opportunity was lost to the world by his not being a passenger in the Ark. What a regret it became to me that it was not wrecked! We invited him to dine with us every evening; he invited himself to breakfast every day, to lunch, and to accompany us on our evening walk. He was entirely one-ideaed on his own subject and a master of monologue, and on all these occasions we became one large pair of ears into which was poured the detailed anatomy of birds, beasts, and reptiles, whose names one had never heard before, and whose bodies one might happily never encounter.

Personally I am content to love animals without knowing anything about them, which made it more trying. Also, we had a cheery young soldier with us, who had come to buy horses for his regiment, and who was full of entertaining chatter. But he, too, became a large ear.

> Young, strong, and so full of life,
> When the agony struck him dumb.

I sometimes wonder how Shakespeare or Sir Walter Scott, with all their wide humanity and genius, could have borne some of their own creations—Mrs Quickly or the Antiquary, for instance —if they had met them in the flesh. Eternal sources, no doubt, of laughter and delight on the stage or in print; but could they have suffered them gladly for an uninterrupted week of seven days in the narrow confines of a tent? Could Miss Austen have rejoiced in Miss Pratt in a desert?

My father used to say that true Christianity

and good breeding were equally expressed in courtesy to every human being, because they both sprang from consideration for others. I adore those loving natures whose hearts, too big to be exclusive, can find a place within them for the evil and the good, who shine like the sun in heaven upon all humanity, and can find a point of contact with every living thing. Do you remember dear old Mrs R.'s comments on an unsatisfactory neighbour : 'Oh yes, I know, I know he's a greedy, selfish, lying brute. But I love him.' 'Ah me, how easily things go wrong' with some of us. It is easier to endure some vices than some voices! Perhaps when I am old and deaf I may be able to love Mr Z., when he, too, has lost his memory a little bit about animals.

'Aw, we're very gay in our part of the world. I've gotten a Waliagi Herisidos all to myself in the compound. It's a kind that is rarely met with ; its tail is a yard and three inches long, the stripes on it fully an inch and a quarter wide, and its claws on the forefeet prodigious. Have ye ever seen a Waliagi? Aw, but ye must look out for it. I'll see if I can point it out to ye in our evening promenade. The eyes of the creature's a dark - brown colour, mingled with green, and ye'll easily know it by its method of walking first to one side and then to

another.' Then would follow detailed accounts
of specimens to be found in Kashmir, Valparaiso,
or Timbuctoo, till I wished once again for the
hundredth time that the Ark had been submerged
along with its neighbourhood.

J. used to take him away after dinner to smoke.
Once I left them in the dining-room portion of the
tent after breakfast, and sat in the further end of
the drawing-room to meditate on solitude and the
silence of the grave, to speculate if the nebulæ
were inhabited, and to ponder upon all those edi-
fying subjects which tend to distract the mind
from magnifying trifles, when I realised that my
poor crushed worm had turned at last. He had
begun to read aloud an important extract from
the newspapers. Mr Z. interrupted him with an
extract from a naturalist journal, which he prefers
to any newspaper. J. went steadily on reading
aloud. So did Mr Z. Alas, J.'s extract was
finished soonest. Mr Z. was left as usual in undisturbed possession of the field! Well, he is
now in the Salt Range looking for the imaginary
Armadillo. Who knows? perhaps its scales may
be poisonous. In any case, before he returns I
think we must visit America!

These unconventional meetings are characteristic
of India, where there are metaphorically no locks
or keys, certainly none upon hospitable front-doors.

There are hardly any to fit office-drawers; only one kept sacred for the safe custody of certain important official documents, which flit through the Empire to demand the opinion and advice of experts, just as Bills are discussed by the Cabinet before they are printed and eventually become law.

There is little, in fact, hidden that may not, with or without provocation, be revealed. Even skeletons in the cupboard have more chance of an airing in India than elsewhere.

The hospitality of the country is proverbial. To be a stranger, above all to be in difficulty or in trouble, is the surest passport to possessing a friend. I have never heard of the road on which a good Samaritan could not be found in India. To have a common acquaintance with the country is to dispense with any other introduction. At railway restaurants, in hotels, in dak bungalows, in clubs, strangers talk to one another with a frankness which is more characteristic of other races than taciturn Britons. Sometimes this absence of conventionality has its amusing side. A friend of ours was lunching with some of his fellow-passengers from England in a hotel in Bombay. In the course of conversation he hazarded the conviction that he could tell anybody's nationality at first sight, and was enlarging on this theme when he was interrupted by a stranger who was sitting at a neighbouring table, and whose accent bespoke an acquaintance with Aberdeen.

'And whatt would you take *me* for, I would like to know?'

In a spirit of levity Captain D. studied him for a second and then said meditatively, 'I should imagine that your mother was a Spanish princess and your father a Dutch baron.'

'And do you know whatt I would take you for?' was the answer. 'I would say you was a most notorious ass.'

So ended the discussion upon pedigree!

SHAHPUR, 1890.

DEAR A.,—Is there anything in the world so entrancing as dancing, granted a perfect floor, a perfect band, a perfect partner, and a spirit tuned to happiness? Whether you are in the body or out of the body you know not, only that you are a part of the music and on the wings of song, near the secret of life, with no before or after, only an immediate Now.

We have had the loveliest holiday. It is over now, but the air seems full of happy memories. To begin from the beginning, dear Mrs B. was the good fairy who asked us to come to Jhelum and her dance. I persuaded Jim, with all the eloquence at my disposal, that a moral holiday would be the best preface ever conceived for dealing tenderly with the question of the peasants' obligations in land revenue to the State. *Kurz und gut*, we left all care behind us, and started a week ago at midnight from Khushab, with the world before us and any adventure welcome that might come our way.

The only episode on the journey was that Mrs Y. joined us about midnight, also bound for Jhelum and the dance. She had a young sister under her wing, who had just arrived from Paris, where she had been studying art to some purpose. She looked quite Parisienne, with a French figure, a long waist not intended to bend, an ivory complexion, expressive dark eyes, and a general air of mystery which was most alluring. I expect many moths will singe their wings at that candle.

Mrs Y. was also extremely well dressed, her bonnet composed of violets, a violet bloom on her cheeks and a bronze tint on her hair, which very much suggested that our whilom friend had, under the influence of her sister's Parisian education, learnt to paint. Perish the thought, but let me first give it expression! After all, the end in this case fairly justified the means, for she looked perfectly charming. I admired her spirit and pluck, for she was in a plight which could only befall us in India. Her husband, who is in the Indian Army, has some kind of inspecting appointment, which carries him here, there, and everywhere. Owing to some unexpected change in his plans, to a variety of unforeseen visits which have carried her too from place to place, and to some miscarriage of the post, she has not received one of his letters since Christmas, and is really worried, despite her brave front.

I am afraid I am not a true patriot, as I thank God daily I am not a soldier's wife. My poor husband would so soon be a widower and his wife in a coward's grave.

I must, however, arrive in Jhelum, where we were met at the station by our padre host, and at the door of their house by his dear wife. Next day we called on Mrs B., who has all the attractive charm of the Trenches, and an English home in which Indian servants seemed an anomaly. She carried us off to a conservatory, that opens off the drawing-room, which was at that moment being transformed into a ballroom.

Such a ballroom it was, too, with such a floor —hung on chains,—so you can imagine the swing. You must now also imagine us in it, in the haven of our desires; Jim's being limited, however, to square dances and attendance on an old lady, whom I called 'The window in Thrums,' for she sat stolidly in an arm-chair perfectly happy, armed with her pince - nez and ear - trumpet, conscientiously estimating the contents of the room, the ladies' dresses and jewels, and their partner's pay and financial prospects—a cross between the questioning spirit and a public valuator, — Jim perfectly happy in his own way too, for she was helpless and old.

Everybody, as a rule, has a superfluity of partners in India, especially in garrison - towns like
Jhelum. Old and young take the floor and waltz
with a will through their programme. I think
the only people besides Jim and his dame who
did not dance were the surplus men, and two
couples : one of them newly married, and so intense
that they would only dance with each other or
mutely sit in shades; the other our Parisienne
débutante and such a good-looking young captain,
with whom, for the first half of the evening, she
alternately danced and disappeared.

After the supper dances a change came o'er the
spirit of their dream. You should have seen his poor
face when she first gave an extra and then three
of his precious dances to an old general, a hero
riddled by shot and shell and held together by
rivets, yet dancing as if he only lived to dance.

It quite spoilt that bit of the evening for me,
for I was all for the captain and his good looks
and gallant air, and always as I danced I saw
him standing near the ballroom door, hypnotised
and dazed, a study in despondency. The band,
oddly enough, played as one of the waltzes the
queer old air which the street fiddler has played
so often at night through many a year, till it has
become to me like the glad and sad refrain of our
lives. I wondered if he would always remember

it too.   But who can tell what any one of us will always remember, or whether love itself will live or die ?   What do we know about anything ?   I suppose all of us have loved some one best in our lives, but who could exactly say why ?   Have you ever had an insane impulse to ask your unknown host at a dinner-party, over your soup, why he proposed to his wife ?   Could he always inevitably tell you, even if he would ?   Some microbe settles on the brain, the victim calls it his or her ideal, but would the very mother of the microbe recognise her mite beneath our magnifying-glasses ?   Yet heroes and heroines also have been moulded by such dreams.

All my sentiment backs the Captain, my 'age and sad experience hand in hand' the General, who, I hear, is now her shadow.   That little head, if I am not mistaken, thinks in battalions, not companies, and the long downcast eyes are not even half asleep, but look up and down and round all corners.

However, we often waste our pity on people long after they have ceased to be sorry for themselves. When my Captain, in years to come, has his blond laddie—the very image of his darling mother —on his knee, and hears, perhaps, that old sad air, I see him smile and sigh, and then methinks I hear him thank his stars for the best wife and mother of his bairns that ever blessed a Colonel on half-pay.

How my pen runs on, but our dreams about life are a part of our life, and you must just take them as that, along with the happy reality.

DEAR G.,—Your long letter was quite enchanting. This will not, I fear, be a very consecutive answer, as I am trying to catch the mail, while one of our guests is reading Ibsen aloud!

It has been impossible to find any leisure for letters this week. You can't think how upsetting it is to have people constantly changing their plans, writing one day that they were coming to attend the Annual Horse Fair, and asking if we could put them up, then telegraphing they could not come; their rooms given to other people; then another telegram to say they would arrive the following morning.

Every one, more or less, belongs to some cavalry regiment or has to do with remounts. Mrs B. is also staying with us, and Mr H., a home friend, who is traversing India. Some of the officers are in the Dak Bungalow, and four others are billeted on the Civil Engineer.

Thursday afternoon was a bit of a nightmare. A tennis-party, to which every one in the station

was invited, was to come off at four. At a quarter
to four, five extra officers came to call and asked
if they might have some tea, while a messenger
from Jim arrived begging that some should be
sent to the show-ground at once for another contingent.

Nothing under ordinary circumstances; but we
had three new table-servants, who had been engaged by correspondence from Lahore. One is a
confirmed opium-eater, another in his dotage, the
third in his teens. At this commonplace juncture
they entirely lost their heads, and chasseyed from
one spot to another like mice trying to evade a
rat-catcher. It is all very well to smile at a distance, but picture to yourself being saddled with
three maids-of-all-work who have never been in
service, and you can perhaps imagine the feelings
inspired by the sight of these dancing Dervishes,
with three consecutive dinner-parties in prospect,
to be sped by their skill.

However, the dinner-parties are, by good luck,
if not by good guidance, successfully over now.
Brilliant talk, obstreperous laughter, a general
clatter of voices, and quite good dinners, although
I question if any one knew what he was eating,
so intent were they on what they were saying
themselves.

Then after dinner Mr O'D. sang Irish songs,

Captain F. some of his own, to the guitar; and one night we had choruses, every one singing from their different corners in the drawing-room. The day before they all returned to their regiments, we had a spirited golf match. So ended our first ' burra tamasha.'

Now we who are left are enjoying the calm which has followed the storm of voices, although it is a distinct change of focus to be discussing the motifs in Ibsen's plays instead of the points of a horse !

GRAND HOTEL, SIMLA, 1890.

DEAR F.,—Are you surprised at our new address?
A telegram, summoning Jim to a conference on
some revenue question, brought us six days ago
to Simla, when we were at once whirled into the
social maelstrom, greatly owing to the kind initia-
tive of a dear lady, and to her husband's injunctions
to her to look after us in his absence.

We found her cards and some flowers on our
sitting - room table when we arrived, along with
an invitation to dine with her on the following
evening and to go on with her party to the
Maharani of Kuch Behar's fancy ball. The Maharani's invitation also awaited us, and has been
followed by others equally kind.

The greater part of each day has been spent
by Jim at the conference. In the gaps between
our engagements I have been chaperoned by—
could you ever guess whom ? — Captain Speedy,
Jane Stuart's old friend, who bore down on us
just before we left Shahpur, looking considerably
larger than life and preceded by a telegram

announcing his proposed visit, although a fanfare of trumpets and a menagerie of lions would have seemed the most appropriate forewarning of his arrival.

We have revelled in his company, and in his stories and reminiscences of his own life in days when, in the East, the canvas was big enough to afford space for individualities and initiatives as daring as his.

A flippant friend has asserted that the 'social headers' of some of our hostesses in India are no less direct, if they are not so alarming as the one burst upon Leslie Stephen by an American at the very commencement of dinner, when I hope the poor man was hungry. Her opening question was 'What do you feel about Life?'

Our critic maintains that we lead our attack by first asking our victim 'Where do you come from?' then 'What are you doing?' and last of all, 'When will you go?' Dear Captain Speedy, who combines in some ways the transparency of a child with the daring, venturesome spirit of our eighteenth-century pioneers, needed no such prompting to give us his best. He began at the very beginning, from the day when he was seconded from his British regiment and detailed to collect, train, and lead Indian irregulars in the Mutiny. Then on to his resignation of the Service, after his return to his British regiment, when his colonel set him, the ex - adjutant, to practise the goose - step along with some recent recruits !

After that we roamed with him through the deserts of Africa, shot lions and big game, and heard *en passant* a lion's roar given so realistically, that an orderly who was snoozing in the verandah staggered into the drawing - room convinced that we had been mangled.

What did not happen next ? For a year and a half he was the guest of King Theodore in Abyssinia; then he commanded militia in New Zealand; was interpreter in Lord Napier's Abyssinian expedition — having a marvellous gift for tongues. He was guardian to King Theodore's son : happily married to a charming Englishwoman, his ideal comrade through all the chances and changes of life. He figured prominently in a minor war between Chinese and Malays, was resident in the Malay Peninsula, and was finally the owner of an ostrich - farm on the borders of Egypt and Abyssinia, from which he had to fly before the approaching hordes of the Mahdi.

Have you often heard of a more chequered career? His great height, for he is six foot five and broad in proportion, his imposing presence, his wild-beast skins, his shield and the mighty helmet which crowned his tawny locks at the Maharani's Fancy Ball, made a distinctly imposing spectacle. You can therefore imagine our amusement when we heard Lord William Beresford, evidently impressed by the *tout ensemble*, gravely introduce our lion to the Viceroy as 'the Cause of the Abyssinian War!'

The Cause was a great source of pleasure to me as we wandered at our own sweet will together through the by-ways of Simla, studying its manners and customs and the lie of the land. A vast panorama of snow-capped mountains forms a far-away background with valleys between us and them. Viceregal Lodge crowns a hill at one end; three miles away, at the other end, Barnes Court, the residence of the Lieutenant-Governor of the Punjaub, lies hidden among trees. Snowdon and the Commander-in-Chief are located in the middle; four or five big hotels at different centres, with bungalows here, there, and everywhere, on the edge of the roads or perched under pines on the hills. The names of the owners of these bungalows are painted on a board nailed on to the trunk of some tree near the entrance gate, a little tin box being frequently hung beneath this board with 'Not at home' written above the slit in its lid, into which cards can be dropped.

I am told that every one calls on every one

else in Simla, including the inhabitants of all the
hotels, and that it is held incumbent on every
householder who receives such a call to acknowledge the civility by an invitation to luncheon,
dinner, or tea, a custom which has survived the
days when conditions were totally different, before
India was dreamt of as an alternative to the
grand tour, or even to a winter in Egypt, and
the population of Simla amounted to about a fifth
of its present numbers. I cannot help thinking,
therefore, that this multitudinous exchange of
hospitalities must have become rather a strain to
both the entertainers and the entertained.

But to return to our irresponsible days. Captain
Speedy and I, having finished our grand tour of
Simla as a whole, shopped all along the Mall
and had sometimes tea in Peliti's balcony, looking
down on the never - ending stream of rickshaws
which passed and re-passed, their owners having
a welcoming smile, so it seemed to me, for everybody, and a bow which was as regularly repeated
as if it had been pulled by a string.

In this way we filled up the blanks between
luncheons and dinner - parties before evenings devoted to dances and plays — hospitalities which
more than confirmed all one had heard of the
kindliness of the Anglo-Indian community, while
they also sometimes make an elderly person

wonder if caterpillars on the verge of their middle age would ever consent to form their chrysalis if they realised they would have to emerge thereafter and begin life again as butterflies.

At the same time, though one feels for the caterpillars, I must confess to having thoroughly enjoyed my butterfly flights in Simla, and we shall go back to Shahpur with many happy memories of our busy days here.

DEAR F.,—In dear delightful camp again! How I love it and the sense it brings of leisure, freedom and a wide horizon.

Think of us in a great tract of country covering three thousand square miles, studded with towns and villages, and holding half a million human beings, for whose wellbeing Jim is responsible. Realise that a thousand men work under him, all of whom, with the exception of the doctor, civil engineer, policeman, and assistant commissioner, are Indian. Then add to that undying curiosity about the whole of them, and judge if monotony is possible for an hour!

I love them all in an unreasoning blind way. The look of their brown villages perched on little hills and built on the ruins of dead homes, has its own note of greeting. The very smell of the village smoke, by which one knows in the dark that these old homesteads are near, is dear to me, and brings with it the sense of elemental things. I love to watch the big clumsy bullocks,

83

driven by a child, lazily swinging back in the
gloaming from the wells they have worked in
the heat of the day, or the ploughs they have
dragged over dusty fields, sure of a place in the
family courtyard and a well - earned meal from
their faithful friends. Just at this hour, so one
dreams, this has happened for centuries. So the
cattle will return to their home in the twilight
centuries hence. Time and change, with the restless woe they bring in their train, do not surely
exist in this land of habit and mute resignation.
The past and the present have both the same
pattern, and have ever been met in the same
unchangeable way, even as the stars in their
courses fulfil their appointed task.

There is an hour in the day, too, which comes
just before twilight, when the village, if it is
large enough to possess a bazaar in its central
street, has its brief space of busy perennial excitement, when we too wander with the little
crowd, and stop before the open shops which line
the streets, to view their manifold contents.

The wife of the headman of the village is
seated on the ground before a butcher's shop,
a bit of goat's flesh on a broad leaf darkened
by flies on her lap, while she haggles with the
butcher over what the price of the meat should
be, and tries to get it for one farthing less than

the day's market-rate. In the next shop a shoe-maker is bending over a pair of crimson-leather slippers which he is embroidering, unaided by any pattern, with coloured thread. They are surely destined for a bride, and will probably spell debt to her father. The next shop anticipates the sequel. It is a grain-merchant's shop. The low wooden counter is heaped up with bright yellow maize, ochre-brown oil-seed and green peas. On the board above the shop the gods of the Hindu pantheon are painted in bright colours, with a sign in red ochre beneath them, which should bring good luck.

The Hindu grain-merchants are also usurers. These money-lenders are often honest men, but equally often they are not. With their quick brains they learn from the village schoolmaster, at a very early age, how to read and write and cast up accounts, and then they hold the illiterate Mahomedan peasant in the hollow of their hands, for his only knowledge is of the plough which he has followed since he was a child. A wedding and a funeral are the two occasions for feasting which an Indian peasant has in his life, and they are pitfalls for debt which may end in the loss of his lands. A big clumsy farmer seated before the grain-merchant's shop is evidently in a tight corner. He is arguing, with a puzzled and angry expression, with the Hindu money-lender, who holds a bit of paper covered with figures in his supple hands. It is probably the old story. The interest of the debt has been paid in cattle, cotton or grain. The Hindu has reckoned these at much less than their market-price. The debt, with the interest due, is bigger than ever. There is only one end to the argument. Threatened and bamboozled, the farmer has at last added his thumbmark to the account as it stands, and accepted all that it involves.

Down the centre of the street runs a stall, covered with all kinds of incongruous articles. Indian ornaments, rings, bracelets and anklets of silver and coloured glass, made in Germany, enamel ware, glass tumblers, combs and soap from the same energetic market; Indian toys and coloured pictures of their gods, with portraits of our Royal family, and strange presentments of French, Italian and Spanish Roman Catholic Saints, are all there in indiscriminate confusion.

The street is crowded. Men are carrying their little sons on their shoulders, dressed for the occasion in tinsel coat and skull-cap, and eating sugarcane. Women chatter to one another, as they wait for the scones an old hag is baking for them in an oven. There is a jingle of sounds, the clang of the blacksmith's anvil, the wheeze of the bellows

which keep up his fire, the tinkle of the bell which
the sweetmeat-seller rings behind his gay stall.
A wild-looking Fakir, stupefied by bhang, with
matted locks, powdered face, and a long iron
staff, repeats the name of his particular god with
rapid insistence, and is given alms by his followers.
A village postman, with bells attached to a stick,
rushes past on his way to some outlying homestead.

To me the sounds and the stir of the living
panorama are a never-ending delight. And yet
I know it is only at the framework of this life
I am looking, and I have a sad feeling that themselves I shall never understand ; that as far as
the East is from the West, so far are we removed
from one another. I realise that I am face to
face with a sphinx who is not dumb, but who
remains an eternal enigma. Why ? you may ask.
I cannot tell. Perhaps it is because with univer-
sally good manners, these people have an inborn
reticence which you can never plumb, hardly con-
fiding to a brother, so they say themselves, the
cherished wish or the secrets of their heart.

I sometimes fear that one's ignorance rests on
something deeper, more elemental and impassable
than their reserve. I remember sitting when I
was a child at the window of a house in the street
of a busy town, and still recall the moment when,
with a wave of awe and wonder, I for the first

time realised that each of these busy passers-by was to himself an I and the centre of his universe. Hours passed as I tried to guess by each face and form what the I was like, if it was sad or happy, good or bad, loved or lonely. It was invisible, and yet it was the essence of the man.

Men speak of not believing in the Invisible, and yet, when all is said and done, it is on nothing more or less than it that we finally build our knowledge, love and life. It is the invisible atom, Kant's 'thing in itself,' which no one has ever seen or handled, which is yet the basis of every scientific deduction and the hidden secret of force. It is the invisible I in us all which is the final reality in life. It is the invisible I in people that we love or hate, trust or fear, even when the outer and visible man may be passive, inactive and dumb. To it we speak, on it we rely, for it we would live or die : just as it is with that we sometimes cannot get in touch, about which we have no intuition, which remains an impassable secret to our tentative endeavour.

Well, it is just this old invisible I, which to me is shrouded in mystery in this mysterious land. Not always, but often, I do not know, I cannot guess, I am entirely uncertain what I am addressing, behind these passive, courteous, inanimate frames. However, such experiences are common to us all everywhere, and of course only sometimes occur here. What does not come by intuition may arrive through knowledge. So on one goes asking a thousand questions about everything one sees, and trying to arrive at the life which lies behind. I often visit the women in their homes. I believe they quite like it, and are as curious about me as I am about them, as many of them, in lonely places, have never seen a white woman before.

Shall I tell you about my first visit to a village ? They are all very much of the same pattern. This village was in a lonely bit of country, originally barren, but transformed by the peasants into spreading fields of wheat and cotton. Just as bees might gather round a field of wild flowers and build a new home in a bush, so do these people, when they find water, settle near it, make a pond, a well, and then a village. And as every hive has its own workers, so these settlers carry with them their workers too, their carpenter, potter, blacksmith, shoemaker, barber and sweeper, who are paid in kind or in mutual services.

All their wealth and sustenance come from their fields and cattle,—

> ' Grain and cotton and milk,
> Milk and cotton and grain,
> This is the blood and the breath of their life,
> And all that they live to gain.'

At the apex of the village is the headman, at the
foot the village watchman, both, from time immemorial, the servants of their landlord, the Ruler
of the day, the headman acting as hyphen between it and the feudal lord; the chief difference between their past and present history
being that their new landlord takes a tenth of
the peasants' produce, where their old one took
the half.

If I pause, however, on the way like this to
give you useful information, I shall never reach
the village! It was built on a mound, and rose
like those villages in Italy, which in olden days
were refuges from the pirates of the Mediterranean,
but had none of that mosaic of colour which one
associates with those old spots. Everything connected with an Indian village is mud-coloured,
beginning with the water in the pond at its
entrance. The mere sight of the pond was enough
to give one enteric by proxy. For buffaloes and
oxen stood chewing the cud in its murky water.
Boys swam in it, washermen thrashed the clothes
of the village on its brink, and women stood near
it in crowds, with earthenware pots on their heads,
which were to hold the family drinking-water!
Such have been the manifold uses of a pond from
time immemorial, and yet thousands survive to
utilize and enjoy it to-day.

Up! I went on my Spiti pony, escorted by a
lordly chaprassi in scarlet, through the steep little
street of the village on my way to the headman's
house. On either side were low stone walls,
enclosing courtyards surrounded by small mud
houses, out of which women came with smiling
faces to salaam to the stranger. Some of them
held up their babies for me to see. Others let me
look at the pretty dresses they had just been
showing off to their neighbours. They were
destined, they told me, for a little cowering bride
in the background, who was to start next day for
her unknown home, with her beautiful painted
bed and her glittering pots and pans, and her
plentiful good-bye tears.

My hostess and her little girl received me in her
one-roomed house. She was a tall handsome
woman with regular features, dark eyes and a
slow smile, and was dressed in a long dark-blue
sheet, which was tied tightly round her waist and
hung in loose folds to the ground. Above this was
a short little close-fitting striped jacket of cotton,
with short sleeves, and a space between it and the
skirt. A long white sheet covered her head and
person. The little daughter had her front locks
plaited tightly down each side of her forehead, her
mother wore her front hair in two rolls.

All the family savings, converted into silver

ornaments, hung in silver rings from her nose and
ears, and round her neck, arms, and ankles. They
represent the provision made by her husband for
herself and his sons, who live in the houses surrounding the courtyard, and help him to till his
field. No woman, however, entirely enjoys the
prospect of sharing the whole of her silver income
with each and all of her daughters-in-law, without
ever a surplus for her own particular self. And so
I have heard whispers of other ornaments which
she possesses, but which never see the light of day
in her husband's lifetime. They are bought by the
cowries saved by her from the household purchases,
and are safely hidden away in a hole in the ground,
and only dug up as a widow's pension, when the
head of the house is lying in the Mahomedan
graveyard, under his stone slab, and with his face
looking towards Mecca.

Poor things, their luxuries end with their ornaments. There was very little furniture in the
room, only a few wooden bedsteads, with the quilts
which form the bedding rolled up at the foot, a
certain number of jars, like those in the pictured
editions of Ali Baba and the Forty Thieves, holding
grain and meal, and a few boxes, in which, I was
told, were the gay clothes worn by their menkind
on great occasions, such as fairs, weddings, and
funeral feasts. The iron rings in the roof were for

the ropes of the baby's cradle when it was swung to sleep, and the little shelf was for the bowl of milk, to keep it out of reach of the cat. Her sons and their wives lived in the houses round the courtyard. They helped their father in the fields he held from their landlord the Government. And so on we went, through all the hours of the day, from the moment she rose at sunrise, cleaned the grain in the home-made trays, and ground it and churned the milk, swept the room, brought water from the pond, cooked the breakfast in the court-yard over the two stones which enclose her fire, till she took her husband's scones to him in the fields at midday, and massaged his body before his supper at home at the end of his patient work. I could realise the round of monotonous labour from sunrise to sunset, and could not sufficiently admire her thrift and resource, and the praiseworthy order which reigned in that barren spick-and-span room. I wish that many a cottage I have known in the Highlands was half as tidy. But 'oh for one hour of Dundee!' and Mrs Macgee's warm-hearted loquacity! I really think I have got more of the 'feel' of their lives from a little Missionary, who lives in her Dispensary for women in one of our towns, than I have from a score of such visits.

She is a kind little human woman, who used to live in an Indian village, talks their dialect, and has often sat beside them playing with their babies while they carded wool, or spun in the company of their neighbours at the side of the roads. From what she tells me, I have come to the conclusion that Zenana prattle is very much the same all the world over. We are the same birds with different feathers. Can't you imagine it all, that little meeting with its mixed feelings and very human developments, as Miss M. described it to me?

There they are all perched on the wayside like a covey of white-winged doves. At first the cooing is soft and melodious, the different motifs, which stand for felicitation on each other's good looks, good clothes, thrift and devotion to husband, home and family, are interwoven and repeated by different voices in an Andante graziosa.

These poor doves, however, have been terribly pecked at home by that proverbial crow, their mother - in - law. Their nerves have been jarred by her time - worn croaks upon laziness and disobedience, their bodies have felt her claws. Some counter-excitement is needed to relieve the tension.

No soft suggestions or allusive phrases are used by the Indian orchestra. They attack their subject con amore. The Allegre vivace, Scherzo prestissimo and Finale con fuoco, which follow one another with lightning rapidity, hardly require a printed explanatory programme.

The listener can discover for herself that the subjects have passed from the Andante grazioso, through such phrases as 'C. is never at home,' 'it is not respectable to gad as she does,' 'she does not know what it means to work from morning till night as you and I do,' to the Scherzo prestissimo, when modified suggestions of the Andante grazioso are heard in the minor key, with grotesque variations on the original theme. 'Your looks and your things are not as good as mine,' 'my clothes and most of the things I possess are much better than yours,' 'you must be a thrifty woman or you would let your husband give you at least one ornament,' 'God knows it is his fate to be poor,' '*my* husband gives *me* ornaments in spite of his meagre fortunes,' these, with further developments of the original motife are treated with dash and spirit till, with a clash of magnificent discords the Finale con fuoco closes the concert.

Miss M. tells me that the most beautiful feature in Indian home-life is the passionate love given and returned by mother and son. A wife drudges for her husband. She only eats the scraps left of the food she has prepared for him, when he has done, and in some spot apart from him, like an inferior being ; she walks behind him on the few occasions when they are abroad together. They may or may not love one another. Her son, however, is her son and lover while she lives. Our saying

> My son is my son till he takes him a wife,
> But my daughter's my daughter all her life,

is reversed in India. The daughter leaves her mother for her husband's home when she is a mere child. The son brings his bride to the family courtyard, and she must obey his mother as rigidly as he does himself. So deep and sacred is the filial devotion, that it lends a romance to the country's attitude to our beloved Queen.

This blind devotion of the son for his mother is returned tenfold by her. If her husband committed murder she might never forgive him. She would go, if she only might, with her boy to the scaffold. I have seen myself, in my limited experience, what her love means. My ayah asked for a month's leave not long ago, and left me for that period. When she came back I literally did not know her. She was an old, bent, toothless woman, her smile dead, and with such a look of 'helpless, hopeless, broken - hearted grief,' that I took her at once to my room to hear what had happened.

'My son, my son, oh! Mem Sahib, my boy,'

she said with tears pouring down her poor old shrunken face, 'My son, my boy is dead. He was so big, so strong, so beautiful. But he took ill, he died. There are terrible words which we mothers must say to our sons when they are dying. We must say them thrice. He was my only boy. I had to say them thrice. "I your Mother who bore you, I your mother who fed you from my breast, it is I who bid you good-bye." I had to say these terrible words while he looked at me, and when I was saying for the third time "It is I who bid you good-bye," he died. His wife could stay in that place, she could look at the things he had looked at, she could smile. I sent her away. I sent her home. As for me, Mem Sahib, I am still raw inside.'

Ah yes, when all is said and done, the same heart beats in every human breast, and we wept together.

L. B. has arrived, the dear thing Jim knew when she was a child and who is quite, quite charming. Her father was the well-known artist, and we have already discovered mutual acquaintances in Edinburgh in Sir Daniel Macnee, Herr von Lichtenstein, Madame Hopkirk and other musicians and artists.

She looks radiantly innocent and happy, with a shy and rather impulsive manner, wears a rough blue dress that just suits her colouring, has auburn hair, with the eyes and complexion that generally go with that, and is like a picture of Autumn.

At one time L. had an ambition to be a professional musician, and was a favourite pupil of Leschetitzky. I wish she had carried out her ambition, for her music is quite ideal. I carried her off to call on our neighbours yesterday, and when we came back I asked her to play, and it was 'late, late in the gloaming' before she ended. It was such a pleasure even to watch her playing. She sits looking down at her notes, no attitudes, no flourishes, so entirely unconscious, as if she were listening herself. She played Chopin and Bach and Beethoven, and something by an unknown composer that was full of sadness, the sadness that lies in the sense of the Beauty we can never hope to hold, or really possess on this side of the veil. I call it now 'The Song of Summer.'

You are the only other being, darling, whose playing is just what hers is to me. I remember crying as a child when I listened to it, from an indefinite sense that you must have known sorrow to play like that, although it was *Beethoven's* great sonatas you played, with no maundering misinterpretation of his time or spirit; only, your soul was in your dear finger-tips.

L. rather misses an artistic atmosphere in Anglo-India, and loves playing to any one who really cares for music. By the way, you will be pleased to hear she is fond of the song I made, after hearing the Spanish Gipsies sing in Granada. We both think it curiously like Indian music, whose Oriental Spirit Rubinstein caught in his 'Ach wenn es nur immer so bliebe.'

Every one of our neighbours is coming to hear her this evening, and we have just finished arranging the flowers for the dining-room table. Woe betide anybody who speaks while she is playing! Once before, when we had some music, I heard a lady say to her neighbour in a pianissimo pause, '*How much do you pay for your mutton in Calcutta?*'

He is here, darling Mother, our own little son, fast asleep on a pillow beside me, as cosy as cosy can be. A little dove has flown in through the open window and is cooing just like my bird. And I know now the joy of a world of Mothers, and just what that moment of bliss means to them, when they first lay a little bundle in their dear husband's arms, and call it 'our child.' Only two weeks ago did that happen, or was it ages, and were we ever without him?

Every evening Jim comes to play with his dear, pink, little curled-up toes. How I long for you! But you must just dream yourself back to the time when you had your first-born in your arms, and know what I feel about mine. Your picture and my father's, and one of each and all of my darlings are where I can see them. Even the quaint pencil-sketch of Geddes is hung up among them, with the funny little figures of the boy in the wood, in a peaked hat, and the girl in a straw poke-bonnet, because I think she might possibly be you.

The days are sometimes a little long while Jim is in his office, for old Mrs B., 'she who must be obeyed,' will not let me have the pet always, and I may only write to-day for the first time to you for an hour.

L. comes sometimes from Mrs M. and plays to me in her lovely way, too lovely, for if Mrs B. only knew the meaning of 'The Song of Summer,' I suppose she would stop that too.

Then M. comes in with Babs and holds forth in her native Doric, and brings down the temperature to normal conditions. She is an amusing creature. Her wrath over the old Swiss woman's pecularities must find a safety-valve periodically, so she pours out all her pent-up feelings to me in a tirade on her 'foreign ways.'

'She wears two white paitiecoats under her nightgown, Mrs Wilson. That big black and white chaik's one of them. Now, how can she but think but they'll gather the dust all day, and what a state the bed'll be in or she's done with it. It's perfectly true, Ma'am, and no to be laughed at. That cover affair on her dressing-room table too is just a pairfect sea of ink. It is indeed. She puts down her pen each time she's thinking what she'll say next, when it's full up with ink, and leaves it there.

'At meals too, she just turrns me. Fancy her

drinking her tea out of the bowl! and up she
holds it in one hand, and jist powers and powers
the milk in till it flows over the whole table-cloth.
She's always drinking tea. And when she's at
dinner, she says the tableman stands wi' his arms
folded and stares at her, jist to torment her,
because he knows she's no gotten any back teeth,
and canna chew wi' her front ones, and up she
jumps and runs out of the room with her plate,
and says she'll eat in her bedroom. Oh, it's no good
speaking, if it's to make you laugh, Ma'am, like that.'

But with every sentence in the dear old Doric,
and every fresh disaster, what can one do but
laugh? I am quite devoted to the old lady,
foreign ways and all; she is always spick and
span when she comes to see me. She is thin
and volatile, and like a little ruddy crab-apple,
with short-cut hair, so clever, so loving and, in
spite of her temper, so good. Such a plucky
cheery old thing too, supporting a tribe of grand-
children, with old age, debts, and perhaps the
poorhouse before her, yet singing her cheery Swiss
songs, as if all was well with her world. I call
her 'a good, dear, plucky, heroic old vixen!'

Here she comes to forbid me to write any more.
And Babs is awake and must be spoken to, in
his very own particular language. So good-bye,
and God bless you.

DEAR A.,—Last week an old soldier acquaintance paid us a visit. Little did I think, when I last met him at a London crush, that our next meeting would be in an Indian bungalow, in the wilds of an Indian district.

The space of an Indian background is so much more becoming to everybody than the crowds in which they are more or less swamped in England. It is as if a picture were to be transferred from its row to an easel, or a lion from its cage to a desert. Our desert was certainly most becoming to our guest, who would however be somewhat of a lion wherever he went !

It was most interesting to hear what he thought of us all in India. He is immensely impressed by the Indian Civil Service, the greatest field for our administrative powers, he upholds, that the world has seen. He compared India to the Roman Empire and the government of its Colonies, and said our Indian Government compared favourably with that. We certainly have a knack for administration. We abuse our system of education, and vow it neither trains men nor women for the actual life they must live; and many a public school-boy has told me himself that he did not know English history or any other language than his own, nor could he remember even a smattering of whatever branch of science he had worked up, a year after he left the sixth form. Even the stiff examination, which has to be passed before entering the Civil Service, has little bearing on a civilian's future duties. Yet, thanks to the national common-sense, general gumption and sense of justice, put any young Briton in a country that has to be governed, and he takes to it all, like a duck to water.

It really is rather wonderful, when you think of it, what one solitary Englishman and his subordinates can accomplish. Some young creature of twenty-six, it may be, is put in charge of a district as large as Perthshire, while its head has gone home on leave, and behold him adjusting himself to the situation in no time, as if to the manner born.

His most important duty is the maintenance of law and order in his district, in which the criminal courts, the police and gaols are all under his general control. He supervises the Government Treasury and keeps up the registers, in which are recorded the rights of the people in thousands of petty holdings. He has to supervise schools, hospitals, dispensaries and public works. He must watch the state of the crops, the course of prices, and the export and import of grain, everything in fact which can in any way affect the wellbeing of his district. And he does it, although it leaves him little leisure to do anything else, fighting, it may be, with overwork, till it becomes an exciting problem as to which shall be conqueror, and whether the piled-up papers on his office-table shall be read, commented on and dispatched, or he succumb to their numbers.

The Juggernaut car of Duty becomes his idol, beneath which he is willing to die. Woe betide him if he has to fight famine and pestilence too. He rises to it, however, as a bark might rise to the billows which threaten to overwhelm it; and if he is overwhelmed, he wishes for nothing more than to be held worthy, in his own small place, of that humble epitaph that is inscribed above a grave in Lucknow, the grave of a man who 'tried to do his duty.'

Of course the Indian Army came in for its meed of enthusiastic praise, and he repeated the Emperor of Germany's conviction that every British regiment came back the better for having been in India, which, with its mountains and plains, was such a splendid camp of exercise for its efficient and practical training, and quoted his encomiums on the Sikh and Gurkha regiments, as amongst the best in our service.

Then turning to the more superficial aspect of things, he spoke of the influence of climate upon character, and the light-heartedness of Anglo-Indians compared with people of the same class at home.

Young Englishmen in India had more individuality than he found in England : Englishwomen less. They all seemed to be of the same age, to have the same social pursuits, to live as it were outside of themselves, to be without a background or shadow. Even the children, he thought, were much more excitable than English children are. He had never yet met a stolid, silent, *rostbif* type of English boy. Every woman and child seemed to be pitched a note or two higher than they would be at home. He supposed it was the effect of climate on their more susceptible nerves.

It was extraordinary how soon the change was effected, and he cited an extreme case which had greatly amused him. He had met some old acquaintances, whom he had known at home as a douce, middle-aged couple, leading a humdrum, unobtrusive life. A temporary appointment had brought them to India. They had only been here two or three years. What was his amusement therefore to find the lady pirouetting at a Fancy Ball as the Queen of the Fairies! Far from thinking it the Land of Regrets, he was inclined, despite his limited experience, to think it the land of none.

Of course I cannot pretend to know much more of Anglo-India in our quiet corner than he does, or to say whether he is right or not. I must confess, however, that the shadowlessness he spoke of has sometimes struck me too. I can never forget my inward amusement when a cheery Eurasian mother got mixed over the order in which her children died. 'I had seven and I lost three,' she said in her staccato voice. 'First of all Marjie—no it was Robert that died first; and then Mar— and then Vickie died; and Marjie was the last that went. Three out of seven, Mrs Wilson!' As if it was quite an achievement.

Dreadful things have happened since I began this letter, and it seems so heartless to leave it as it stands. It will show you, however, how shallow and limited our impressions may be.

I must have told you about our good kind-hearted doctor, a man who began life as a ticket-collector. He married early in life a simple, kindly Eurasian, who worshipped the ground he walked on. He saved enough money, somehow, to go home and pass his medical examinations, and was so proud and pleased to find himself at last as Civil Surgeon here, with his wife and two boys in a comfortable home. We all liked them so much, they were so true and kind: and the doctor was always eager to work day and night in his cheery, clever way, as far as his many duties would allow him, wherever he was needed.

He came one day, after our friend left us, looking so ill, and indeed having so unmistakably that grey, pinched, doomed look on his face, that I bade him promise to go home at once and to bed. Jim telegraphed to Lahore for a doctor, then when he had to go, for another; finally for a nurse, who thought Dr M. would soon recover, so Jim went into camp. That day he suddenly died.

In Jim's absence I had to do everything, with that rapidity which is so tragically necessary in India. Our kind Scotch engineer, Mr Fraser, a dear friend, wrote to say that he had already arranged much, and that all would be ready by evening.

I went to see the poor distracted wife, prayed with her, and took her boys home with me. Poor little children, they were not old enough to re- alise what had happened. Their innocence went to my heart when one of them said quite happily,

'Two things have died to-day, Papa and a bird.'
How little they knew how defenceless and helpless
they were without him !

Jim hurried back from camp. In the evening
we met in that desolate house. The coffin had
not been closed ; in it she had put her photograph and his, a Bible, a bundle of letters, a lock
of her hair, and her hopes and happiness. When
Jim had finished reading the funeral service, she
went to look at her husband for the last time in
life, and in a sudden paroxysm of grief she threw
her arm over him, with her face on his body,
and there she remained.

I stood beside her until she was quieter and then
supported her out of the room, and stayed with
her till the torchmen, the cart, and its burden
and followers were far away.

We felt that she dared not remain even with
the companionship of a French friend in that
desolate home. In less than four days, everything was packed up, every bit of furniture sold,
and she and her boys had set off, practically
penniless and homeless, on their way to some
relation in Bengal.

I try to think of him as he now is, and Time
will wipe out these ghastly memories. But was
it not terrible ? For days afterwards every time
I went in the evening into any dark room I saw

that face as I had seen it last, as distinctly outside of myself, in mid-air, as if it were really there. I wonder if she sees it too?

I leave the rest of my letter as it stands, as a comment on superficial criticism.

DEAR L.,—I have never told you about one of our nearest neighbours, Malik Umar Hayat Khan, who lives with his tutor in the bungalow next to ours. He is a ward of court, which means that the Malik's father having died when his only son was nine, his estates were taken in charge by Government and administered by the head of the district, with the aid of an Indian manager, who has done his work well, looking after the Malik's interests to such good purpose that a considerable fortune awaits his attaining his majority.

The pity is that these boys are so young when they come of age that they are too often the prey of the flatterers by whom they are surrounded, who egg them on to squander away their fortunes and strength by emulating their forebears' vices. There are of course splendid exceptions, but too many sink under the ordeal.

Once on a journey to Shahpur we put up at a Nawab's house, which had been placed at our disposal. Bedrooms, drawing-rooms, dining-

rooms were resplendent with mirrors, glittering
chandeliers and gilt furniture, but every room
haunted for me by the portraits of the last
owner, such a good-looking boy, dead in his
prime, his poor bedrugged eyes meeting one at
every turn, with the hopeless look of a soul in
prison.

An Indian, who had been his court-physician,
told us it had so wrung his heart to see his Chief
succumbing to his temptations, that he took his
courage in his hands and put the case boldly
before him. The boy thanked him, and asked him
to repeat all he had said when he next saw him
drinking. But, of course, there was a scene when
he took him at his word at the next carousal, a
tumbler thrown on the ground, and the order
given to his old friend to leave his presence, and
never again to repeat this insolent display of
authority.

At night the door of his bedroom was opened,
and the poor boy came and sat in the dark on
his bed and begged him to forgive him. 'But
nothing you can do,' he, said, 'can be of any
use. My father drank himself to death, and his
father before him, and I shall follow them.' 'He
is dead now,' the doctor added, with tears. If
only the age of attaining their majority could

be raised for these hapless creatures, it might give them a chance.

I cannot say we have any forebodings, on this head, about Malik Umar Hayat; for he has far too much individuality, enterprise, brains and ambition to succumb to temptation of that type.

He has the good fortune to have rather a re- markable man as a tutor. K. S.'s father was cup- bearer to Maharajah Duleep Singh's mother, and he was taken by the Maharajah as a boy to England to be educated, with some vague idea of his re- presenting his interests in Parliament. That idea was given up, and K. S. returned to India highly educated and quite denationalised, not even know- ing a word of Hindustani. When he first got this post as tutor to the Malik and they settled down in their bachelor quarters in Shahpur, he used to spend his leisure hours reading Dante and Faust in the original with two cultured Englishwomen who were in the station. He has lent me a book of German philosophy, which he sometimes comes to expound with all the mystical subtlety of his race and the accent and manner, to boot, of an Oxford don. 'His outward presence doth belie his soul's immensity,' as he is short and square, and more like an athlete than a scholar. When I tell you that he also sings Schumann and Schubert's songs in a flutey tenor,

you will realise that the Christian descendant of
Queen Ranjit Singh's cup - bearer has developed
on lines that his grandfather could hardly have
foreseen, and on which he probably would have
hardly bestowed his blessing.

The only occasion on which I detected hereditary instincts was when some Indian musicians
were singing one afternoon to the beat of the
drum, and K. S.'s toes kept time in their golf-
boots to the bewildering rhythm. It reminded
me of that point in ' Blackwood's Magazine ' story
of John Reid, the African missionary, educated
at Oxford, who heard the call of the blood in
the strains of his people's war-dance.

Poor K. S.—what will his future be ? For his
particular type is not always the one best fitted
in any country to tackle the battle of life. With
a nature peculiarly dependent on sympathy, one
cannot foresee where his niche will be, with either
his own race or ours, and the chances are that
between these two stools he may fall to the
ground, and be doomed to a life-long loneliness,
worse really than death.

A sad, or happy, as you choose to take it,
chapter in his history particularly interests me.
One evening, I don't remember how it came about,
he told me of his attachment to a girl he had
met at home, some of whose friends I know. He

said that in heart and spirit, in their interests
and ideas they were at one, and that they had
drifted into an attachment, which with him would
last through eternity.

It is, I know, a mistake to venture to play fate
in any one's life, but in a sentimental hour I
wondered if such a marriage would be quite an
impossible experiment for this particular woman
to try, if her heart was in it, and if the two were,
as he said, essentially kindred spirits. Life can
be so barren for some of us, and a woman of
character can make her own fate, if she has chosen
it with her eyes open. Such a marriage might
mean social ostracism, — it generally does, — and
nature shows too, by her stamp on the next
generation, that she is opposed to the venture.
Still—there are exceptions to every rule, and I
think most women would elect to be given a voice
in the ultimatum, and the chance of counting
the cost and determining if they are ready to pay
it, and adventure their life with their heart. I
have seen just such a marriage succeed.

In a gambling moment I asked K. S. if he would
like me to get to know his friend, when I went
home, and learn by the unspoken language, which
most women understand, if her feeling for him was
permanent. His answer interested me, as it is
not the first time I have known men who have

deliberately come to the same conclusion, and who have wedded themselves to a dream. He said she had become an ideal, influencing the whole of his life, and he preferred it should remain as it was, an inspiration which neither time nor circumstance could alter.

Louis Stevenson has embodied the same idea in 'Will o' the Mill.' It is the motive, too, of one of Ibsen's plays and the theme of Browning's poem, 'The Statue and the Bust.'

Quite apart from the probable wisdom in this particular case, of K. S.'s decision, the corroboration of this point of view, independently held by another human being, gave one food for thought. Has it its roots in cowardice or courage? Are such natures afraid of the corroding influence of cold bacon at breakfast, or 'toothache again, Maria,' and the hundred and one prosaic contretemps of daily life? Or have they just not enough imagination; or the wider, deeper insight that foreknows the halo homely custom wears, the comradeship that outlives mistakes, the advent of the mellowing, comforting, advancing years, when nothing matters much beside the fact that 'John Anderson, my Jo, John' and his mate have climbed the hill thegither, stumbling sometimes it may be, to rise again, but never separated at heart by any folly, nor could they be parted, even

when the hour comes for them both ' to sleep thegither at the foot,'

> ' Their dust at rest in the quiet earth's breast
> And their souls at home with God.'

Do these wan lovers prefer an anodyne to the
realities of life ? They risk less, but what might
they not have won ? No one can take the scales
out of their quiescent hands nor weigh for them
their wisdom or their folly. Poor K. S., perhaps
he is right in his own circumstances, perhaps he
is wrong, but there is no perhaps about the fact
that he is thoroughly unhappy.

Dear P.,—Two delightful hours have been spent this morning by me, in extracting tales of his grandfather from Malik Umar Hayat Khan, who is one of the Chiefs of the Tiwanas. We have been burrowing in the past, rehabilitating old ghosts, and living through days that are for ever dead.

I could imagine myself again in Saddel, harking back to half - forgotten things, and listening to the dear old Laird's tales of bygone ages, so different from these, but with their own peculiar charm; to the story of the misty Isle of the Judges in the western seas, where for three hundred years there was never a generation which had not a bard or a poet in it; the adventures of the Jacobite refugee in the Isle of Mull, who eluded his pursuers and saved his life by borrowing an old woman's cap and spinning - wheel, but who never saw Calderwood or the Borderland again.

Then came Uncle Neill Campbell's experience

119

when he was Governor of Elba and in charge of Napoleon, and his own mother's recollections of the death of Marie Antoinette. How the old man delighted to talk, and hand on his memories to a new generation.

Do you call such voyages into the past a mere waste of time? But if we forgot our own dead, who upon earth would remember them? Is it folly to rescue from oblivion those ghosts once vital as ourselves? For my part, I believe that the love of the past, which is felt by so many, has elemental roots to be cherished by us all. That Janus head, which ' looks before and after, and sighs for what is not,' is but an emblem, after all, of that passion for continuity, that instinct for immortality, which, starved though it may be, is yet inherent in the race, the earnest of its ultimate fulfilment.

To me it is part of the glamour of this land that, just as an old oak is reflected in a lake by whose shores it has spread itself for ages, so the past is reflected for ever in the people who live beneath its shadow. Different hordes have swept the country, but different though they may remain in every particular, they have one thing in common, their tenacious adherence to their individual customs, their transmitted routines, eternally repeated day by day. Their bards they have always

with them, like some clock that chronicles the ticks
of passing hours. Traditions cannot die, when
every village has its minstrel, every important
family, whether Hindu or Mahomedan, its hereditary
bard, to commemorate its homely or distinguished
history, its holidays and religious festivals, feuds
and factions, its humours or its pain.

More important even than such chronicles in
rhyme of customs or events, are the bard's responsibilities as the family registrar. He is the hereditary
custodian of his patron's genealogy, upon which
hang his social status, his claims to the family
inheritance, his aspirations for successful marriages
for his girls and boys. What an important factor
the bard may be in the family fortunes, at some
critical moment of its history, the family only
knows. Wonderful discoveries may be made by
these tried poets, which may alter a man's whole
future and the future moreover of generations yet
to come. To take one instance out of many. The
inflexibility of the caste system is proverbial. Only
certain castes may intermarry : outside of their
own boundaries they may not go. There are
loopholes in the prison walls, however, which a
friendly poet may discover. If a man belonging to
a prohibitive caste has made a fortune, if he has
risen in the world and wishes to rise still higher by
marrying a well-born bride, then any bard who is

worth his salt should be clever and energetic enough
to make his exit from the prosperous present, to
trace the family roots through tortuous roads,
hidden by *débris*, concealed by alien dust, till he
discovers at last the family-tree in all its pristine
glory.   The future father-in-law is satisfied, the
marriage is a *fait accompli*, and the bridegroom
takes his place hereafter amongst accredited castes.

The Tiwanas of Mittha Tiwana, however, Rajputs
by descent, Mahomedans by choice, established in
their grim old fort from the beginning of the 15th
century, did not need the offices of any friendly
bard to trace their family history.   It was written
in blood from the Salt Range to the Western
Borders of Northern Hindustan.

The family history, in these good old fighting
days, was one long record of hostility with their
neighbours, and as full of blood and battle, fire and
rapine, as the Border Ballads or the Book of Kings.
Sons fought against their father, brother against
brother, every man's hand was against his neighbour, and intrigue, treachery, and slaughter were
the breath of their nostrils.   It was, in fact, as
palatable to them to whet their appetite for breakfast by bringing down a few Awans, their own
immediate neighbours in the Salt Range, as it
would be for an Englishman to pot one or two
partridges on his evening stroll.

To give you the history of only one of these stalwart fighters, let me tell you how Khan Mahomed Khan, who lived at Nurpur, treated some of his friends. He had been paying a visit to the Chief of Khushab, rightly or wrongly suspected his host's son-in-law of treachery, and started at once for Nurpur to make ready for war. His host the Chief, however, had always considered himself a faithful ally, so he followed him at once to his mud fort, and with him were his wife and son.

They came to assure him of their friendship and as a pledge of peace. Think how earnest that pledge of peace must have been, which brought a woman all that weary way, urged by it to desert her lifelong seclusion, her refuge from a restless world, bringing with her, her boy. But Khan Mahomed Khan was not to be cajoled by any woman or child. Father, mother, son were marched back in front of his army to Khushab, where they were tied to the front of a cannon, as a target for the enemy. And at the end of a successful siege, these three prisoners, who had neither, so they maintained, done nor wished him any harm, were killed by him in cold blood.

And now to tell you something of his dealings with his brother Khan Sher Khan, a giant as fond of fighting as himself. Their lives were one long shooting-match, with death as the stake to be paid

by the loser.   Their first round in the struggle
was when Khan Mahomed Khan, returning from a
short absence from his home, armed as usual with
a pistol in his belt, a matchlock and a long curved
sword slung by his side, and followed by the
inevitable rag-tag and bobtail retinue, found the
gates of the old square tower closed, matchlocks
pointed from the loopholes of its mud walls, and
his brother established there as Chief.

Then troops collected, a march, a siege, and this
brother thrown into prison.   He was afterwards
released, with pledges of docility for the future,
which were naturally made to be broken.

So the merry game went on, till finally, just
about a hundred years ago, the great Sikh Ranjit
Singh, the conqueror of the Punjaub and its acknowledged ruler, for the sum of £7000 pledged himself
to trap the younger brother.   The different acts
of the drama were arranged between ruler and
subject at the Fort in Lahore.   Ranjit Singh
marched into the country, our friend leaving the
coast clear by a feint of flight.   Out came the
recreant brother to pay his respects to the mighty
Rajah.   He was caught, made over to the head of
the house, and by him murdered.   Ranjit Singh
then took the tribute-money due to him and
returned to Lahore, after which the mighty Chief,
at last the undisturbed possessor of his lands, was

overmastered by his own son. So he too was laid with his fathers.

Does it not remind you of the doughty deeds of the old fiery heroes of the Borders, Scotts and Elliots, Humes and Armstrongs, with their raids and counter-raids and hereditary feuds? Now, with the Pax Britannica, our neighbours' swords have been exchanged for the ploughshare, and these turbulent spirits only fight one another in the law-courts; a deadly ruining duel it sometimes is too, with suave pleaders, as Indian advocates are called, as indefatigable and applauding seconds. For good or evil they have ever had a reputation, however, as valiant fighters, and were the faithful allies of our Government in the Sikh wars and in the Mutiny.

I saw about a dozen of these famous Maliks this year at a Darbar. The Darbar I must tell you is an assembly of District Notables held annually on New Year's Day. On these solemn occasions Jim has to make a speech in Hindustani from his däis at the end of the long narrow tent. In it he had commended all the District Notables, beginning with those who sat on his right hand in the front row of chairs. They were the large landowners, on whose influence and power as landlords the well-being of their tenants so largely depends. After them came the District officials who sat on his left, the English policeman with half a dozen of his chief Indian subordinates, the Scotch Civil Engineer with one or two of his men, our Doctor with his Indian Assistant Surgeon, the Tahsildars, who are at the head of the three large divisions of the District, and the five Indian Judges and Magistrates, who all came in for their meed of praise.

These men constituted the Assembly. In addition to them there were a few onlookers, who stood in the surrounding passage or sat on the grass. Alas! they were not yet qualified to sit on a chair in such an august assembly; and what bitterness lurked in their hearts under their gala dresses only the owners knew. For to be given the right to sit on a chair is to have reached the first rung in the ladder ascending to glory.

Curious, is it not, the little symbols of glory for which a man will work, will fume and fret, or disregarding, win? With us it is a star or a ribbon to be pinned on his coat, initials to be added to his name, or best of all, a special corner for his dust. Here a ruling chief is satisfied if a few more guns than are boomed for his neighbours are added to his salute, as he comes or goes; and a commoner is content if he may sit on a chair in official assemblies, and more than content if his Darbar seat is higher than that possessed by friends who are present. I thought of Burns' lines as they all

streamed in, and sat down with their eastern
dignity.

> ' A King can mak a belted knight,
> A Marquis, Duke, and a' that,
> But an honest man's abune his might,
> Guid faith he mauna fa' that.'

But these men, who sat on Jim's right hand in
the front row of the Darbar, had something in
them which is different from honesty—they were
heroes.   It was they who led the way in the
stream that passed before the däis, pausing before
it to salaam to the representative of the British
Government, and to present a handful of silver
coins, gravely returned with an answering salaam.

First came Malik Futteh Sher Khan Tiwana, the
son of a famous free-lance, Chief of the District
Imperial Darbaris, a stout old gentleman with
bent shoulders, a dyed beard and ominous eyes.
Then came Malik Sher Mahomed Khan Tiwana,
a tall gaunt old figure with a long face, long nose,
long beard and a pair of fierce dark eyes.   His
brown surtout of Kashmir cloth was embroidered
with gold, his white turban crowned with a gilt
pinnacle.   He was followed by Malik Hakim Khan
Nun, a man of sedate and dignified carriage, with
a well-earned reputation for uprightness, honesty
and sound judgment, the owner of five thousand
acres of valuable land, a popular landlord, and a

good old country gentleman of the best type. Others followed whom I do not so far know.

These men when young once fought beneath our flag. They earned their row of medals at many a bloody fight, at the head of their Tiwana horsemen, with Edwardes at the siege of Multan, and through the dark days of the Mutiny, when they tendered their services to John Lawrence to a man, and that at a time when it was not certain on which side victory lay, and when to espouse our cause was to brave ruin. Now in their old age they rest upon their laurels, proud of their title of Khan Bahadur, and of the goodly acres added by the British Government to their already large estates, content with the comfortable pension which swells their own not unsubstantial incomes.

Malik Umar Hayat Khan, who told me these old tales, is the only child of one of the best of the Tiwana Chiefs, Malik Sahib Khan, Khan Bahadur, C.S.I., who only died nine years ago. Sir Donald Macnab, who paid us a delightful visit a short time ago, lived in this house when the Mutiny broke out. Mr Ousely was then the Deputy Commissioner of the District. A body of mutinous sepoys was reported to be on its way from Jhelum, when Malik Sahib Khan rode over from Mittha Tiwana. He stood before Mr Ousely, salaamed, and offered him the handle of his sword,

with the point directed to his own body, and said
'I have fifty horsemen and I can raise three
hundred. I can clothe and feed them, and if no
questions are asked, I can find them arms too.
They and my life are yours.'

He was a prince of fighters, and tales are still
told of his prowess in many an old campaign, of
how he captured nearly two hundred mutineers
before a single shot was fired, and of his adventures
with General Napier in Central India when the
Mutiny was suppressed. Best of all was his peaceful
life in times of peace, which distinguished him in
a family famed for family quarrels, a predominance
in virtues which won for him the Star of India.

Well, those troubled times are over, and if
these old heroes shared with us 'the dangers
and the glory,' it is good to know they also share
'the peace and comfort now.'

So ends my long history of the Tiwanas. You
must not however run away with the idea that
India is peopled with Tiwanas, any more than it
is populated with the creatures of our childhood's
dreams. India, according to our imaginations,
was a vast level continent of enormous heat and
size. The palm trees and thatched huts, which
graced the frontispiece of 'Little Henry and his
Bearer,' formed the background to a swarm of
figures. Some of them were Mahomedans by faith,

others Hindus, but they all bore a striking family resemblance to one another. They had all lithe, slim figures of graceful proportions, sparsely clothed in white and scarlet, and dominated by marvellous, slumbering, almond-shaped eyes, into which slaughtering fires could creep, the Mutiny Sepoy fires in short, with which our old nurse used to frighten us in the nursery.

It would be hardly less accurate, however, to picture Europe as a sandy desert inhabited by Turks.

The old-fashioned, sedate, conservative Madrassi who prides himself on being a Dravidian and the oldest inhabitant of the empire, is more diametrically unlike, more fundamentally opposed to the subtle, eloquent, excitable Bengali, to the sturdy, shrewd Mahomedan peasant, or to the fighting Sikh, than an Italian is to a Swede, or an Irishman to a Cossack.

There is no comparison between the two continents which does not illustrate the greater disintegration of the Eastern races, as compared with the bonds which hold the Western together. Give any two of these Orientals, belonging to different eastern races, the choice of the other Oriental or of an Englishman as a Judge, and I think you would be surprised by the result.

It would be nearer the mark to picture the population of this country as a bundle of sticks, each stick possessed by the ambition to belabour the others, and only held together in external unanimity by the British flag!

SHAHPUR, 1894.

DEAREST G.,—L. B. is here again, a child of the house, and such a pleasure and delight to us all. We have passed beyond the stage of the 'unwritten language' when the busy hostess asks her guests 'what they are going to do?' adding 'I think I am going to write letters myself'; to which you reply 'so am I, and I think I can dispose of them quickest in my own room,' where you stay for at least an hour, and probably two, if she further suggests that 'the housemaid must light the fire.'

I tell Lucy my theory that no feelings can ever be hurt, where there is no ambiguous mystery, and that as there are a hundred things to be done, amongst them finishing the book she wishes to illustrate, she must just entertain herself.

So I leave her quite to her own devices, in the morning, when she reads, walks, sketches, or pays a visit to Babs in the nursery, and vows she is perfectly happy.

We generally play tennis or golf in the

afternoon, and her music in the evening is heavenly, awakening those unheard melodies that haunt the silent air and the sense of all beauty.

I think, in fact I feel almost certain, that she has awakened another chord in a kindred spirit. We have a delightful young civilian near us just now, who has been appointed judge of the District, and it hardly needs spectacles to see he has lost his heart. Of course, if they were wholly 'modern,' this might mean nothing; for the young generation seem to be supplied with very large hearts and very short memories. But these two are made of different fibre.

She went with Mrs E. this afternoon to a picnic, while he asked if he might be allowed to drive her home, and I await her return with maternal solicitude, as we are fond of them both.

Ah yes, my dear G., it was just as I thought and hoped. 'Late, late in the gloaming Kilmeny cam hame,' and 'with a smile on her lips and a tear in her ee,' she needed no words when my arms were around her.

So, when we come back to India after our time at home next summer, perhaps we may have L. as our hostess in this dear house, if good fortune brings Jim again to inspect his old District.

DEAREST A.,—When I arrived before Jim from camp this morning, and found the mail letters on the table, and read the glad news they contained, I was *ausser mich* with delight. I walked up and down the drawing-room addressing the ceiling to find a vent for my feelings. '*Nein, das ist Himmlisch! Ich sage nur! Nein, das ist doch wirklich reizend!* A. in Calcutta! And this is the end of the three-volumed romance. Could anything be quite so delightful?' And when Jim heard the good news you can imagine his pleasure, for you know how devoted we both are to F.

It is already arranged by us both. You must come back with us in autumn, when we and the Babs return from our time at home, and be married in this little station-church. We shall write to Calcutta to-day, and announce that we have heard the good news. More upon mail-day, but this must be posted now. I could not wait five days longer to send you our blessing.

I DARE not think how long it is since I wrote
to my dearest F. from Shahpur. Our six months
spent in that beloved retreat on our return from
furlough were so monopolised by a hundred absorbing interests and duties, beginning with Jack,
that my letters found their way to but one address. Six other months have passed since we
sent off our household gods and our goods and
chattels in a gigantic railway van, arriving in
our new quarters close on their heels and settling
down in this charming house, surrounded by a
garden where roses climb up the trees and hang
from their branches, and mignonette and sweet
violets pervade the air with their perfume.

Shahpur and Rawal Pindi are at opposite poles!
There the sense of lonely wastes awaiting our
tents : here the enclosing arms of mountains.
There, counting our English neighbours by units,
here by hundreds. There all the romance of
India : here all the romance of a garrison-town ;
the coos of the doves, the shrieks of the parrots,

135

the sounds of the village-stir, exchanged for the tramp of seven British and Indian regiments and the call of their bugles at all hours of the day.

Don't ask me which I love best; one can love both. If India has half of my heart, with all that is left of it I shall dote on the Military as long as it beats!

We are peculiarly fortunate in being linked, so to speak, to both the 4th D.G.'s and the K.O.S.B.'s by the fact that one of the dear 'Clan Sellar' is in the first, and a son and nephew of our beloved Mrs Sellar in the other. Add to this that, as it so happens, quite a number of the Gordons were at Fettes College with B., and you can perhaps understand why these three regiments have given us such a delightful welcome, calling upon us *en masse* and, the Scotch regiments especially, quite accepting us as 'belonging to the family.'

There is always a mental holiday in learning the language of a new kind of 'shop,' when you have mastered your own. I have inherited our father's love of military history, always provided it has maps, so that one does not get lost on the battle-fields. The Colonels of some of these regiments have therefore, by special request, given me their regimental histories, with another thrown in by Colonel R., not the history of his

own Indian Regiment this time, but that of the
42nd Highlanders, whom he adores.

'I'd rather be a *Jock* in the 42nd,' as he puts
it, 'than a *Major* in the Staff Corps.' A spirit
of mischief tempted me to tease the dear old man.
When I had read about a hundred pages of his
treasured history, I asked him to lunch with us,
and told him I could not quite understand his
enthusiasm, for, as far as I had gone, I had only
learnt that quite a number of the 42nd had
deserted on their first march to London : that
after that they had been distressfully beaten in
the Low Countries, and had not won a single
battle in Canada!

You should have seen how his face fell, till I
hastened to assure him that I was certain they
were going to do well in the future, if he would
still entrust their history to me till I finished it,
and could glory over their proverbial success.

There are such dear women, too, in Rawal Pindi.
The one I perhaps especially appreciate is Mrs
L., the wife of the Colonel of the 4th Dragoon
Guards. Before we knew her we often used to
see her in our evening walk, in her lovely garden,
under her archways of roses, or moving about in
her wilderness of flowers, herself the 'fairest of
them all.'

Now I know her in her own home, where everything speaks of her love of beauty and her personal charm. There she is amongst her books and her pictures, devoting her life to her husband and children, a living refutation of the wholesale assertion that every woman in India is a gadabout and a butterfly.

Mrs T., our Commissioner's wife, is charming too, in fact fascinating, and you should see Mrs R. in her studio and look at the result of her labours, and hear Mrs C.'s violoncello performances, if you want to appreciate the other side of the shield, and count those women too who are all in all to their husbands and children, treasuring every hour that precedes the one when they must part with their pets, and pay with their tears for our Empire in India.

Of course we have our share of frivolities, polo, football matches and races. There is a public club in grounds of its own, on the Mall of Rawal Pindi, where tennis is played every afternoon, and dinner-parties and dances are given every Saturday evening. The 4th Dragoon Guards, the King's Own Scottish Borderers, and the Gordon Highlanders, each gave Regimental dinners to their friends this winter, followed by dances which we greatly enjoyed. In this club, too, the K.O.S.B. string-band plays every week upon Tuesday afternoon. So there we meet quite a number of kindred spirits and enjoy an hour of heavenly music together.

Every one is so good to Jack, especially the young things in the Regiments who come in batches to lunch or tea, when he is almost as good as a puppy! To see them together you would think them all of a piece.

Was it best, do you think, to be young? Lovely, no doubt, to remember, but don't you think we forget the impossible hopes, the blind disappointments, the days that had no to-morrow? Every age has after all its own advantages, its own particular joys. The horizon grows wider as we mount to the top of the hill. It may be that there comes a time, sooner or later, for all women, when they must bury something that is very elemental in their nature, and that they share with all created femininities. Nature planted it there, and they have to read the burial service over it. But from that grave there rises a disembodied spirit, that can enjoy something much better than ever it knew before, for it is reborn a Mother.

Speaking for myself, I certainly see Jack more or less, as he may be some day, in every young creature I meet, and I think they see their Mother in me, for we have actually been privileged to sit by one or two of our laddies in bed after a long spell of fever. What impresses me most perhaps, in our talks about everyday life, is the tyranny of Public School 'form.' It is not more characteristic of soldiers than of civilians or any typical Englishman. 'The trail of the serpent is over them all,' and they go through their short spells of life with their tall hats as the armorial shield of 'good form' held carefully over their hearts.

An Indian said to me once, 'If the Sahibs would only talk to us about themselves. We are a sentimental people. We could be so easily influenced, if they would only tell us what they think and feel, and let us understand their ideal.' 'That they will never do,' I assured him. 'You may guess what they think by what you see them do. They will work for you and die for you, and if you were to cut them up, you would certainly find India written on their hearts. But they won't talk about it, and if they were more emotional and did, they would have different natures and lose something by the exchange.'

One sees the same thing in the army. They would die for their country or Regiment and long for a chance to prove it, but it is not 'good form' to say so, or to talk apparently about anything when they are together except polo, polo ponies, dogs and sport. They must all be of the same pattern, and woe betide them if they have a hobby of their own, outside of the regimental routine. It must be hidden in a napkin that is never produced at Mess!

I am certain the result must be very monotonous, and the 'leave-out' days, when they dine elsewhere, a distinct relief. The young ones say so, the older equivocate, if one other soldier is present! As for talking about their own lives to each other, not while the tall hat has a bit of brim left to hold on to. A batch of youngsters came to lunch one day, for example, bringing a black-bordered letter of regret and explanation from one of their number. 'Was he really in trouble?' one of them said with surprise. 'They thought he had only been sulking in his hill-tent.'

Such are the functions of a 'tall hat,' and yet I sometimes wonder if it is not just this traditional 'form' and its code, the only certainty that a boy carries away with him from his years at a public school, which will land him successfully at the North Pole or help him to rule the inhabitants of the Equator.

I don't think the tall hat is quite of the same pattern or always held in the same place on our side of the Border, although it may 'arrive' with its owner at the Pole and Equator too. Perhaps it is the slight variability in its size or position which has earned us the adjective 'quaint,' and a tendency to believe that our young men of fashion must wear tartan, and play the bagpipes at public dinners, for who knows what may not happen when people are 'a little *different*, don't you know?'

Like the proverbial woman letter-writer, I have kept my very best bit of news for my postscript. Who do you think commands the Northern Army, with his headquarters at Rawal Pindi? No one less than Sir William Lockhart, the only one of his beloved family I never until now met, although one used to gaze at his photograph, as a schoolgirl, when A. and I paid our first visit alone to Milton Lockhart.

Everybody has some memory, I suppose, which they cherish as long as they live, just as dear Grannie Macleod used to talk on her death-bed about her beloved Lady For-bes, as she called her, Sir Walter Scott's love, and that dear Lady's long-ago visit to Aros and all that she was to her, when she went to her 'finishing' school in Edinburgh. 'I forget everything now' she would say. 'But there is one person you never forget.' 'And who is that, darling?' 'Lady For-bes.' 'Have I forgotten, can I ever forget her?' and then all the old stories were told again, with the old undying devotion.

I think that I too may babble about our visits to Milton Lockhart and Mauldslie, in my old age. I babble about them now to Sir William, who has all the family charm, the humour, reserve, the half-veiled kindliness, with the same power of touching the imagination, and of comprehending all the strange elements, the pathos, the weakness and strength, that go to make up human character and run through the web of life.

He is adored by soldiers, and well he may be, the hero of so many successful campaigns. But it is not of these we speak, when I have the good luck to sit next him at dinners, but of people we both knew 'before the flood,' whom nobody else, I daresay, in India knew, except Lady Lockhart—and whom not many others in Scotland may possibly remember, but whom I, with my 'resurrectionist memory,' love to dig out of their graves.

DEAREST M.,—Miss M., Jack's new governess, has
been one of the household quite long enough
now to inspire us with the peaceful and certain
conviction that she is a treasure. Her personality,
as well as her ways and habits, create such a sense
of security. She is short, with a dear, homely
face, kindly little grey eyes, which beam on you
through spectacles, dark hair tightly drawn back
from her benevolent forehead, a tiny nose, a sweet
little mouth, and a spare figure, which is generally
clothed in frugal alpaca. She is well educated,
speaks with great par-tic-u-larity, and continues
her studies of an evening in large volumes which
deal with history, geography and other subjects.

She knows India, as she was for eight years the
governess and devoted friend of a well-known
missionary household, and has already arranged
to teach in a Sunday School here, contributing a
' natural second' to any hymns that are sung in
Church, a talent which one almost anticipated.

Patient, unselfish, full of common-sense, and not

above her business in any way, she has volunteered to darn the household linen, to arrange the flowers, and to make cream cheeses! She is devoted to children, has just the temperament and patient wisdom they need, and often quotes her mother's advice, 'Always remember that a child's brain is like a bottle with a thin neck, and don't attempt to pour too much into it at once.'

Jack is devoted to her. I heard her saying to him last night, 'Now, darling, you have been very good to-day and so you have been happy. You cannot expect to be happy, you know, if you are not worthy,'—Jack open-eyed and meditative.

Dear Miss M. ! I have been trying to introduce her to one or two neighbours of the kind she will find most congenial, which I hope may result in little engagements, as the strain of being with a child needs an alternative, which I do think mothers should sometimes remember. For un-broken days of unadulterated Jackies can some-times prove just too much joy for even *their* fond hearts and nerves.

Miss M. says 'Jack is all in extremes. He is the most loving, the most artless, and the most self-willed child I ever knew !' He is in the angel mood at present. His dog, Jack, is his infatuation. He generally pays me a visit in the morning, when I am having tea, and yesterday was dissolved in tears. 'What *is* the matter, Jack?' I asked him. 'I'm crying because Jack can't come to heaven. I don't want to go to heaven, Mother, if Jack isn't there.' 'Perhaps he may be, we don't know.' 'But dogs and beasts haven't got souls.' 'But then Jack, you see, is such a very good dog. He is always so obedient. You had better take care. It may be you who aren't there.' 'I want him to be there in the form of a little dog, and I as a little boy. I don't want to be an angel, Mother.' 'Why not?' 'Because I'd have to play a harp, and then I couldn't pat Jack. Mother.' 'Yes?' 'Mightn't another mother be there who might think I was *her* little boy?' 'Oh no, Jack, I am sure I would know, and then we could be together.'

This morning his greeting was in a whisper, 'I love Miss M. better than you now.' 'Do you, darling?' I said without a tremor. 'Yes, she gives me medicine and holds my nose.' 'Oh,' cheerfully, 'I could do that for you some day too.' 'She tells me more stories than you do' (I should rather think she does, as she happens to read herself hoarse every day). 'Does she, pet? How many days is it since you loved her most?' 'I don't, Mother, I don't.'

He does all the same, but I am so glad he is happy, I could not be really jealous.

MURREE, 1896.

DEAREST M.,—How I wish you could borrow the
carpet of the Arabian Nights, even just for one
evening, to look in on us all and put a crown to
our happiness. Jim is reading the newspapers
beside a log-fire, Jack on the floor at Miss P.'s
feet, her slave like all the young generation, and
A. is writing her daily bulletin to Calcutta. I
know they have both written to you themselves,
to tell you about their respective journeys by sea
or land. Already it seems as if we had never
been parted.

It has been a week of arrivals, for hardly had
the house settled down after these two exciting
events, when a telegram came yesterday from
Colonel and Mrs H., who are making the grand
tour of India, asking if we could take them in
for a night on their way to Kashmir, as all the
hotels in Murree were full.

I had just made the grand tour of their rooms,
to see that everything was in its right place,
when Mrs H. arrived looking wan, her maid look-

ing wanner, followed by Colonel H. escorting the
luggage—'faint but pursuing.'

Mrs H. longed for a cup of tea, her husband
for a chop, and both for oblivion. They revived
after dinner and amused us all by their tirade on
the 'smart phase' at home, the Colonel vowing
it had ruined society, and been the death of all
old-fashioned courtesy, and that its presence in a
room affected him as a cat affects others! They
had been shadowed by it, even on board the P.
and O., as a girl they had been asked to look
after was under its spell, ignored their existence,
and became engaged to a penniless subaltern
before they reached Suez, on the strength, they
supposed, of a twin passion for *ties!*

They went on to Kashmir this morning, and
we have resumed the even tenor of our ways,
and are all three reading Flint's 'Philosophy of
History.' With that as a *pièce de résistance*,
combined with the gossip about nations supplied
by the daily papers, and the gossip about friends
supplied by ourselves, the days slip happily past.
I am afraid we prefer the monotony of monotony
to the monotony of so-called excitements, a sign,
I suppose, of 'age and sad experience hand in
hand.' It requires a little imagination to idealise
some things, a little more to realise them, and
she who has dreamt in her youth of the romance

of a moonlight picnic, realises too well by her thirties how cold the moonlight may be and how long a *tête-à-tête* under its beams, with perhaps a comparative stranger, ever to dream of a moonlight picnic again except as a possible nightmare!

I hear a voice in the hall, at this moment, asking if the Memsahibs and the Miss Sahib are at home, the voice of a faithful friend Major H., who promised to look in this evening to show us his sketch - book, and let us hear some of the topical songs which are to be sung in an operetta he is bringing out.

'Jack the dog' is at once on the *qui vive* for a romp, and 'Jack the boy' for some more stories about Major H.'s 'twins' and their latest delinquencies.

So farewell to mail letters and 'theories.' There are so many delightful and loveable people here, I foresee we shall soon be immersed in the Maelstrom, and even involved in Gymkhanas!

DEAR G.,—Another nice week has passed and
Miss M. continues to be a comfort and joy. She
is such a quaint survival of an old-fashioned
generation, whom one associates with the peaceful ticking of an eight-day clock, a kettle singing
on the hob, Pussy purring on her cushion, and
a cheerful acceptance on the part of John's wife
that 'John always likes to nod in his arm-chair,
poor man, after his six o'clock dinner, which
gives his wife a chance to get on with her
stocking!'

Miss M.'s reasons for leaving England were
the restlessness of the age. She felt so agitated
by all the new ideas she heard in her corner of
Norfolk even about grammar. 'In her young
days she was taught to say "spoonsful": now
every one said "spoonfuls," and so on and so on.
She could never become accustomed to it.'

She divides her days into regular portions,
devoted to special occupations, darning, knitting
vests for Jack, baby's bootiekins and such like

150

demurities. Then a little sketching, a little
scanning of the newspapers, a little reading of
Chambers's Educator, and a devout perusal of
her Bible.

She tells Jack Bible stories every day, which
he applies in his own childish fashion. ' Do the
Angels kiss one another, Miss M. ? ' 'Perhaps
they do, darling—why do you wish to know ? '
' Because I'd like to give them a kiss, too, when
I see them. May I show them my doll ? Perhaps they will let me take it to them, if I hide
it under my arm.'

His doll, which he calls Queen Victoria, consists of a head, with a hat on it, which he decks
with every imaginable scrap of tawdriness, including the flowers he brings back from his daily
walk. It has five or six long knotted streamers
of yellow cotton to represent limbs and body.

Miss M. teaches him history and geography
with infinite patience, and his mental arithmetic
in penny and farthing edition is her special ex-
hibit. She vows that monotony suits her, but
I tell her she shan't have too much of that. I
know one is too apt to treat every goose as a
swan, but I really think that this time we have
secured some one who is a bit of an old-fashioned
angel, and I think too we almost deserve comforting after our previous disappointments.

Alas! N. S. left us last week, for which we need comforting too. From the moment I met her at the railway station, when she told me she had lost her travelling ayah, whom she had engaged to be her comfort and stay but who had wandered off into space at some junction, where she had relied on the ayah shadowing her, we seem to have laughed intermittently, 'comme on rit à vingt ans.' Intermittently — for we have had our quiet hours too, in our arm-chairs by the fire, when we have read and talked and remembered, gathering the threads together which have united our lives.

N. has enjoyed everybody and everything, including a K.O.S.B. sergeants' dance, where we were initiated into the mysteries of the 'De Alberts' and other portentous solemnities, and she has naturally been greatly appreciated, not only by our own particular *côterie*, but by all who have met her. It is delightful to find we are at one in our absorbing interest in India; in our sense of its beauty, its unfathomable mysteries, its gigantic problems and far-off horizons.

DEAR A.,—What an impossible hope! You wish
me to tell you about the religious life of the
people? You little know how much I long myself to be within the veil, and fathom the mystery
that lies behind it, and how incompetent I am
to lift it for you.

Shall I ever reach the point of being able to
flatter myself that I can even imagine what any
single Hindu feels upon the most indifferent subject, far less guess what the preponderating idea
is in that curiously elastic mind of his, which
can apparently accept two contradictory statements at once as equally credible, to the point
of giving you, for instance, the scientific explanation of the eclipse of the sun with the gentle
addendum, 'at the same time a demon is eating
it up'?

The knowledge I seek escapes me, like the will
o' the wisp vanishing into mist. Some philosopher comes to our tent at night, and tells us
how he suppresses his breath till his thoughts

153

are centred on God alone. I cannot *feel* what
he means, and dare not announce my remoteness.
Some villagers come to our camp and act by the
light of bonfires and torches, with crowds of onlookers weighing down the branches of trees. I
see what they think of their neighbour's foibles,
which is always something, and how we appear
to them, which is something more. Of themselves
I have not a glimpse. I wander through their
villages, visit them in their homes, play with
their children. We invite ourselves to their
village fairs, sit in their temple courtyards, listen
to their hymns. The veil which falls between
them and us is not for a moment lifted.

With franker manners, their reticence is deeper
than ours, and I can well believe what a Hindu
friend told us, that it would never occur to him
to share his thoughts with his brother. That
seems to me, however, rather lonely and sad, and
makes me wonder if it is not on the whole better
for poor transitory mortals to give themselves
away, than never to give themselves at all. We
are but birds of passage after all. Why not sing
our little song while we can, to cheer the passer-
by, even if it is not a very remarkable twitter?

I confess that the absence of the song sometimes makes one feel such a stranger in a strange
land, that I have known what it was to be grateful

to poor lonely lepers for the genuine joy they displayed at the sweetmeats we thought they might like, and gave them on Easter Sunday. Perhaps we felt outcast together.

Baulked in my endeavours to make the people tell me 'more more, about themselves,' I have fallen back on their literature, and read some of the Vedas, Brahmanas and Upanishads, the Laws of Manu, as well as bits of their great Epics, the Ramayana and Maha Bharata, which are practically the Bibles of the people, recited by their bards and acted at their village fairs and festivals.

The mere sight of the Vedas and Upanishads held me spellbound. Only to handle them seemed to bring one in touch with the people who thought them three thousand years ago, just as one used to look with awe at Kish the Jew, as a living link with his ancestor Saul!

To read them was a mixed pleasure. The Rig Veda consists of hymns largely in praise of different gods. The Yajur and Sama Vedas borrow from it freely, for their own sacrificial and ritual purposes, while the Atharva Veda might be called a Witches' Manual. About the Upanishads and their philosophies I shall try to tell you later. The Vedas are what I read first.

Sometimes the hymns in the Rig Veda are beautiful, especially those addressed to Varuna, the

encompassing heavens; sometimes they are ob-
scure, often they are simply baffling. There is
a monotony in the attributes of the gods which
is very confusing. You find one god called the
only god, till you pass on to the next hymn and
find another is the only god too. Each in turn
is praised as absolute. Five different gods stand
for the sky, and the same story is fathered on
several deities. Then there are hymns to Mitra
and Varuna, who is next called Mitra Varuna, and
finally, as if with an effort to correct the mistake,
'two Mitras' and 'two Varunas.' I think I must
have transmigrated from a Rishi, it is so like me
in my worst-of-memory days! Some gentle com-
mentator tells you 'these are the products of
simple men.' So comforting to know that is
what it is called: I should have stumbled on
the conclusion that in this case it was the result
of a prevailing endeavour to wed Polytheism to
Monotheism, with Pantheism holding both in its
embrace. It is in fact very difficult to understand what is meant by writers who contradict
one another and themselves.

Wiertz of all artists could have given us the
Pantheon on his large canvas, Indra in the centre
seen through mist, a thunderbolt as his weapon,
the rainbow as his bow, quaffing Soma while the
Apsaras dance before him, defying the anger of

his wives. Rudra the Howler and the three sixty stormy Maruts, whirling their axes, and cracking their whips in clouds ablaze with lightning; Ushas the beauteous Dawn fleeing from Surya the Sun, and vanishing as he seeks to embrace her; Vishnu (the sun again) striding through the firmament in three steps. Then the manifold Deities in their coats of mail and armed to the hilt, traversing the heavens in their chariots drawn by horses or goats, giving battle to the Rakhshas demons whom the three-headed Agni, enkindled by flame, seizes with his teeth. Don't you think that the brush that could give us Napoleon in Hell and the sensations of a decapitated head, might have done justice to such weird conceptions?

A few bold strokes would be needed to bring in the worshippers on earth; the donors of the sacrifices, the crowds of lookers-on, with Brahmins as sacrificers, Brahmins as chorus, Brahmins as earthly deities. All the necessary stage properties in the foreground of the picture, the posts to which the sacrificed goats, oxen, horses, sheep, and human beings are tied; axes, knives, a tub, a butcher; pots for the meat, for the melted butter, for the soma wine, for all the offerings in short which are to reach the gods, as parcels are delivered by our Indian Value Payable post, with the request that their value may be returned by the receiver.

And everywhere demons, godlets and personified magical powers in the rivers, trees, mountains : in the sacrificial post, the drum, the metres, the ritual, the oblation compelling the gods.

But to give a pervading note to this inharmonious medley, there must be above, and as if enfolding it all, Varuna the greatest of the Vedic gods, he who alone amongst them all is the upholder of physical and moral order, he who beholds all the secret things that have been, or shall be done, who witnesses man's truth or falsehood, whose wrath is raised by sin, who yet is gracious to the penitent. He spares the suppliant who daily transgresses his law, and is gracious to those who have broken his commandments. There is no hymn to Varuna in which the prayer for forgiveness does not occur, as in the hymns to the other deities the prayer for worldly goods. He and no other must preside over a picture filled with much that he alone can comprehend, and with which he alone can deal.

So much for my puzzled, disappointed, inadequate perusal of the time-honoured venerable Vedas. I read them because I had hoped and longed to be able to understand the thoughts and minds of their dead writers, and through them perhaps the thoughts of their living readers. Perhaps you may ask, however, if there could be any connection between the thoughts and acts of those people, who lived three thousand years ago, and their descendants of to-day?

Go to Benares if you want an answer, and see the men who have crawled slowly with prostrate bodies over every inch of hundreds of miles to reach it. See them lying on their face in the mud of a dark temple before a cow, and worshipping in the monkeys' temple, or in the street where sacred bulls are reverenced, as they move from one grain-shop to another, if you wish to know something of their mixed deities. Stand on the steps of the sacred Ganges lined by Rajas' palaces, and by a thousand temples filled with the multifarious images of the gods of their Pantheon. Watch the enormous Brahmins under umbrellas, making the same idol-images out of mud, breathing on them, mating them, and selling them to crowds. Look, if you can, at the poor corpses lying in the holy river, till their fires are ready, the living corpses seated near them; Yogis with their eyes fixed on the tip of their nose, reiterating 'Om'; Fakirs with mad drugged eyes, matted locks and ash-stained bodies, calling out 'Ram' without a moment's intermission.

See the crowds who stand up to their waists in the river, holding up its sacred waters in brass bowls as offerings to the sun, or dipping their poor sick children in its bosom, and ask if the people's thoughts have changed throughout long ages.

If human sacrifices have ceased to be offered, it is because the laws of the British Government have dubbed them murder. Till then women—mothers — gave their first-born babies to the Ganges, though why they did not rather choose to be damned for ever, I cannot imagine.

I proposed you should go to Benares, but on second thoughts I believe you had better not, if you value sleep, for I lost mine.

Yet Varuna, the all-encompassing sky, still looks down on Benares and hears its faltering prayers, ' He knows, He knows,' and remembers that we are dust.

These strange conceptions, however inconsistent, contradictory and impossible they may be, are what the people have always heard, what they associate with every object they see, every bit of work they do, every habit of their daily life. They are in their blood. No outside influence ever reached them. If the polytheism of the Roman Empire had been arrested and never known change, what might our own case have been now ?

Even as it is, one feels faint traces of the primeval Aryan blood in one's veins, and a strange fascination in some of the odds and ends of philosophic booklets which one comes across. They are

such an extraordinary medley of profound speculation and sudden collapses into impossibilities,
that I could imagine the writer as a metaphysical
genius, bound body and brain like a Siamese twin
to a brother who had never grown up, and whose
mental development had been arrested by constant attacks of fever. When his temperature is
high, it affects the genius, who begins to wander
too, and to babble about metres that have magical
powers, and notes of music that evolve spirits,
and what not.

I know the mood myself, without the compen-
sating genius, when my astral twin perhaps has
lapses, and I fall to apostrophising my midnight
pillow as a *confidante*, who knows everything and
has comforted me through life; bless the dying
embers of the fire for transforming weariness into
peace; feel my helplessness when hooks elect to
be malign and attach themselves to everywhere;
and the horrors of the periods when Time shrinks
and when half an hour becomes ten minutes. The
only difference is that I would hesitate to embody
these aberrations in my creed.

Yet what a monument the deepest Hindu philosophies are of the gropings of the human mind and
spirit after God, and of its longing to pierce the
darkness which veiled His presence! The old
Hindu sages were amongst the earliest philosophers

in the world's history and, with all their contradictions and obscurities, had the power to stamp
their impress on the ages. Through Pythagoras,
the later Greek Philosophers, and the gnostics of
the Middle Ages, they have influenced the development of European thought until the present day.
Their pessimism was the greatest consolation
Schopenhauer knew upon his death-bed. It is to
them our Theosophic Societies owe their birth.

How difficult it is, however, to disentangle the
true from the false, and knowledge from assump-
tion in their metaphysical reasoning, and to avoid
getting lost in its mazes!

If you wish to study their philosophies for yourself in their most pleasing presentment, you ought
to get one of the editions of the Bhagavadgita,
translated by English admirers. It was written
about 200 A.D., embedded in the national epic, the
Mahabharata, and is considered the gem of Indian
literature.

The form of the poem is the dialogue favoured
by the old Upanishads. The poem itself is char-
acteristically Hindu in the elastic welcome it gives
to the varied co-existing beliefs of the people. The
central figure is Krishna who, immoral on earth,
reappears in these pages as a Divine embodiment
of all the virtues, and an incarnation of Vishnu, the
favourite god of the Hindus. As the discussion

with the epic hero Arjuna advances, he becomes the spirit of Pantheism, pervading mind, matter and the All. He further discourses in the Brahminical vein on Caste and its duties, on the Sankhya and Vedanta philosophies, and the Yogi system, and it is all so subtle and so full of an indefinite grace, that you are no more disturbed by the varied transformations and ideas than you would be by a delicate transposition in an overture from one key to another.

One is also grateful to the poet for not dwelling too much on the lonely Self and the wandering soul, for when one hears too much about either, it only makes one miserable and long to comfort them both, and assure them they will wake from their dream to find that it too was Maya.

Perhaps you feel by this time like the old woman who said 'She had read the *notes* in the " Pilgrim's Progress," and, please God, she would read the text soon.' Let me then give you a very abridged résumé of the Vedanta Philosophy, the creed of educated India. It will be more like the summary placed at the heads of chapters in old-fashioned books than anything else. Still it will help you to realise for yourself its ' inwardness.'

The creed is epitomised in three words of an old Upanishad, which are translated as 'One only without a second,' and for mortals ' Thou art That.'

That One is the Universal Spirit, or as He is also named, ' Brahma,' ' The Self.'

He is the one Eternal Essence, who is Being, yet only conscious of Being : Thought, with no object of thought : Bliss, with naught in which to rejoice : true Being, and at the same time true Nothing.

The world on the other hand is Self, and yet not Self : Thought, yet Ignorance ; Verity, yet Error. It is in short Mayà, Illusion. And how did this Illusion arise ? By the sport of Brahma the great Magician, who by his magic evolved an illusive wraith of himself, which we in our ignorance call the Universe.

Then the great Magician, the Universal Spirit, wandered into his Illusion, and so we have the Universal Soul in matter and in man. The cosmic entity is unreal, as opposed to Reality, yet it is Real, for the light of the Self falls on it, and the Cosmos is the shadow cast by that light.

Only by wandering back through Illusion to Reality, through Ignorance to Knowledge, through Error to Verity, can the soul return to Being, and at last become Nothing.

This wandering is called Samsara or Transmigration. The soul, still a part of the Self, wanders from birth to birth in three subtle sheaths. On the highest of these sheaths is stamped the imprint of all the thoughts and actions perpetrated in the body which the soul inhabits. Upon the merit or demerit attached to these imprints (Karma) depend the punishments or rewards apportioned to the soul in its next embodiment, whether that be in a plant, a mineral, an animal or a human body. Hence the apparent inequality of fortune, which is really the just portion of the new embodied soul.

If you asked any single Hindu or Indian the first question of our 'Shorter Catechism,' 'What is man's chief end?' from one and all you would have the same answer, the sigh from the heart of India, 'Mukti,' *i.e.*, deliverance from the 84 lakhs of births that lie before him. How can he escape from them? Action only multiplies existences, and existence is suffering. It is Desire which precedes all Action: so Desire must die. Moreover, since life is but Illusion, why desire it? True knowledge lies in recognizing its undesirability, in abstaining from action, from liking and disliking, from loving or hating, from all sense of separate existence, and so, freed from Illusion, returning to Being and the Universal Self.

To be a Yogi is the Way. Ascetics by paralysing their faculties come to cease to be. There is Kriya Yoga, to be sure, the Rule of Action. A man should fulfil the duties of his Caste. But who would lightly engage to fulfil the first preliminary

Rule, and retain a mind empty of all desire, while his body acts; to do, yet remain detached from the deed, detached from results, and thus detached from his fateful Karma?

The Raja Yoga is the better Way, the Kingly Rule. With the thought fixed upon some physical point, to train it to steadfastness, the Yogi must keep 'an even tenor of conceptions in a state of concentration' till he entirely loses self-identity and consciousness. To be in a cataleptic trance is the physical and mental state that is cited, as the nearest approach to the union hoped for with the Universal Self, when the endless fear of endless lives will end in absorption in the Self, and the reunited soul be alone with It in Its solitude.

Have I understood these mystical writings? I know not. I only know that I have tried, that I share their sadness, and from my heart feel for the millions who are mentally bound to their terrible Wheel of Life.

Even the dear Buddha, with his beautiful soul and his beautiful ethics, and his vision of the brotherhood of man, believed in Karma and Samsara, and the soul's necessity to wander through a weary round of 136 hells and multiplied existences, without the hope of God or Immortality at the end. Into Nirvana and extinction the purified soul at last evaporated and was 'blown out.'

Discarding the Universal Self, and disregarding consistency, he, as well as the Vedanta philosophers, held on to subsidiary gods, who had to take their turn with their neighbours and transmigrate like the rest. And the Hindu Brahmins held on to their *clientèle* and received their fees, and kept a vigilant eye on the prison doors of Caste.

I have written till midnight. The stars are all out, and the Southern Cross is shining somewhere down on the earth from the all-encompassing sky, and I seem to hear a voice, that was ever gentle as the spirit of Peace, saying to the tired world, ' Come unto Me, and I will give you rest.'

DEAREST M.,—The last Jirga has come in and the Tirah campaign is ended! Heaven grant we may never be so near the seat of war and its horrors again. It is one thing to read about battles in newspapers, translated into the sporting phraseology of the war correspondent, quite another to be at the base of operations.

It seems more like eight years than eight months since we used to watch on our evening drives the long trains pass filled with soldiers, such young things some of them were, singing with their legs dangling out of the window and their coats thrown off in the sultry heat.

Then good-bye to old friends, and an empty cantonment, save for the presence of brave wives left to search the newspapers every morning to follow the fate of the war, and visit the Club every evening to read the last telegrams.

One day some poor stricken father arrives to ask Jim to secure him a tonga and relay of ponies, to take him without any delay to a half-way bungalow where his boy is certainly dying. There were creatures straggling back from camp hospitals on the convalescent list—one of them half silly from sunstroke, the other minus an arm. So many have been prostrated by fever, Sir William Lockhart amongst them, but riding it off.

When the war was practically over, and the troops encamped in the Bara Valley, non-combatants joined us in camp upon ten days' leave. Soldiers never tell one such grisly tales as they did, murdering sleep.

The Military Hospitals in Rawal Pindi were filled with the wounded, who liked to see a new face, so the nurses said, when they had reached the tedium of convalescence. 'We were fighting not men, but mountains,' a man in the Hampshires put it; 'up the sides of them we went, seeing nothing but rocks and stones, to be rolled over by the bullets of the enemy we never even caught sight of. It wasn't war as we had known it before.'

But I am not going to tell *you* tales. The campaign is ended, and I have accepted an invitation from A. to stay for a month in Calcutta to try to return to normal conditions. E. is there and R. H. B., but I am afraid it will be quite impossible to wait for the wedding, as I ought to return, in less than a month, to 'flit' the household to Murree.

Darling M.,—We came into camp for a draught of solitude, and some spirit of mischief bestowed on us coughs and colds, followed by a note from a poor little person who lives in an abode of perennial heat, saying she would like to show me her little sister before she returned to school '*because* she has a full-mooned face.'

Poor things, of course we are sorry for them and their uneventful life, and tried to make it an exciting visit, teaching them golf, and Miss M., Jack and I playing Old Maid, Beggar my Neighbour, and Grab with them at all kinds of un-seasonable hours. Still I cannot say I hailed their desire to show me another brother, *because* he is six foot three, with anything like flattering delirium, as the family is a large one, and the 'becauses' threatening!

When they left the spirit of mischief took pos-session of Jack. The things that boy has been doing all day! ending up by nearly hugging Miss M. into nothing, while she called him the

Octopus, and every evangelical bad name, between spasms of noiseless laughter.

God cannot give us mirrors, but He gives us children in whom we can see our own faults, and Jack did not inherit his self-will from his father! And how can the self-will be fought in a country where every Indian obeys the whims of the Chota Sahib, and even the tonga-driver resigns the reins of a pair of boisterous horses into his childish hands? He has had a boy of his own age, the son of a delightful couple we know, to work along with him in the schoolroom all summer, and they have had one or two excellent fights. But it is well for his sake we are going home next spring, for India can never be the home of our children, sad though that fiat be.

I have come to the conclusion that camp would suit you most beautifully, not life in tents, perhaps, but in nice rest-houses such as we are in at present. To arrive to find all your pet things in their pet places, a cosy fire blazing in the grate, to have a silent ayah, like a slave of the camp, to do all your behests, and then to know that when, after breakfast, you have issued your brief orders, all the day lies before you in which to possess your soul in peace; this surely would spell joy to you too.

Do you know, I think that Celts are so made

that unless they dawdle sometimes, they die. I have been so terribly systematic lately that life was nearly robbed of all joy : but now we can have a spell of dear, delightful, mild bohemianism and return to old Shahpur days.

I am glad that our good Miss M. appreciates it as much as we do. At each new bungalow she says, 'How nice this is; I am sure we shall be very comfortable here,' and sets to work herself to arrange her own specialities, a happy contrast to the muttered asides of the thrawn A. 'Eh me! mair o' this tinker's life again!' For Miss M., as for us, 'neither time nor custom can ever stale its infinite variety.'

When Jim's work is over in the evening we set off for what Jack and I call 'an adventure.' His first was to discover a magnificent toy-watch in an Indian bazaar, displayed amongst the Indian bracelets, nose-rings and ear-rings, with which one of the stalls was covered. The hours of the watch were numbered. The mainspring was broken before bedtime. Jack thought it might be restored if left quiet all night. Next morning found it no better! by noon it was worse, for the knob came off. He bit the glass, but assured us most solemnly that he had not swallowed the pieces. The chain and pendant have vanished, to be followed by the case in due time. For once dear Miss M. has failed to discover in these experiments any symptoms of genius.

We drove to a Buddhist tope to-day, and I bought from a peasant a Greek woman's head, probably sculptured by some follower of Alexander the Great, as he was once in this neighbourhood.

On our return to the bungalow we found some guizars had come from a neighbouring village, dressed up to represent different figures in Hindu mythology. The performance ended by clever representations of one or two of the familiar figures, who play a part in their life. There was the blind beggar who can see when he likes; the famine-stricken suppliant, transformed from a well-fed man into a skeleton; the thief who tips the policeman; the old woman who wishes to pay for her railway ticket in wool; and the village official, who swears he will enter the peasant's bare fields in his book as covered with crops, the shouting, indignant peasant, the outstretched hand of the threatening official closing on five rupees, with the change in his tone thereafter. All greeted with laughter and shouts from the audience of villagers, while Jack, in high feather, stotted up and down on his chair like a new india-rubber ball.

The bungalow in which we are now has a dark

grove of trees behind it, in which is a walled-in
enclosure, where the grave of Lalla Rookh stands
beneath weeping willows. Near it is a Sikh
temple, which we visited yesterday. It is built
on the steps of a tank, the home of gold - fish,
who expect to be fed with bread - crumbs. The
sacred book of the Sikhs, the 'Granth,' lay on a
dais in the little temple, and was covered with
gorgeous gold embroideries, while majestic figures,
like those pourtrayed in the Arabian Nights,
stood over the Granth, fanning it with long,
silvery, white - haired tails. In the foreground
men sat cross-legged, playing violins and singing
Sikh hymns.

While we were having a romp in the evening
with Jack after his tub, we heard, to our amusement, the familiar sounds of the bagpipes proceed
from the temple enclosure, the player, so Akbar
informed us, an Indian soldier at home on leave.
You can imagine how incongruous to the occasion
the 'Pibroch of Donald Dhu' sounded, followed
by 'Up wi' the bonnets o' Bonnie Dundee.'

Last week a venerable old man came to see
us, who had been Nicholson's orderly when he
marched from Peshawur to Delhi. He knew him
first as a child, when Nicholson was Deputy-
Commissioner of Rawal Pindi, and elected to live
amongst his people in a large mud - house, now

in ruins, and not a hundred yards from this bungalow.

It was interesting to hear some of our visitor's comments on his hero. 'Nowadays,' he said, 'rulers were feared without being loved. Then they were loved as well as feared. If Nicholson had one hand of iron, the other was filled with milk and honey. He never zigzagged : he must be obeyed, but he was kind to those whom he knew to be the friends of Government. If there was a funeral from their house he wrote to them in their grief : if there was a marriage, he sent a present to the young couple. His father had fought the Sikhs and had his village burnt down. Nicholson never forgot that, and showed him unfailing kindness.' This old man came to him as a boy, every day, to repeat his Persian lesson. If he made a mistake, Nicholson used to send him home with a message that the teacher would be flogged by Nicholson Sahib, if the pupil made such a mistake again !

He was his orderly in Delhi, and wept when he told us he had waited on him till he died. Nicholson's mother sent him some photographs of her son's portrait to be given to his Indian friends. He insisted on my accepting a copy, in which his hero looks more like a poet or a musician than a soldier.

You shall see it when we come home next year. That point is settled now.   Jim will return to India in six months, and I six months later, when Jack will be eight and will begin his school - life.   I remember your advice not to think of the separation but of meeting again, only the thought of the parting is not in one's brain but in one's blood.

One other point we have decided is that I shall go home every year for three months, to be with him in his summer holidays.   We have heard too much of the sad results of divided homes to accept such possibilities, if they can be avoided.   One mother told me her boy had ceased to write to her because he said 'he had forgotten what she was like.'   And a dear girl said that after dreaming for years of again seeing her mother, something snapped in her heart when her mother came to her school and did not know her, and that the sad fact was she had never loved her again.

Many parents feel as we do, and some of the mothers, to meet the expenses entailed, remain with their husbands in the plains during the hottest months of the year, instead of taking a house in the hills, and go home when the monsoon breaks.   Anything better than to be told by her child, as one mother was, that 'no one had ever looked at him as she was looking now for three years.' That would never be our laddie's fate I know, in any case, but yet I think you will endorse our decision to mitigate as far as we can the unnatural situation.

HYDERABAD, 1898.

DEAREST M.,—I know you will be glad to hear that I am with E., who is getting on capitally. Her kind and capable doctor is thoroughly satisfied with her progress.

The hour of arriving in a new place is not exactly the one you would choose for an illness. Nothing unpacked, the drawing-room empty and gaunt, its scanty furniture 'under the weather,' swollen or shrunk as the case may be, possibly even damp or mildewed; nothing beguiling to awaken the smallest desire to recover and make its further acquaintance.

I felt the moment had come when what she most needed was to be womaned. For not the very kindest of men is just like a woman, at least the best of them aren't. They cannot, for instance, unpack our best dresses for us, and hang them up in just the right way, or gossip about nothing till we forget we are drinking our beef-tea: or even always know when a well-directed and fulsome compliment might possibly work wonders. No,

178

we may employ a Frenchman, when we wish to secure the most perfect cook, a butler as best attendant, a tailor or Worth for our best-fitting dresses; but when we are ill, although we summon a doctor, I fancy we shall always cling to a woman as nurse.

E., looking so pretty in her white muslins and ribbons, is promoted to the drawing-room now, and watches her pictures and curtains being hung, her books put evenly into the bookcase and her china and other femininities ranged. R. reads aloud to us in the evening, Chamberlain's great speech on Tariff Reform last night, and then a chapter or two of Jane Austen's ' Emma,' a book we adore. In fact I have taken the vows of the marriage service over Emma, and promised to love, to cherish her, and to laugh at her well-meant mistakes till death do us part.

Speaking of books, I have sometimes wished lately that Dante's ' Inferno' could be brought up to date, with a special circle reserved for the inventors or perpetrators of shrill, intermittent noises. The canto would be written with zest by any one who had occupied my room, for the last three consecutive nights. Many disturbing elements have combined lately to make our nights hideous. A small group of Indian huts runs parallel to our garden wall. In one of these huts a poor man died, and during three long nights his dirge has been sung by shrill-voiced women, to the accompaniment of a vociferous tom-tom. Add to this that wild cats dash in succession through my bedroom door, left open to catch the tepid night air. They perch on the top of my wardrobe, from which I vainly attempt to decoy them, and there they caterwaul to the tom-tom with all the power of their lungs.

Neither the tom-tom, the dirge, nor the cats' concert is half so perturbing, however, as the conversational powers of two little brown women, who are my punkah-pullers. There are pauses in the dirge, the beat of the tom-tom, the wails of the cat, which perhaps only accentuate the recommencement, but they are better than the punkah-pullers' never-flagging eloquence.

One night I tried to explain to them that I could dispense with their services, and that they might return to their homes. Alas! they only retired to the further end of the garden, where they wakened their babies, and continued their confidences.

And this while mosquitoes hummed round one's head! How I longed for my old friend in Rawal Pindi, who is as noiseless as night, except when he invokes his God Hari's protection against demons invading his throat when he yawns.

There are crowds of these little brownies who would figure effectively in some of our modern processions. They are the porters, gardeners, grooms, and punkah-pullers of Hyderabad, a few even forming a company of Amazons in a Hyderabad Rajah's regiment, and some others employed by him as one of his military bands. What a feature they would be in Trafalgar Square on a suffragettes' field-day, with 'Vote for the Amazons' inscribed on their banners!

E. is going to have her first drive to-morrow, in one of the commodious carriages in which I have already enjoyed seeing some of the sights of this unique place, one of the most advanced Native States of India. It is an understudy of our British administration, in its system of education and civil and criminal administration, although as old D. used to say, 'there's nae man pairfect; I'm no pairfect mysel',' and you need only see the collection of instruments of torture and other poisonous weapons, which Mr H. the police inspector has captured from dacoits, to realise that much still remains, to bring some of us just into line with the millennium.

Hyderabad is much appreciated by one of the unfortunate classes of the community. It is the Earthly Paradise of Eurasians. Here they have not the submerged look they too often have

elsewhere. You realise this with the first sight
you have of them, as you crawl past their
bungalows, when entering Hyderabad in the little
carriages of the State railway. There they
are, stretched on their long cane-chairs, taking the
evening air as exercise, the menkind in nonde-
script garments, the ladies in dressing-gowns, their
lively laughter and continuous chatter speaking of
minds at ease. You see them, too, dressed in their
best bright-coloured dresses, and fly-away hats and
feathers, overloading their dog-carts and forming
a part of the long procession, which drives through
the Hyde Park of Hyderabad in the cool of the
evening—a sight that might be called 'Isis un-
veiled.' For the carriages are filled with Hindu,
Mahomedan, and Parsi ladies enjoying themselves
en plein air with their husbands and children,
some friend perhaps riding beside them, passing
the time o' day.

The Eurasian contingent fill their own particular
Church—where they have a Eurasian pastor, such
a good little man—and a choir composed of Eurasian ladies, dressed in white surplices with under-
graduates' trenchers crowning their heads. I like
to see them all looking so happy, and so contented
and pleased with themselves.

We see a good deal of our Aryan brother here,
both in his own well-appointed bungalow and at

various functions, for a social fusion of the two races exists in Hyderabad which possibly anticipates a century elsewhere, the military element predominating, as this is one of our largest cantonments in India, and the Nizam and many of his nobles have also their independent troops.

At a large luncheon party given the other day by the Prime Minister to the Station, I sat between my host and an Indian General, both very pleasant companions. The two races meet also at balls. The Nizam deports some of his most favoured protégés annually, to be educated at English Universities, and I am told that those who have added a London season to their educational advantages are distinctly *précieux* in the selection of their Hyderabad partners, with memories of the graciousness of London Ladyships still haunting their imagination. A story is current, although I cannot vouch for its truth, of a lady asking her host at his cosmopolitan banquet what he would do, if he was ordered by the Sultan of Turkey to join in a *jehad*—a religious war. 'Cut off your head' was his ready but startling reply, a warning to her, let us hope, not to lay snares for an alien sense of humour.

I made the acquaintance of one of those fortunate protégés of the Nizam on a night which I shall never forget. It was the evening upon which the great annual festival takes place, called the Lungar, when the horse-shoe of Mahomed's favourite horse is worshipped! At ten o'clock on that evening R. and I drove in the State carriage, with an escort of mounted cavalry, to the Nizam's empty marble palace, which stands in the busiest part of the town.

There from a marble balcony we looked down on one of the strangest scenes I have ever witnessed. But, before I tell you about it, I must give you the benefit of a trivial little episode which occurred in our balcony. We had as companions in this balcony three of the Nizam's A.D.C.'s, very pleasant-looking young men, dressed in evening suits, which were a credit to their London tailors, and innocent of turbans. They had the excellent manners of their countrymen, and did all that was possible to add to our comfort and *bien aise*.

Personally, I confess to having a predilection for old-fashioned manners everywhere, especially when they are the outward expression of a genuine *politesse de cœur*. If the traditional manners of any man's race are perfect, why should they ever be dropped, or exchanged for the base imitation of those which belong to any one else? These opinions were not, however, I regret to say, shared by another of the Nizam's protégés, who sat in the front of the balcony beside me. He was a barrister, I believe, dressed like the A.D.C.'s, probably of the same age, although his embonpoint and beard made him look much older. He had a twitch, poor man, in his right eye and shoulder, which added an air of familiarity to his most trivial remark. Our conversation was a brief one. 'Quite like the Lord Mayor's show, eh?' was his first essay at acquaintance. 'I am sorry I have never seen the Lord Mayor's show.' 'Never been in London, what?' 'I have been in London, but never as it happens just at that time. You know England?' 'Yes, I was educated at Cambridge. Ever been to Cambridge? We're very proud of our Backs at Cambridge.' 'They're very beautiful, aren't they? Which College did you join?'

When I turned to catch his muttered reply, I noticed that his feet were crossed on the top of the balustrade before him, and as I had not sufficient nerve for the situation, I deserted it, and adopted my A.D.C. neighbour as guide to the extraordinary scene, which now unfolded itself in the street beneath us.

The narrow pavements were packed with men, every one of them armed, many of them intoxicated, and the whole mass on fire with religious excitement. The centre of the street was thronged by the procession, made up of a strange mixture of bizarre elements. The great families of Hyderabad were represented by companies of their troops, amongst them wild Arabs, African negroes, Abyssinians and Copts, followed by family retainers carrying flying pennants. These retainers surrounded enormous Tazias, hollow, pinnacled erections of honeycombed white stucco, shaped like minarets or domes, which are ultimately offered to the river, with deafening cries and shouts.

Behind the Tazias came gigantic edifices, which supported household furniture, gorgeous gilt four-poster beds, surmounted by canopies of precious stuffs, gilt arm-chairs, such as might have graced an Empire drawing-room, State carriages of magnificent proportions and enormous mirrors, all greeted by the clash of trumpets, the rattle of drums, and the babel of the surging crowd. Excitement reached its climax when the horse-shoe of Mahomed's favourite charger appeared, held high above the crowd on the summit of its pennant, and was carried by a horseman into the Central Courtyard of the Marble Palace, where all the retainers representing their Chiefs made their obeisance to it, lowering their pennants to the ground, before its sacred power and might.

The whole scene was perhaps the weirdest one had ever witnessed, with the exception possibly of the dance of the drugged fanatics in Morocco. The lure of such spectacles is the old longing to understand things from inside, to lessen the gulf that separates us from each other, to catch some glimpse, it may be, of the hidden nature which makes us all akin. They are a part of the challenge of life. For I believe that the whole of nature pursues the same goal, although some or us may follow the false duessa, guised as the fairy queen, and seek in the poisoned goblet the elixir of life.

KASHMIR, 1899.

DARLING M.,—I have had a hideously busy week, settling accounts, making arrangements for our time in Kashmir, with people at dinner, or us dining with them every evening. Tell 'Miss P.' I had twelve boxes made, small enough to be strapped upon mules, and holding all we wished we had taken with us on our last adorable flight into Kashmir. Four servants this time, with two Swiss-cottage tents for ourselves and two tents for them. We are going to spend three months wandering from place to place, and I can't see why we should be uncomfortable, when it is not necessary.

I shall always think the four days' drive to Baramulla one of the most beautiful in the world, followed by the tow up the river with the look of reeds, long grasses and swooping birds, and banks carpeted with wild flowers, shaded by orchards and shadowed by mountains. Then the first glimpse of Srinagar like an Eastern Venice or Bruges, with every house a Swiss châlet, brown wooden temples with glittering spires, and the buzz and colouring of swarming humanity.

We have pitched our tents beside the dear M. S.s' camp, and shall be here for a week. I think Miss M. would like to spend the whole of our short three months on the Dal Lake, attempting to sketch the floating gardens of flowers, and the Palace where Shah Jehan dreamt away days with his Nur Mahal. It would challenge the genius of Turner, however, to reproduce the unearthly beauty of the sunsets, when sky, mountain and lake are bathed in gold, succeeded by purple, then blue, fading at last into ghostly grey.

It was rather an anticlimax to our enthusiasm to hear some one say as we passed his boat, coming home, 'Well may they call it the Dal Lake, for I have never felt so dull in my life!'

Jack is replete with energy, and will not go without protests to bed, 'in case he should not see something,' nor take off his boots, 'in case we might wish to walk somewhere': but he is now in a dreamless sleep.

August 19*th*. Still thoroughly happy. The long days spent in the open air are so life-giving. Jack is sunburnt crimson, Miss Mayes is dark brown, Jim mahogany, and my nose has caught the sun and looks intemperate. We start on our ride up the Sonamarg valley immediately after breakfast, when the camp goes ahead to our next halting-place. We follow at leisure, passing homesteads and cornfields, then forests of fir-trees and birches, with purple heather and ferns fringing the roads, and a very blue river roaring beside us most of the day.

I wish we could march for many more days, only I daresay we should get tired of eternal cold chicken for luncheon. To-day we have 'struck' and are going to have 'Army Rations.'

I should like to sketch Hari Singh, our invaluable roly-poly orderly, in his various aspects. He looks like one of the Hindu deities, and I would like to draw him as 'Hari Sing on a lotus leaf,' 'the all-conquering in action,' 'the subduer in repose.' He has a passion for work, and enjoys making others work too, knows everyone's name, and shouts as if he were a general in the thick of battle.

By the way I wish to strike a bargain with Jim, which is that I shall pronounce all Hindustani words correctly, in Kashmir, remember everybody's name and official title, and recollect dates, if he will only promise to do the opposite; but he won't close with me. It would give his brain such a moral holiday ; I am afraid his ethics could never be blunted !

August 27*th*. We are now in our standing camp, where we shall be for three weeks. Our tents are pitched on a little plateau, fringed on either side by pines and birch-trees, and facing a wide and verdant valley, surrounded by mountains, some with rocky peaks and eternal snow, others green as Ireland. Our foreground is covered with wild flowers, while we are within reach of a glacier and can hear its smothered roars.

Miss M. has undertaken the housekeeping, to give the finishing touch to my content, and to hers, for she is an enthusiastic housekeeper. She takes under her special protection the butter, milk, jam, cakes, pickles, sardines, anchovies ; everything, in short, which servants in India sometimes love 'not wisely but too well,' and is keenly interested in their preservation.

This morning she intercepted Jim, and I heard her addressing him with a slight tremor in her clear voice, ' I was going to ask you, would you *mind*, I mean to say, would you have any objection, I mean would you dislike *very* much, if we had some good skim milk for our porridge this morning ?   We have hardly any cream left for our butter.'

Jim acquiesced with a smile, and forbore to suggest 'a rider being sent into Srinagar, or a boat for that matter, to let us have plenty of milk and butter, whatever else we may do without.'

All the recipes she acquired in Paris, for soups and pasties, are brought out of her little dispatch-box to good purpose, and she has reached that stage when *she is the dish!* I thought she was laughing at an amusing incident this morning at breakfast, but it was only at the way the bacon had been served ! Bless her for a conscientious little treasure.

Hari Sing has accomplished a swing, hung from the sturdy branch of an oak, and we have a bonfire every evening, in which potatoes and apples are roasted, under Jack's and my supervision.   I have heard that family parties even 'paddle in the burn,' in lonely places in Kashmir, but that sounds quite too undignified, doesn't it ? Could you ever imagine it happening ?

You can at least believe that we are loving our holiday.   It reminds me so much of our summers in the Highlands, alas, how long ago, yet only yesterday in the memories of my heart; and I think of one who seemed to me then, as he does now, like a giant of love, who was never too tired to become a child again with us all, so human, so kind, so amusing, yet with eyes that could look so sad. As far back as I can remember anything, one felt as if he knew and understood every one, with a sense later on that he loved, hoped, trusted and waited for all that was best, like some brave pilot in stormy seas, who would never acknowledge shipwreck, while one plank was left for the crew.

September 15*th*. We are now back at Baramulla, after a week spent in the Gurais Valley, which leads to Gilgit. We had a misadventure there, that might have been a tragedy, but which, thank God, ended happily.

One morning, about six o'clock, Hari Singh came to our tent, to ask if he might engage coolies to clear away the snow, which had been falling all night. Hardly had Jim given his consent, when we heard a dull thud, followed by Hari Singh's shout of ' Jack Sahib.' In an instant Jim, who had realized what had happened, was out in the snow. The tent, in which Miss M. and Jack were, had fallen under the weight of the snow, and whether either or both of them were under the heavy tent-pole, no one could tell. Every servant in camp was shovelling off the snow. Not a sound came from inside the tent. At last, after what seemed an eternity, but was only a few minutes, they cleared the tent-pole of snow. Hari Singh hoisted it up on his broad shoulders. Jim crept in and came out with Jack, whom he perched on his shoulder, followed by little Miss M. in her brown checked dressing-gown. The pole had fallen between their rooms, and neither knew what had happened to the other. Both were chittering but, as Jack said, 'only with fright.'

Of course we could not remain in our tents, and after breakfast all our goods and chattels were removed to two wooden houses, whose previous inhabitants were escorting the newly arrived political agent so far on his way to Gilgit. As luck would have it one of his party, who had lived in our rest-house, returned that evening while we were at dinner, but he established himself in the second bungalow.

Hari Singh informed us that neither his luggage nor servants had yet arrived. So Jim, with the informality characteristic of India, sent him a note explaining the situation, and proposed we should send him some dinner, while suggesting that he should supply him with a complete set of dry clothing, both of which offers were accepted with gratitude. We enjoyed his company every evening after that, till we left, which we had to do with unexpected rapidity, for a telegram came from Simla, offering Jim the vacant post of Chief Secretary to the Punjaub, which had to be filled at once.

Jim welcomed the prospect of the new responsibilities which belonged to the post, and telegraphed he would arrive in Simla as soon as he possibly could. So snow or no snow, we had to pack up at once. Our road down to Baramulla led us along precipices, where it was often safest to walk, ankle-deep in snow. Our luncheon was taken under the shelter of some rock, and our nights spent in small wooden rest-houses. Thanks to Hari Singh's generalship, there was no hitch in the necessary arrangements for food or fuel, and we quite enjoyed the experience. We felt some commiseration for a couple we met. He, from his general bearing, was evidently a soldier of the age of a Major. She was much younger and, from the inexperience of Indian conditions revealed by her dress, was evidently a new-comer, probably a bride. Poor woman, between sun and snow she was crimson, and I feared, from the expression of her eyes, and the fact that her pony was led, that she might be snow-blind.

I knew not for whom to be sorriest, herself or her husband, for she was apparently in that stage of impotent rage against circumstances, that seemed to accuse him of being responsible for them! I longed to address her, on the strength of being another woman in those solitudes, but I positively had not the nerve. So in silence we passed them, with a tentative bow, which she probably was not able to see, and many unuttered regrets for her plight.

LIEUTENANT GOVERNOR'S CAMP, 1898.

WELL, dearest G., you have learnt no doubt from other mail letters that we joined the Lieutenant Governor's Camp some weeks ago, and are now established in our three tents which include Jim's Office.

The Camp is certainly a most imposing sight, consisting of an army of tents, a small company of Infantry, another of Cavalry, with elephants, camels, and bullock-carts as 'transport.' The principal tents form three sides of a square, a flagstaff, surmounted by the Union Jack flying, in the centre, sentries pacing up and down, with a goodly array of chaprasses. When we are not encamped near a large station, involving much entertainment, the party at dinner usually consists of the Lieutenant Governor and Lady M. Y., his private Secretary, the A.D.C., the Commissioner of the Division, the Deputy Commissioner and Police Officer of the District, Jim's Under Secretary and ourselves.

I accompanied Lady M. Y. on a visit she paid

yesterday to a school for Indian girls. The school
was started by a Parsi and his wife, who are
Christians. It is largely supported by them, and
carried on under their supervision. The girls are
taught to read and write, and to do ordinary sums
in arithmetic. Besides this they are taught to do
everything thoroughly which is connected with
household management or their own requirements.
They sweep out their rooms, make their own beds,
cook their own food, make their own clothes, and
have themselves spun the cotton of which the
sheets on their beds and their dresses are made.
Everything connected with their daily life they
have mastered, and are capable of doing, and
each girl has a little child to look after and
tend.

How I wish our working-girls at home were
educated on such practical lines! What people can
do well they generally like doing, and nothing impressed me more on our tour together in Holland
last year, than the love the Dutch women had for
their daily work. It was the same thing in
Brittany too, both with men and women. To see
the women at market, studying a cabbage before
buying it, with their heads on one side and a loving
smile, made you think they would end by patting
it! And when some man had polished up a brass
pot on his doorstep, whistling while he rubbed it,

he was as proud as could be that he had got on the right glitter.

If our girls were only given the chance at the outset to learn how to do things, why should they not get the same pleasure out of doing them well? And think of what a world of difference it would make in their homes and their daily lives, to themselves and to every one in the household. As somebody has said, 'I don't wonder so much at what men suffer, as at what they lose.'

By the way we had rather a melancholy visit from K. S. Circumstances have been rather too much for him and his will-power has snapped. A host of indigent step-relations have planted themselves on him and 'sat down,' as they say, in his house : several step-brothers and one of his step-mothers, all waiting for him to find them employment or support them himself.

He is now in the Provincial service, with not a very large salary, and little or no connection or influence with the employers of labour. He has found work in a factory for two of the men, and would be content to have the little old step-mother always under his roof, a peaceable soul who sits on the floor in a corner of his dining-room, sewing in silence. She is there to come back to, he says, and lessens the sense of loneliness, which follows him everywhere. But the unemployed, eternally visible step-brothers are always there too, and have become nightmares from which he can see no way of escape. He has, in short, lost all 'whip-hand vitality'—as you put it, and is a prey to impotent hopelessness.

The Lieutenant Governor had a talk with him. I think we were able to brace him up a little bit too; and Jim is arranging to transfer him to Delhi, where some good folks will be kind to him and keep his head above water. But he is a sad edition, at present, of the K. S. of Shahpur days.

DEAR P.,—The parting is over between Miss M. and Jack, a sad wrench for them both. Miss M. broke down hopelessly, having cried through most of the previous week, and ending by being ill.

Jack crept up to me on the morning we started, with a piteous face, and whispered 'I know what it is. I know what it is. Don't cry, darling Miss M., come home with us. Mother wants you to come home with us. Say good-bye to India for ever, but don't say good-bye to me.' 'Oh, but, darling, it would only be parting at the other end. I should have to return to India, to work and fulfil my duties.'

He craned his head out of the window in the train to look at her, till the little figure, with the tight hair and the big white hat, had disappeared, then 'still to see where she had been,' and then inconsolable tears.

Life is rather hard on the Miss M.'s with

mothers' hearts. I am glad our dear, good and faithful friend has at least promised to spend every Christmas holiday, that can be spared from her new little family, with her boy's father and mother.

DARLING MOTHER,—It is over now. The channel
has been crossed and sunny France traversed, and
now the ship will soon be on her way to take us
to the other end of the world.

A dreadful thing happened to me the last night
I was in England. I was sitting in a small inner
room in the big London hotel, only one other
woman there, and I meant to be so brave, when
into the room there rushed a boy, just like my
own boy, the same age, the same height, with
the same radiant joyous face, the same dear loving
eyes. He came with arms outstretched, and calling
'Mother,' threw himself into the arms of the other
woman, and covered her happy face with kisses.

Then something touched those elemental depths
which, thank Heaven, are not often moved. A
sense of the anguish of a thousand mothers, who
pay for India with their babies, like birds dropped
from the parent nest before their wings have learnt
to fly, swept over a lonely woman, and there, in
the sight of all that happiness, she wept.

One thing you must promise me. If you ever hear Anglo - Indian women called shallow and frivolous, if they ever seem to others to be vain pursuers of the empty bubble of an hour, will you remember there may be another side to the shield? I know that there is an alternative, to shirk no suffering, which brings with it understanding, the strength to endure, and that strange possession, peace. Only do not let any one be too hard on them. It may be cowardice, or it may be their own kind of courage, that makes them shut their ears to baby voices, or turn their eyes from haunting baby faces, to be resolutely gay.

> ' For even yet they dare not let it languish,
> Dare not indulge in memory's rapturous pain.'

ON THE FRONTIER, 1901.

DEAR G.,—I came back from the mysteries of the untraceable footsteps, queer lights and noises of our old-world quarters last summer, to find we are to have no home at all this winter, as Jim is now Settlement Commissioner, and we shall wander all over the Punjaub in tents, and only settle down when the heat drives us in May to Simla.

But don't pity us. It is the kind of life Jim likes best in India, for he has an elemental love of the soil in his veins, combined with a paternal affection for every Hindu and Mahomedan farmer; and as for me, I adore every hour of each day in camp, and wonder each morning what may happen before evening. We have had plenty of experiences lately, and I have evolved a new conundrum, which you must help me to solve.

Can you explain to me the subtle power that is possessed by some towns, places, or bodies of people? Why does an Englishman, for instance, who lives for a few years in the wilds of Australia, come back an Australian to all intents and purposes, with even a pronounced nasal twang, when his only companions may have been merely kangaroos, sheep, or cows?

What is it that makes Oxford turn out one type of man, Cambridge another, when the successive generations that come or go may never have met or known their predecessors? What is the spirit of the age which touches people *en masse*, who have never heard of it? How do regiments, too, acquire a traditional character, one eschewed because it is always extravagant, another because it is haughty, a third chosen because it is always well to the fore? The last campaign may have riddled the ranks of the regiment, and left a wholesale vacancy amongst the officers, but 'from its ashes rise its wonted fires' and its habitual spirit.

Towns such as Nuremberg, Bruges, or 'Grey St Andrews by the sea'; the solitudes of the New Forest, the lonely glens and mountains of the Highlands; whole countries such as Kashmir, Brittany, Morocco, have a *geist* of their own, which we find an all-sufficing companion.

We are on the frontier of India, and these questions flit through one's brain, because many of the stations in this part of the country are so comparatively new, and yet their *geists* are already in full possession. The British and Indian regiments and political officers, with their wives and children, are seldom stationary for any time. Yet the character of their quarters remains the same. Bannu is slightly jumpy, Dera Ishmael Khan proverbially dreary, Kohat unalterably gay. The same people meet at one or other of these places, in perfectly different moods, taking on the tone of the tutelary *geist* — as chameleons adopt the colouring of their surroundings—and disliking or liking the fate they foresee.

Everywhere, however, there are two presiding spirits that overshadow all others : the one the Shadow of Death, the other Indomitable Courage, and no one can afford to forget or neglect either. Every story one hears, or history one reads of this wild bit of country, turns on danger, victory, tragedy, valour, murder and treachery, dominance and power.

The frontier province lies side by side with territory that is non-Indian, and is inhabited by Pathans, Afridis, Waziris, and other independent hostile tribes, with the growl of the British lion as our watch-dog.

The country itself is in the mood of the play. The Pezu Pass, through which we travelled yesterday, is like the valley of Apollyon, bereft of hope. Dark, desolate, with barren peaks and deep abysses, gloomy caves and giant boulders, it is the natural background for murderers and robbers, who know no law but the dagger and hereditary vendetta. The jirga of the Afghan tribes is the old *panchayat*, written big, of the Indian villages— a council of wise men to whom disputes are carried. It represents the people in their dealings with other tribes and with our Government, but under its shadow hereditary blood-feuds are carried on, from generation to generation, and will never end while the last murder is still unavenged, or until the last woman carried off has been paid for by a kindred theft.

No Englishman can tell at what moment one of these wild creatures may win a place in Paradise by his death. We are prepared as far as possible for off-chances. In Baluchistan, on the rocky pass through which the railway slowly creeps to Quetta, we saw our Indian soldiers, armed to the teeth, patrolling every station, and the Khyber bristles with our forts.

I am alone just at present. The Dak bungalow, in which I am, is surrounded by high fortified walls. For, on the other side of the road is a low hill, beyond our territory, on which Waziris live. Our camel-men were thrashed by some of them yesterday, and I saw a dead Waziri carried past on a bed this morning. He was a dacoit who had been shot by a policeman.

The police-stations are fortified too. A few months ago, our nearest one was attacked by nine armed robbers, who carried off the police rifles, killing two men and wounding another in the struggle. Ten armed policemen guard this bungalow, and last night they were joined by some Pathans from the village. Yet I cannot say that it has ever occurred to me to be afraid, thanks perhaps to the *geist* of the place! and also because, in the present instance, there is really nothing to fear. Our walls are high and strongly built, the gates are iron and strongly barred, and there is no reason why our wild neighbours should ever desire or attempt to surmount them.

The log-fire is blazing cheerily in the hearth, a store of novels is waiting to be read, and my friendly ayah is curled up cosily like a cat—asleep on the door-mat. I rather envy her for having such old deaf ears, for I distinctly object to the noise the Pathans make all night, coughing, laughing and talking, which gets mixed up with one's dreams and gives one a headache.

Jim is meantime inspecting fields and villages, where the roads are again too rough for the tonga. Last week he had to be absent for the same reason, so I seized the opportunity to pay a visit to our dear Mrs C. and her beloved General at Peshawur,

which let me see something of the Kohat and
Khyber Passes, both quite new experiences.

I enjoyed my time at Peshawur so much, for
both my host and hostess are amongst the people
we most appreciate in India. He comes of a stock
that has always given the army distinguished
officers, and she is so pretty and such good company and so kind to everybody, including the
people who fail. But to return to my drive
through the Kohat and Khyber Passes, both drives
covering forty miles each. We made the roads,
but we pay to be allowed to pass over them, for
the country belongs to the Afridis and is not under
our Government.

On the whole, I was almost most impressed by
the Kohat Pass, although it is of less historical
interest. It was a day of cloud and sunshine. I
had a splendid succession of good and well-trained
horses, who simply flew like the wind up the steep,
zigzag road. We looked down on Kohat behind
us, lying in an oasis of green fields and blossoms.
The hills we ascended were stern and wild, and the
people we passed were all Afridis, cut-throat looking people, almost all armed, even the women and
children carrying long curved knives.

The Afridis, whose clan we had been fighting
three years ago, were working in their fields, and
came to help the coachman to harness a new relay

of ponies at the half-way inn. They seem to be a cheerful people. They and their wives, who flocked to see the tonga and the strange Memsahib, have the Mongolian type of features, with small slits of eyes, high cheek - bones, and sallow complexions. The women's hair was tightly plaited down each side of their round faces. I wondered whether their husbands preferred the security ensured by peace to gather in their harvests, and the good wages they get from us for keeping the road in order, to shooting us from the top of hills. Possibly the call of the blood and the love of other people's cattle is more alluring to them than any prosperity paid for by monotony.

I had a talkative Pathan as coachman on my drive up the Khyber, who chattered in Hindustani about the tribes and the Pass.

'Every race had fought here, but no one had ever conquered the hill-tribes. Hari Sing, Ranjit Sing's great general, had fought and conquered all over the Punjaub. But that was his white tomb beside the Fort at the mouth of the Khyber. The Angrezi kept it in order and paid a man seven rupees a month for sitting beside it.

'The Afridis were like animals; they flew from rock to rock in the hills, and disappeared from sight. No one could catch them. They not only fought with their neighbours but among themselves, father against son, brother against brother. No day passed without two to nine murders being carried out on those hills. I would see no village. They could not trust one another enough to build them.' 'How did they live?' 'They ate mud; they were animals.' I said, 'Oh, nonsense! They have plenty of rupees. How do they get them? What do they do? They *must* have houses, food, clothes.' 'They sold wood and grass in Peshawur, which was work good enough for jungle tribes. They lived in the earth and ate mud.' And he pointed out holes in the sides of the hills with curtains of tattered rags before them, and into one of these I saw an old hag disappear.

Meantime, as we neared Ali Masjid, the Fort beyond which we were not allowed to go, we passed long strings of caravans, under the protection of perhaps six armed Khyber Rifles in khaki. Such strange-looking people from Kabul they were, on shaggy Bactrian camels, men with their wives and children, some quite fair, others like Chinese, others like the Lost Tribes, wearing sheepskin coats or patch-work clothes of every brilliant shade of rags, with big blowsy trousers. (I noticed, by the way, that the wooden boxes on the camels had come from Sweden, Austria, Germany, Switzerland, but never a one from Britain.)

Arrived at the Fort, the coachman told me I

must be ready to return to Peshawur in an hour, as every visitor must be well out of the Pass before sunset. Until he returned with the tonga, I sat at the entrance of a roomy cave, with the charred remnants of a dead fire in its centre, and surrounded by bleak peaks and barren crags, and the most desolate landscape I had ever witnessed.

In this eternal silence our soldiers on their march to Kabul found the frozen corpses of thirteen thousand men, women, and children, who had been killed or had died from cold and hunger on their long, weary march from Kabul, where Sir William Macnaghten and his staff were murdered. Sir Arthur Trevor, whose father was with Sir William that day, told me he remembered his brother running in terror from the window to his mother's arms, having just seen his father assassinated, and the night when they and their mother fled to the British Afghan Fort for refuge. So it began. You remember the stories our governess told of her Uncle Brydon, the sole survivor of the host whose bodies lay in the Khyber Pass.

In one way or another we have certainly paid with our blood for the peace of India. We still carry our lives in our hands on this side of the border, as our Afghan neighbour does on the other, he losing his as if it were not worth a wager. There, it is exactly as if the Reign of Terror had been protracted through centuries, till the *sang froid* of the prisoners in the Conciergerie had become hereditary.

We have heard some odd stories of the national stoicism from people who have been in Kabul. One of our Indian envoys, for instance, told us that it is the unwritten law of the country that, when a man is murdered, his wife, brother, or nearest relation may avenge his death by cutting the murderer's throat, always provided the man is caught. Our envoy saw one of these sentences carried out. The man said his last prayer, lay down on his back, stretched out his limbs without a tremor, and calmly accepted his fate from the avenging hands of the widow.

Their rulers, he said, were well fitted to train men to accept the inevitable by the fates they might have meted out to them any time. The Amir's baker, for example, had a trick of making sour bread. For the first offence he was fined, and warned that for the second he would be baked himself in his oven. The bread was a failure a second time, and the man was actually baked! A slower method of punishing a miscreant is to sew up his mouth. But I shall not inflict any more tortures on you! They remind me of Morocco, where one used to see blind and crippled objects on the Tangier Sok, witnessing to the same ideals of Oriental justice.

Some Indian students were enterprising enough to go, not long ago, to study the administration of Persia. When they were asked, on their return, what had most impressed them, their somewhat inconsequent answer was ' the British Government.' Perhaps a visit to Afghanistan might prove an equally useful object-lesson, and the country has the advantage of being nearer home.

It is near enough to our Frontier Province, and its subjects wander in sufficient numbers over the boundaries to test our powers and courage.

There are no characteristics which more appeal to Orientals than dominant personality, vitality, and power, especially when they are combined with the grand manner and human sympathy. Nicholson, Edwardes, Neville Chamberlain, and all those old heroes are still household words, and stories are still told of the gallantry of the Guides and Frontier Force, by the children of men who fought against them.

Englishmen for their part love the Frontier, and have a soldier's admiration for the valour of their foes, and heartily appreciate their chivalry, their frank, jovial manners, their songs and their humour, and their stoical indifference to danger and death.

I wish I could give you all the details of the siege of the Fort of Gumatti, and of how seven men in a mud tower held out for a day against two regiments. They were outlaws, with a long record of murders, thefts and devilries to their account, and a price upon their heads. Yet when the siege of their rough stronghold was preceded by a parley, Mr D., who was our political officer, walked alone up to the tower to come to terms with its inmates, and what was more significant was that, when his terms were rejected, he turned his back on these outlaws and returned to the ranks of their enemies, confident, because he knew his men, that not a shot would be fired on him as he retreated.

Two regiments against seven outlaws, a long day's siege, and two of our officers killed before the tower was taken. And when the end was near, one of the last survivors was heard singing a brave song of death. How could we fail to admire such enemies?

Yes, death and courage are the shadows and lights on the Frontier skies, and if no one can afford to forget or neglect their presence, no English man or woman I have ever met here has failed to grow stronger beneath it. Are they inspired, do you think, by the Geist?

DEAREST A.,—Where do you think we spent yesterday afternoon? Nowhere else than in the Boer camp, talking to one man and seeing them all!

To let you know all about it from the very beginning, I must tell you that for days we have been watching the preparations made for the Boers' arrival, with the greatest excitement: 'we' being Jim and I, a young civilian, Mr W., and his two nice sisters, just arrived from England; all of us settled together in a dear old bungalow, beneath the shadow of hills, and blessed by the radiance of spring.

Every afternoon E. and M. W. and I have sallied forth in the direction of the Boer camp to see what we could see, just like Jack and me in search of adventures in the summer holidays!

One day we heard that two privates of the 60th Rifles had arrived to guard the camp, so I wagered E. and M. that we should have a talk with them before the day was done. And a talk we had!

begun by our taking them an 'Illustrated London News,' which happened to have pictures of incidents in the siege of Ladysmith. This led up to their telling us about the last days of the siege, the short commons, and then to the appetising points of a mule's ''eart.'

'You see when you've got but a pound of meat in the day, Ma'am, without vegetables or salt to it, wy, it's soon over, Ma'am. So wen a mule was shot down we'd make for it, and the 'eart was wot we relished!'

Next adventure, a talk with the Indian camp baker, who was building his oven with bricks against the Boers' arrival, Jim as interpreter, as the baker's dialect was not always intelligible, and some chuckles when the old man told him 'the Boers' clothing was very homely, indeed it was no better than the Sahib's!'

Then came the day when all the tents were up and ready, and the Boers might arrive at any moment. We stood behind a high hedge with gaps in it, at the foot of the garden and edging the road, waiting for them to come. Then we heard their tramp and shuffle, and when eight hundred of them straggled past, I cannot describe to you the 'awesomeness' of the sight. To think that here in India were these men, as prisoners of war from Africa, to realise the great expansion of the Empire that foreshadowed, the responsibility, the power for good or evil it involved, was almost oppressive.

Could we ever be fused into one people? The Boers were so foreign, and so varied in type. Some of them looked like pictures of old Biblical patriarchs, with hooked noses, long white beards and old-age dignity. Others were like German burghers or farmers, well set up, well clothed, well to do, *tüchtig;* and then there was a third type, more like the submerged classes met in the East end of London, with sloping shoulders and slouching knees and no foreheads or chins to speak of; and there were little children, poor dears, hopping and running happily along, beside the others. These mites had fought beside their fathers and lost them on the battlefield. Far from their homes and penniless, they had thrown in their lot with their friends, and stuck to them when taken prisoners, and come on to India. In the rear of all the mixed masses of Boers came a crowd of Indian camp-followers with their paraphernalia. So you can see that it was a strange medley, and one full of speculation for the small audience on the other side of the hedge.

That same forenoon Major Kinloch called officially upon Jim in his office-tent and asked him to bring us all to tea in his camp in the afternoon.

I wrote to ask him to dine with us in the evening. When I saw his handwriting in the note accepting our invitation, I knew at once he must be a son of mother's 'dearest Lady Kinloch,' for his was a facsimile of her clear, well-formed 'hand of write,' and when he came to meet us in camp, the family likeness was beyond a doubt.

This made it a great pleasure to us both to meet, and in the evening we had such a gossip about old friends, the balls we must have been at together one winter in Edinburgh, with all the subsequent histories of our old partners. Time flew. When at last we came on to the present, and he told us what a great political opportunity he felt this time with the Boers to be, for mutual understanding and good fellowship, we felt sure they must end by loving him too. One had such a sense of his gumption, tact and kind-heartedness, combined with the best traditions that are in the blood of a race who have always been leaders of men.

To return, however, to the events of the afternoon. The little Boer boys in the camp delighted me, they were such imps! jumping up and down and making absurd noises when we came near them, and then throwing themselves down on their faces, giggling with pride in their childish pranks.

Major Kinloch introduced us to a very good-looking Boer, a tall slight man with a soft brown beard, a gentle voice and the dreamy eyes of a poet, very like those pictures you see on a yellow-back novel of a man in checks, with a gun at a stile, talking to the exquisite heroine!

He spoke English slowly and as if with difficulty, and said he had had no idea India was so big, miles and miles to go over in the train, days and days to arrive and always people. He did not know about it and would like to know, to tell his friends.

Jim said he would send him one of his own books about an Indian District, to let him know how it was governed, and asked if there was anything else he would like to have. He said he had no writing-paper and would like to write to his wife, and that he had nothing to smoke and he missed it. So he is to have paper, his pipe and tobacco.

While we were talking to him, we heard a strange eerie sound—long, low notes, as long as the notes of a German Chorale but different, more like the music we used to hear in the Jewish Synagogue in Dresden, minor, and as sad as what the Jews might have sung when 'by the waters of Babylon they sat down and wept.'

We looked in the direction from whence it came, and there we saw a great crowd of the oldest amongst the Boers standing with their heads slightly upturned, reminding one of the prisoners in Beethoven's 'Fidelio,' who turned up their faces to greet the sun with a song.

Major Kinloch told us the Boers always sang a metrical Psalm at the end of the day, and added that they used to sing another at three in the morning, till he had suggested they might postpone it till five!

So ended our afternoon in the Boer camp. Next day it was empty and deserted, for they had all trekked up the mountain road towards Abbotabad, where their permanent camp is to be. From there Major Kinloch has promised to write to us, every now and then, to give us news of their welfare.

Dera Ishmael Khan, 1901.

Dearest P.,—It is hardly a week, but it seems more like a year, since we heard by telegram that the Queen is dead. We were alone in our camp in the hills when the telegram came. When Jim opened and read it, there was something like tears in his eyes. He said he had always felt as if he were working for Her, and there must be thousands of Her subjects who have had the same inspiring devotion.

She was worshipped by Her people in India, who identified Her with their gods, and to whom She was an incarnation of Motherhood. For it was not only Her political sagacity, Her unerring judgment and grasp of affairs, that won Her admiration and reverence. There was something deeper than that, which added to reverence love. Something which far less gifted beings might dream of possessing, if they only had a spark of Her genius for sympathy, Her gift of understanding, Her infinite unwearying impulse to give it expression, to comfort the distressed and bring hope

223

to the broken-hearted.   She will reign through the ages for the things that are never forgotten.

I shall ever cherish the memory of Her kindness, when she asked mother, J. and me to come to see Her in Holyrood, on Her last visit to Edinburgh, as the greatest honour of our lives and the last proof of Her goodness to three generations.

CAMP, 1901.

DEAREST M.,—A wonderful piece of news has just reached us from G., which would really seem too good to be true, if one had not long ago recognised how swiftly the Spirit of India responds to all goodness, as a sensitive plate to each ray of light that touches its surface.

To grasp its significance, you must remember the hostility which has smouldered for centuries between Hindus and Mahomedans and periodically bursts into flames. Remembering that, can you believe what a number of these two races now do, every year in G., as a tribute to the influence of a homely Scotch padre, who has lived amongst them for years ? They meet at a Love Feast, which they hold as a sign of peace and goodwill. If you quite realised what that means, you would think it incredible, but then you don't know the padre as they do, nor just what he has been to them.

They knew him, you see, as a boy, when they too were young and attended his Father's School, as their sons attend his ; so the padre has been their friend for more than the half of their lifetime. That is one point in his favour. Another is that he is a Scotchman, and I am inclined to think that Scotchmen, despite their proverbial caution, fraternise better with alien races than either Celts, like ourselves, or Englishmen do. Perhaps it is their dry sense of humour, which is more amused than perturbed by differences, or their bent for philosophy, which makes them welcome the chance of an argument. Whatever it be, they seem to accept human nature in all its variety, more as a matter of course than an annoying surprise.

This is a generalisation, however, which does not wholly account for the padre's popularity, for it is really his gift of loving which has won him his people's love. In the School where he teaches they have learnt to count on his patience and justice. In the hospital, built by his efforts, the padre knows just what they suffer. The farmers, smoking their hookahs on their circle of stones in the cool of the evening, rise to return his salaam when he stops to discuss, in his homely fashion, their crops and the state of the weather, in the dialect he learnt as a boy. He is a part of their daily life and every one's friend.

And as for his influence. Is the secret of that different in one part of the world from what it is in another ? To do good anywhere I fancy you must, in the first place, be good yourself. These people see that he who counsels goodwill is kind, that his peace surpasses their patience, that for creatures of fear he is full of hope. Then, children as they are in spite of their guile, he knows that, like most of us, they can only learn to walk after many a fall. He holds out a helping hand to them, just where they are, and takes them on further, recognising all that is good in themselves or their faith, and that half truths are part of the whole. They grope in a darkness lit by the only lamp they possess. He does not extinguish the flickering spark, but waits for the flame. He rejoices whenever he sees it, for he knows there is only one Light.

He knows they are victims of fear, and that what we all need most is Hope. ' We both love God,' he says to some gentle soul who has seen, in his longing, the Vision. ' Now let us work together to lessen the evil that is still in His world. Don't set yourself tasks, only say " I will love," and all the rest follows.'

There is really so little to tell you, however, about his work, for it is all on a homely scale, just the things we might all do if we chose, only we don't. Nothing voyante or melodramatic, nothing much more remarkable than kindness and common-sense, and what Wordsworth calls ' the best part

of a good man's life, his little unremembered acts
of love,' although why he should call them unremembered I shall never be able to understand, for
they are just the things that we never forget.

Our friend's homely straightforwardness suits his
surroundings. Woe betide any man who ventures
on subtleties if he is dealing with the subtle Hindu.
Far better to let him know just where you are,
although it may take him some time to believe it.
And because he trusts them, he is now trusted by
many of that reticent race as a father. 'I think
you told me you became a Christian at first,
because Englishmen are patriots and you wished
to be a patriot too?' he said to a public-spirited
Indian. 'Yes,' the man answered, 'but now I
see deeper, and I am a Christian because I love
Christ.'

Boys, who come to him Christians, are sent back
to their homes to be good sons and brothers, and
somehow their people do not seem to resent it to
any apparent extent. 'You owe me nothing for
what I have done when your children were ill,' the
Hindu doctor said to their mother, 'it is I who owe
your Husband everything for what he has done
for my sons.'

Of course life would be unendurable in an Indian
village if it was not enlivened by feuds and fights
and other primeval excitements : but against that

you must put their latest tamasha—the Love Feast.

To let you know how that originated, I must leave the Indian quarters, and pass to the Civil Station and to the closed door of one of our country-men's bungalows, behind which lay a tragedy too sacred to be wholly laid bare. Suffice it to say that a poor man had lost his wife, to whom he was entirely devoted, and with her his home and any desire to live. The Hindu doctor arrived at the Manse one evening, to announce that unless he was watched night and day he would get his own way and die. So the doctor sat by him, while Mr P. stuck to his school work. For the rest of the day and night the padre was nurse.

Naturally that could not go on for ever. Days passed and anxiety deepened; the want of sleep was beginning to tell on the watchmen. Then a dear old man, who was head of the district, came to the rescue, and with him the judge. They insisted on the day being divided between them, and on their being allowed to mount guard and to watch the patient by turns.

And so, by slow degrees, the poor broken creature was brought back to a life which he no longer wanted, and was thereafter sent homeless Home.

Soon afterwards, under the doctor's orders, the padre took furlough too. It was then that the first Love Feast was held in the Hall, the head of the district as chairman, Hindus and Mahomedans as guests. At the end of the evening a casket was given to the padre by his Indian friends, with their chairman as spokesman. For by that time he too had learnt to believe in Missions, and as long as he remained in the district he presided at the Annual Feast.

DEAR E.,—At last I have found the magic key that has opened the door, behind which brooded and dwelt the impenetrable mystery of the hidden spirit of the people of India. Where has my search not led me? To the tents and caves of jungle-tribes, to solitary villages, to crowded towns, to the homes of philosophers or country squires, to busy fairs and temple precincts, only to remain a lonely spectator, or like a stranger who has learnt the words of some language by heart, without ever reaching its sense. And to think that in all these wanderings the magical key lay hidden, where for years it seemed least likely to be !

Sometimes in the night I have heard a far-off sound like an alluring call, elusive, arresting, fading again into silence; the song of some wanderer in the hills, who was warding off ghosts or evil spirits by notes that vibrated like a broken sob, and seemed the essence of loneliness and hopeless despair.

Yet why follow up this haunting challenge?

Not there could the magical key be found. For all that I otherwise knew about Indian music at that time was only repellent. In fact, when any band of musicians came with violins, drums, or pipes, and essayed a performance, it seemed to me simply synonymous with pandemonium. The discordant yells of the men, whose appearance suggested the extremities of toothache, only tended to induce insanity on my part.

Several years passed without anything occurring to dislodge my prejudices, or alter my opinion, until one evening I heard a man playing in a field beside our tent. He was playing a violin, with a drummer beating an accompaniment, and as I listened I thought I had never heard anything more beautiful. It reminded me of the music one hears in the Highlands of Scotland, which are like stories told, with only the hills to hear them, until they become a song; or of the melodies I had heard gipsies sing in Spain, or the wild airs Hungarians improvise. But this was sadder even than those, fuller of a monotonous despair, as if it carried in it the burden of the world's woe, and was the voice of the old and endless ' still, sad music of humanity.'

We sent some one to find out who the player was, and learned he was a man whose days were chiefly spent sitting by the grave of a renowned

Mahomedan saint, a shrine visited by crowds, to whom this man was accustomed to perform.

He came and played to us, and as I sat listening to him under a clump of trees, with dark fields of wheat before me, and beyond a stretch of barren, arid plain, which met at last the starlit sky, it seemed to me that I had at last discovered the hidden secret I had sought for years, and that this was the unconscious expression of the heart of the people. I heard in the music the history of vague longings after the unseen and the eternal, of dull resignation to unalterable fate. Then there came strains of vigorous cheerfulness and rustic humour, alternating with hysterical emotion, feverish passion, undisciplined excitement, hatred and despair, and then again monotony and enduring hopelessness. For me it was that evening as if the dumb had found a voice and deaf ears had gained the power of hearing.

Gulab Mohamed remained with us a week and had many successors as visitors in our camp. For having now realised the spirit of the music, I was fired by the ambition to master its structure, and to be able to reproduce and transcribe the songs I loved. This was not, however, an easy task. Musicians were our neighbours, it is true, wherever we went, as every village in the

Punjaub contains some of the Mirasi caste, to which these men belong. They wander about the country, like the bards and minstrels of the Middle Ages, are hereditary retainers in big houses and established necessities in villages, where they are in great request at marriages, fairs and festivals, and figure largely in the foreground of everyday life.

There is no dearth of musicians. The difficulty is that the greater number of these men who sing and play, according to the traditions of their system, cannot explain its principles and have not the mental tenacity of purpose required for its elucidation. At one time a Brahmin was my teacher, at another a discharged policeman, who had reverted to his old profession as a wandering musician. A third preceptor was a rather incoherent priest. He explained to us quite frankly that he was the victim of drugs, and his nerves and powers of endurance were so quickly worn out under cross-examination, that we soon heard him beg a bystander, 'for the love of heaven to get his horse saddled quickly to take him out of this.'

Poor men, I felt for them myself, but I am afraid I had also made up my mind that if some one must die of *ennui*, I would not be the victim before I had mastered the Indian Scale! I learnt, however, to temper the wind to the shorn lamb, and to take my lessons in short spells, to spare my teacher the painful discovery that his mother was dying, his house on fire, or that his own unexpected state of health or business affairs demanded his return, at that very day and hour, to his home!

The facts which I gathered in our camp wanderings from those chance instructors were, that the year is divided by Hindus into six seasons. Each season has its own *rag*, as it is called. Having assigned to each season its *rag*, the Hindus next divide the day into six parts, and give to each division its particular *rag*. The people say that only at that time has the presiding deity of the *rag* leisure to listen to it; but it cannot be denied that they occasionally sing it at other times too, when they have leisure to enjoy it themselves.

Certain notes must be used in each *rag* and no other; they are the necessary notes of that particular *rag*. Provided he uses no others, the musician can improvise on these notes at his own sweet will, and *ad infinitum*. This threw some light on one's early sufferings, when listening to Indian music, for the improvisers one came across upon these occasions were, as it happened, 'excessively uninspired.'

But not only must the musician stick to the

use of certain notes in his *rag*, he must also adhere to the prescribed number, and begin and end on the decreed notes. These subtleties, however, were only arrayed when I had the good fortune to become the pupil of the Principal of the Lahore School of Music.

In a fortunate hour we paid a visit to his school, mounting a flight of mud stairs to a room near the roof of the house. The upper end was adorned with every species of Indian violin, sarangas, sitars, tambouras, and vinas. One stood on feet which gave it the air of a large wooden grasshopper, another was like a gigantic banjo, a third resembled a Spanish mandolin, the cases of others were carved like peacocks, and all were flanked by big drums, and little drums, as well as by different kinds of flutes, like pipes.

The room was dimly lit, and the floor covered with students seated cross-legged, who rose as we entered, like a covey of white, scarlet and orange-winged birds. They sang their exercises in unison, after which the old Pandit sang a Vedic hymn, reminding one partly of a German Chorale, partly of a Gregorian chant.

When we went away, we carried with us one of the Pandit's musical primers, which are written in Hindustani and have never been translated, but which he afterwards explained to us, his latest scholars.

Are you as much surprised as we were to learn that the Hindu scale, dating as far back as Vedic times, is the same as our own, although between each of our whole tones and semi-tones it has also quarter tones and a third of a tone, which could only be reproduced by us on a violin ?

In their old Sanskrit treatises on music, moreover, the names of our seven notes of the octave, and of sharps and naturals are given, as well as the equivalents of our semi-breves, minims, crotchets, quavers and semi-quavers. Their timetable, in fact, was practically the same as our own, and in use thousands of years before it was completely accepted in Europe. This, and everything one had previously learned, were comparatively plain sailing. But I confess that when I reached the mysteries of Indian time, as applied to the air played, along with its accompaniment on the drum, I found myself in deep waters without a chart, and am still on the verge of floundering.

First realise that the song is divided into bars, and that while we count multiples of 3 or 4 in our bars, they may also count 5, 7 or 9 in theirs. Add to this that the drum-beat is counted in one way, the air in another, and you will merely begin to fathom the depths of these unknown seas. Taken separately, one can follow either kind of time. But, if not content to enjoy the general impression produced by the two modes of counting, one attempts to analyse and to determine how the two parts belong to each other, how the drum-beat falls, often with irregular rhythm, and how its beats mate with the rhythm of the music, I can only compare it to the impression produced by the effort made by any one to rub and pat himself at the same time, with the additional determination to accentuate some of the pats.

Yet to listen to these novelties in time is like hearing a new rhythm in poetry, with a beauty all its own, elusive, fascinating, incommunicable. I never, as a matter of fact, heard anything quite so expressive as the rattle of the Indian drum, under the hands of a master. The swing, the monotonous reiteration, the vociferous throb of its beats have often awakened the conviction that the presence of Indian drummers might have intensified history in the French Revolution. With a dozen of them accompanying the Marseillaise, and leading the Sansculottes, the country would have been not half, but wholly depopulated.

My ambitions are limited to reproducing the airs that are played. I have a score of them now you will love. To note them down from the singers recalls the old days when one used to transcribe ' the Bonnie Banks o' Loch Lomond,' and the ' Praise of Islay ' and many another Highland croon, from the boatmen and gillies and old folk in the Highlands, and although 'mountains divide them and a world of seas,' there is sometimes a kindred spirit in them both, which endears the Indian songs to me.

Dear B.,—From change to change our beings roll, especially in India, as you may see by our new address. Our winter wanderings are over and we have taken a house in Simla, which is, I believe, to be transformed into a hotel, and which is meanwhile ample enough for the clan - gathering which it now holds. A. and F. have arrived from Calcutta, E. and R. with their child and nurse from Quetta, and N. from Ferozepore, full of military ardour and musical projects.

We have turned back the wheels of Time, and are all under twenty, with a superfluity of spirits, which finds vent, with only ourselves as audience, in evening dramatic performances, when each one in turn dons one of the masks which A. has brought from Calcutta, and improvises the character. Then N. sings some of his own songs to his own words, and I sing some of mine, and E. reduces us to sentiment with her Hungarian songs, or 'The wind and the day had lived together,' and R. contributes 'Tom Pierce, Tom Pierce,

240

lend me your grey mare.' Care and responsibility forgotten, we are whole-heartedly happy every hour of the day.

I don't know how it came about, I think E. was responsible for it; in any case, we had a dinner-party of twenty. E. had drawn different sketches upon twenty menu-cards, and these were passed round the table, every one having to write in turn on each card what book they thought the sketch on it illustrated, the best guesser winning the prize. This proved so alluring that when half of the party adjourned to the drawing-room, the other half continued to sharpen their wits and their pencils over them—with brilliant results.

They say ghosts of the past haunt houses. I think the ghosts of our spirits must have haunted the air, for when the dining-room door opened, out streamed ten men, wearing our masks! and with these ridiculous heads the Lancers were danced. Their hostess soon left the ranks of the dancers, disabled by laughter and engulphed in the depths of a wide arm-chair, the climax being when a certain high dignitary disappeared for a minute, to return with a tartan plaid arranged as a kilt, in which he danced the Highland Fling as a solo in the centre of the room!

The fame of our menu-cards spread, and I believe that some wits are still racking their brains to find other titles than ' The Heavenly Twins ' or ' The Book of Genesis ' for two babes in their perambulator wheeled by their nurse. But what names could they find for the Lancers ?

CAMP, 1901.

DEAR G.,—We both wished you could have been with us lately in camp, when we have seen a good deal of a Hindu civilian. He is one of the best officials we have met in India, hard-working, hard-thinking, thorough, upright and patient, with a high ideal of justice and truth. If there were more Indians of his calibre, the question of self-government for India would be more easily solved.

He is a Brahmin, with a pedigree covering a thousand years, and a father who was given the title of Rajah as a reward for distinguished services to the State. Our Pundit is tall and well-built, with a sense of humour and a fat laugh, which reminds me of Major M. He has a great many friends amongst young civilians, with whom he has many a game of polo.

It is sometimes a little difficult, when one meets Indians often, to hit upon subjects which have a common interest without being purely official, for so many others are debarred from discussion by Indian etiquette. One cannot, for instance, men-

243

tion their wives, except under the name of their 'household,' or express any interest in many of their domestic affairs, and various other topics must often be excluded because our points of view are so different.

This we did not feel so acutely however with the Pundit, as while he has perfect tact, he at the same time never hesitates to tell you the bald truth about anything; and the equal terms on which we meet make it much easier to express opinions that differ from his, knowing that he is quite able and willing to hold and defend his own.

Still our first essay to enter alien ground was not wholly a success, partly perhaps because of the presence of attendants who understood English, which destroyed some of the intimacy of a three-handed talk. We were dining in his tent, our host arrayed in white muslin, with a yellow embroidered and fur-lined coat, and had for some reason been discussing Napoleon, which led me to ask the Pundit whom he considered the greatest man in Indian history. I was rather surprised when he answered 'Krishna,' as I said I had imagined that he was an Indian god. He gravely answered that he was also a general in one of his incarnations.

This was followed by a full stop. When the

men left the tent, Jim ventured to ask him if he believed it did any one any good to come back to earth to improve his temper, when he had no memory of the ego who had indulged in a bad one?—a smile from our host—or if any good was done to the world by a Fakir who sat in a desert absorbed in inaction? His answer to that was another question. ' Do you not believe in the power of silent, unseen influence, and believing in that, can you not also believe in its being exercised by the people whose lives are prayers?' Yes, we all could believe that was possible, although I confess that such prayers for the world were not what one had hitherto associated with the poor self - torturing Fakirs we had seen in our wanderings.

I must tell you of another conversation we had, as it throws such a light, or shadow, on the problem of a possible united India. One evening when Jim was still trying a case, the Pundit asked if he might join me on my evening walk. I told him of a book I was reading, ' Asia and Europe,' by Meredith Townsend, and asked him if he endorsed one of the writer's theories that East and West cannot easily understand one another, owing to the exclusiveness of the caste system, each caste keeping itself apart and communicating nothing to other castes, until Indians lost the desire to explain themselves to any one ? He said it was perfectly true. A relation of his was more spiritually minded than he, consequently more particular in his ritual, and so much more exclusive that he would not now dine with him. 'And would you explain yourself to anybody ?' 'I should not think it necessary.' There it is—the impossible gulf fixed between each of them and any one else—although perhaps for each of us, after all, 'in loneliness the soul abides,' unknown to ourselves, except in rare moments of insight. But for Indians how much rarer the possibility of outward or ordinary contact, or power of combining in action !

The Pundit has helped me immensely about Indian music, and brought one evening a gramophone to our tent, with records of Indian songs collected by a friend. I have often wondered if one did not read one's own ideas into the music, and seized the opportunity of having some one with us who would not hesitate to set one right, to ask him if I had interpreted the song and the singer correctly.

The result was most encouraging. When I had listened to the first singer, I said, 'This singer is different from other singers I have heard. He belongs to a good caste and is educated. He shows self-restraint in his singing and does not bawl, like the ordinary village-performer, and he is a cultivated musician, for he sings as if he felt and knew the way the song ought to be sung. As for the song, of course I cannot feel certain about Indian music, but if this was an English song, I should say it expressed loneliness, entreaty, and reproach.'

I was delighted to hear both my guesses were right. The Pundit said, 'Mrs Wilson, it is a love-song. The man says, "How can you leave me in solitude like this? How can you be so cruel? I beg you to listen and to come to me. I cannot bear my loneliness, and am wretched as I am now." And as for the singer, he is an educated man and a Brahmin by caste.'

You will be more interested, however, to hear of a power that the Pundit possesses, which is much rarer than to be able to guess the mere contents of a song.

He gave us one evening many extraordinary instances of his doctor brother's hypnotic powers, and said that he too possessed the power to cure illnesses, and had cured his groom of pneumonia, by making some passes over him, laughingly adding it was partly selfishness prompted him to make the attempt, as he wished him to go on ahead with his horses, which the man was able to do next day.

The following afternoon one of our servants came to tell me he had been stung by a scorpion — a poisonous creature that runs about with a turned-up tail and pincer mouth—and he showed me his poor, swollen hand. I sent him with a note to Jim, asking if our friend could do anything for him. The man came back from the healer in five minutes, with no signs of the swelling, and the pain gone. How do you account for the cure?

On the Frontier, 1902.

WELL, dearest, how do you like your son-in-law in his political uniform and adorned by his C.S.I. badge? I rather fancy him myself in that particular toilette!

He is fêted galore in our present part of the world, with arches, fireworks and flags wherever he goes, the climax reached upon Saturday. An Indian potentate wished to give us a *burra tamasha* and feed us. The day therefore began with a ten miles' drive before breakfast. Flags, avenues of red baize, salutes by golas, many brass bands, proclaimed that the drive was ended. Then a large breakfast-party with conversation in Hindustani, followed by a visit from me to the Zenana, when I saw all the ladies' pretty embroideries and jewels and the babies belonging to the different brothers of our host, who live in the neighbourhood.

At four a band preceded us down the red baize avenue, which led to the scene of the *tamasha*, one of the musicians revolving before us, blowing frenzied blasts from his trumpet. Then tent-pegging, races, tugs-of-war, with a crowd of three thousand onlookers.

After dinner at eight and conversation in Hindustani—fireworks; and just as a popular overture generally ends with a clash from every instrument in the orchestra, so did our evening conclude with a concentrated volume of all the separate noises from golas, drums, and rockets whizzing overhead and spluttering at our feet, as if the birthplace of clamours had burst.

Then a drive home in the dark beneath the silent stars to find my poor ayah, who had been at the *tamasha* too, seated beneath a poplar, having her head stroked by an ayah friend, 'to take the tottie pain away, please, Memsahib,' she said, as she tottered to her feet to salaam.

I wonder if dignitaries who go to *tamashas* all the world over would fain have their heads punched too, for the very same reason, when the long day of glory is over?

India in general is given up to *tamashas* at present over the conclusion of the Boer War. When things were at their worst in South Africa, Mahomedans prayed in their temples for the success of our arms, and every one now seems to share our thanksgiving.

We wrote to Major Kinloch to congratulate him

on the end of his *surveillance* duties, and he told us he had a great *tamasha* in honour of the event. Every Boer came to a large tent to have tea and other refreshments, concluded by an ordeal of hearty hand-shakings. Then each man carried a stone to the cairn that was raised on a hill, by their own request, to commemorate the occasion, and Major Kinloch made a speech, the oldest patriarch Boer mounted the cairn and made another, and they all sang a Psalm.

Our particular Boer sent us one or two of the stone Bibles the men had made, during the long days of waiting, with their names written on them. He wished us to have these as a memento of the afternoon we spent with them all. A few of the men have elected to remain in India, where they have hopes of employment, so we may come across them again, under happier auspices; and perhaps give them, too, a *tamasha!*

DEAR B.,—We are now in that tract of Shahpur which used to be the home of our old friends the lizard-hunters, leech-gatherers, cattle-trackers and cattle-thieves. When we left Shahpur seven years ago, it was still a desert. Here and there a batch of camels nibbled bushes, spread like rambling mistletoes, with the tattered low round tents of the camel-owners somewhere near. Here and there a low wide-spreading tree, whose branches touched the ground, and formed a closely-knitted screen for stolen cattle. Everywhere a waste.

Now it is the focus of a hundred interests. The Indian Army has its eye upon it, for it will soon be the centre for one branch of its big scheme for making India and its Army self-supporting. Projects are on foot for establishing gun, rifle and cordite factories elsewhere. British as well as Indian soldiers are already clothed by Indian factories. Now their transport will be found in India too. For this land, which was once a desert, will be peopled soon by old pensioners and new settlers, who will hold the land on the condition that they will keep mares to breed horses for the army, as well as till the ground, and that they will hand the land on to a son, bound to carry on this trust.

But how can these old pensioners till land or raise remounts in our old desert, you may ask. That has already been made possible by the great engineers of India. Here they are in their twelve bungalows, with a railway and a vast network of canals as the visible signs of their powers.

I must really pause to sing their praises!

All of them belong to a body called the Public Works Department, a name abbreviated into the initials P. W. D. These letters somehow carry with them an inglorious sound, while they in reality represent some of the most glorious gifts which the British Government has given to India. They are, it is true, amongst her material gifts. Take them at that : roads, railways, and canals are the saviours of a country which depends for its life upon the regular recurrence of its periodic rains. The failure of these rains spells famine. Their recurrence lies in the hands of the fickle god of the weather. With the engineers, however, lies the responsibility and power of mitigating his fiats.

The Continent of India is too vast, too varied in its climate, to suffer simultaneously from drought. There comes the railway's opportunity — bearing trucks of golden grain, like some forlorn hope to a falling citadel, barely held, so sparsely filled by the famine-stricken, the dying, and the dead.

It would need the genius of a Walt Whitman to apostrophise the potentialities of the railway, the freight it carries, whether it be human or material, altering the destinies of millions, whether these be famine-stricken, beleaguered, or distressed. When one thinks what it alone has done for India in a hundred directions, one's only wonder is that the elastic portals of the Hindu Pantheon have not yet been opened to receive its image.

As for roads, before the advent of British rule there were none in India worth the name. Akbar, the Great and the Beneficent, planted trees at distances to mark the tracks, which stood for roads, in some parts of his dominions. But these tracks were impassable for three or four months every year. Trade and traffic stopped till autumn rains had ceased. Now British India is as chequered by a pattern of intersecting roads as a tartan is by stripes, all made and all maintained by these energetic ubiquitous Civil Engineers. Yet roads and even railways sink into insignificance beside the canals. Roads and railways benefit the bodies of India, canals are its life-giving arteries. What do you think of the engineering powers of men who can carry a river in a tunnel through a mountain, or the bulk of the river Ganges in the nutshell of an aqueduct, as a mere episode in the life of a canal, whose main channel is a hundred miles in length, with a thousand miles of distributaries? What does that mean in the lives of millions whose life depends on wheat? I know nothing in the external conditions of India which appeals to one's imagination like those huge canals. I always feel they might be added to the Wonders of the World, and as a matter of fact travellers do come at times from the other ends of the earth to see those giants.

To return, however, to the Shahpur Colony. The canals are there, but the land is not yet ready for the colonists. At this point enters Mr H. In age Mr H. is little over thirty, young, as you and I would count summers, and he is only one man, although when you hear what his duties are, I expect you will imagine he must be at least twenty different persons.

He is what is called Colonization Officer. The land reclaimed from the desert is half a million acres. It has to be divided into squares and apportioned to people in small holdings. Conceive the responsibility involved in allotting these squares, and deciding the conflicting claims of something like 10,000 tenants with their families sent in batches, when they have been selected by their Colonels from the ranks of pensioned soldiers, or by their District Officer from some distant village. Four thousand mares have to be settled with the right kind of caretaker, in the right kind of place. Roads have to be made, trees have to be planted, post-offices, police-stations, school-houses, dispensaries, villages have to be built. Imagine this responsibility devolving upon one single man, helped no doubt by able Indian assistants, but still responsible for every decision made, and for every order that has to be carried out. Sometimes he works for fourteen hours upon end, hearing petitions, giving instructions, inspecting this, deciding that, planning something else, while the railway engineers clamour on one side, the canal engineers on the other, and the officers in charge of the horse depôt urge him to 'hurry up' the builders at work on the depôt stables. I am sometimes surprised that the mere strain of readjusting his thoughts, and concentrating them again on so many successive subjects, does not turn his fair hair grey in a night!

His wife, a descendant of one of Napoleon's sisters, is made for the situation. She is a fearless rider, a good shot, an excellent housekeeper, and a skilled musician. She thoroughly enjoys her open-air life, and is on good terms with the Indian gentry, who flock in from the neighbourhood to inspect their own squares, and those which are to receive the overflow of their tenants.

I have never seen a prettier tent than the one which is Mr and Mrs H.'s temporary home, with its flowers and pictures and the pretty bookcase and writing-bureau, designed by our host. When the day's labours were over, and another tree had been felled — a form of exercise which has appealed to other hard workers—if anything could be calculated to distract a man's thoughts from their deep-worn channels, and remind him that 'über die Bergen sind andere Leute,' it should be the songs we used to listen to every evening, sung to the guitar, and carrying us back to the blue Bay of Naples, and the peaceful beauty of starlit nights on the Lido.

Well, at least it can be said in Mr H.'s favour that he leads a life which, strenuous though it be, is led in the open air. How infinitely better that is than a later stage in colonization, when a man is chained to his desk in the office-room of his bungalow, we had every opportunity to learn when we were at Lyallpur a few months ago.

It was at Lyallpur that the Chenab Colony was

born with Captain P. Y. as its Godfather. That was
in the days before the railway was made, when the
first colonists streamed in on camels, or on carts
drawn by bullocks ; fathers, mothers, boys and girls,
with their pots and pans, beds and bundles. Some
of them had nothing left to call their own but the
clothes upon their back, and screamed their rage or
wept their sorrow over the loss of their belongings,
which had been stolen from them by jungle thieves,
who would sometimes neither sell them food nor
tell them where water could be found for their
camels or themselves.

While the women and children sat by the
roadside underneath their carts or near their
camels, the Colonization Officer sat in his office, the
bamboo screen on his window black with flies, the
air heavy with the din of hundreds who poured in,
clamouring for the promised land.

In they came from sixteen over-populated districts
from which the District Officer had chosen them,
weeding out the applicants for squares—the rich
who had sufficient land already, the thriftless who
had hopelessly mortgaged what they had, the
decrepit who were too old to work, the opium-eater
with his pallid sodden look, the dandy in his jaunty
dress, whose very hands betrayed that their owner
had never done a day's hard work. Life at first
in new unbroken land would be too strenuous for

any but the physically fit. Men were chosen who were connected with one another by race or blood, and they were told the conditions on which they would hold the land.

In they came, for their 100,000 squares were now ready for them, in an area which covered nigh upon 3000 square miles. In they came, these different human units of nearly eighty different tribes and castes, the Hindus, Sikhs, Mahomedans, with all their subdivisions, with their Mullahs and their Brahmins, their jogis and fakirs, and their different menials in their train.

Captain P. Y. began work as the pioneer of the Colony in the autumn of 1892 and left it in the spring of 1899, with the echoes of a ballad of thirty-six stanzas, commemorating the praises of his rule, as a characteristic Indian ending to his labours.

Do you think he had been idle or had had an easy task? He left the Colony after those seven years with a population of 800,000 people settled in their villages. The town of Lyallpur had been built, lit up by night, shaded by trees by day. There it was, the pride of all the Colony, with bathing-tanks, bazaars, and metalled roads, its Municipal Council, Civil Station, Schools. Best of all, there was a grain-market, piled up with wheat and cotton brought by farmers on their camels or bullock-waggons, and sold by them to the Indian and foreign agents, for export to England, the Continent, and Japan.

And the railway too was there, still bringing fresh Colonists to the land. Mr L. J. had been working strenuously amongst them for three years when we stayed with him in Lyallpur. Oh the voices of those peasants clamouring for their squares! I can speak with feeling, for our room was in a remote corner of the house, but distance could not dull the pitch of their penetrating shouts.

Sometimes there was a moment's lull, when some lordly capitalist or yeoman came through a narrow passage in their ranks, to learn where the ten squares allotted to him could be seen. Bad investments these, for far from sinking money in their land, and living on it as examples to their neighbours, many of their fellows had been so far absentees, whose chief ambition was to stay at home and draw more money from their indigent tenantry. Then the din began again, the nomad of the desert shouting hoarsely, as he established his right to be given a grant on the land, which had so long been his home, and proving this by the records of his convictions for cattle-thefts and other crimes. Shoving past him, shaggy, bronzed Biluchi cameldrivers, who were ready to maintain registered camels for government service as a condition of their tenure, and the succession of their heir, always granted that their pay was ensured to them in war time, and the food and clothing of their drivers.

Each man in the huge crowd was given a piece of paper with the number of his square, very much as the busy agent of some hotel in Switzerland might hand the London tourist bent on sport the number of his room. And just as the tourist might besiege the Manager of the Hotel to have his room exchanged for a better, which he knew to be vacant, so was this crowd swelled by peasants, who had returned after testing their given square to beg for an exchange.

Day out, day in, they came, and even 'the deep and silent night' was broken by their shouts. Outside in the moonlight they were discussing the conditions of their lease. I could hear the word *maurusi* repeated in their reverberating basses and their high-pitched tenors, with that tremor in the tone which betokens excitability. The Sahib had said they were to be permanent tenants, occupancy tenants, as they called it. Government would take six shillings on an acre of wheat, which would include the cost of water, and the Sahib had said if they did well and fulfilled the conditions of their lease, they could hand on the land inalienably to their sons and grandsons.

There was something else that other Sahib had

told them weeks ago, in their old village. Of what it was about some of them had a confused idea, others none.

It was something new, and it takes some time for anything new to penetrate the brains of Punjaub peasants. For I must tell you that there are certain seas upon which some of these Punjaub peasants are apt to drown. Government was going to throw out life-buoys. Would they wear them ? And if they wore them, would they fit ? Would they prove to be too tight, or if they were made looser, would the men go down ?

First and foremost, they were to live on their land, and bring forth harvests. No more sub-letting, no more sales to wily money-lenders, no land speculation, spelling ruin, and a return on the bullock-cart to the old life of squalor and indebtedness. Next they were to fight fever and disease. No more puddles in the courtyard, side by side with heaps of manure. Outside of the village was the place for these. Then they must all, as a matter of course, have houses, and help as their ancestors had done before them to build a well, and lend a hand, according to use and wont, on the village roads. Every village would have its common, open government land, and trees must be planted now that wood was getting scarce and fuel prohibitively dear ; fifty trees, as a reserve fund, on their twenty-seven acres, after that as many as they liked or needed for present use.

All excellent and necessary conditions to ensure prosperity. I sometimes wondered, however, if they did not ever feel as if they were being planted out themselves, to be doctored by the latest scientific aids to development! Lucky for them, at any rate, that the planting was not in the Crown Lands of Australia, where the powers that be, with all their socialistic tendencies, have imposed similar conditions and in some cases have enforced them by severer penalties. It is to be hoped that there is a Sahib there too who, like the Colonization Officer in the Chenab Colony, sometimes rides over the whole country and that, like him, he sometimes too remits the fine.

As far as that dignitary had learnt upon his rides, the Colonists so far were doing well. Here and there was a man with the old primeval, heaped-up, puddly courtyard, or another who had set to sowing wheat and maize upon the Village Common, or had ploughed up a bit of road and sowed it for a cotton harvest. Some of them would have no trees of their own, or preferred their neighbours', or a tree on the Common, which they chopped up for firewood. One or two men were conspicuous by their absence. No house belonging to them was in the village. Some one to whom a man had sub-let his field was reaping where he had not sown. These were the things that had to be stopped. In this case the man must come back or forfeit his land, or in lieu of that must be fined.

In spite of such episodes it was a thriving and prosperous Colony. No farmer ever existed who does not grumble sometimes, and the Punjaub farmer does not differ from his class. As their own proverb puts it, ' He was given a bundle, and he asked for a mule, after that for a man to lead it, for another to put the bundle on the mule's back, and then for a third man to take it off.' They sometimes complained that the trees attracted birds and that the wheat suffered accordingly. They would like to eat their cake and have it, live with one foot in their old home and the other in their new. Above all they resented the exactions of native subordinates. If the Sahib could only be in every place at once, there would be more chance of their not having to pay thrice over to pacify these money-grabbers, with their threatened reports upon every lapse that had or had not been committed.

As a matter of fact, the Colony promises complete success. It is certainly a great experiment, and not the least interesting bit of it is to see how the people have started new plays upon their new stage, and freed from the thraldom of custom, have emerged from old grooves and developed in enterprise. The Colonists were drawn from all parts of the Punjaub. There were men who had known rich soils, rainy soils, dry soils. Here was a soil which depended no longer on the sky above, but on a constant supply of water brought from canals. There were men who had only dealt with particular crops, sown in the fields of their part of the country. Here was a fair field and no favour for all kinds of agricultural projects, and eighteen cereals have now a place in their exports.

A particular wheat wins the prize at the annual Lyallpur Agricultural Show, and whets every farmer's energy. One man shows the way and is followed by others. Cotton-seed from Assam and America has been introduced to the farmers' profit. Naboth inspects Ahab's vineyard in the next village and copies the pattern. Orchards are started and orange-groves flourish, roses for attar and melons for far-away markets.

When the peasants left their old villages, they knew only two kinds of ploughs and one kind of sickle, and could not at first afford any other. Now, thanks to their own prosperity, to the combined contributions of their whole village or to the loans of their Agricultural Bank, every kind of plough, including the latest American invention, is used, and reaping-machines have taken the place of the ancient sickle.

So they go on, while the Colonization Officer guides and commends them, the ubiquitous, strenuous, responsible head under the British Government of three thousand square miles; and I should just like to ask you if you think that England is yet on the down-grade, while she can send out such men as these?

Dear L.,—I have been established in comfortable quarters for the last fortnight in a Rawal
Pindi Hotel, waiting for our tents and camels to
reach Lahore, while Jim is riding from one Rest-
House to another over roads that are too rough
for tongas.

A nice young couple, Mr and Miss U., are my
nearest neighbours. He is a civilian, who has
published some excellent translations of Indian
poems in the 'Spectator' and other home papers,
and their beauty has fired me with the ambition
to translate some Punjaubi songs to mate with
the airs one has already collected.

Mr U. has been good enough to lend me his
literal translations of perhaps fifty cradle, love,
marriage songs, dirges or religious poems and
the originals of little more than a dozen. The
best of them, so far as I can judge from my very
limited experience, have the pith and terseness,
the human notes of elemental joy and sorrow
which are to be found in the folk-songs of every

267

country, with an indigenous flavour all their own. In the cradle-songs the language and ideas are very much what is understood between mothers and babies all the world over. In the popular love - songs it is almost invariably the lady who is the devout lover. Certain similes, such as comparing the loved one's locks to snakes, the songster's bed to thorns and fire, are much favoured, while the prosaic joys of eating and drinking are as frankly introduced into the most fervent, as beer and sausages into the classical smoking concerts of Germany.

The area I have traversed, however, is very limited. Here and there one comes upon bits of pure gold amongst the earthy dross, but as a rule it is only in religious poems that one finds the spiritualising idealism of our own love-songs.

By dint of studying the translations Mr U. has made, and others given me by Indian friends, I hope to be able to adopt some of the traditional imagery. Mr U. will not, however, allow me to use any adjectives as they are unknown in Punjaub poetry. Nothing must be said as it would be said in Piccadilly.

He is of course quite right in this dictum. Either it is an Oriental or an English song. I have not given in yet, although I sometimes think it is making bricks without straw to try

to write without the materials he has amassed.
Most of my models are as elliptical as the Proverbs
of the Punjaub, which leave the central incident
to be inferred, like the instance of American
humour given in the account of the death of a
child, 'Two boys played at William Tell and the
Apple. The funeral was the largest ever seen
in New York.' If one were to use the Punjaubi
proverbial form and adopt it for Anglo - Indian
consumption, one would have to allude to a mere
male man's sense of politeness in this way :
'Have the last of the eggs,' said the husband,
and held it over his own plate, or to a wife's
arithmetical troubles in this : 'The Memsahib
mistook every 0 for a 9, "Oh heavens! I have
ruined my husband!"'

You can imagine, therefore, it is not altogether
an easy form into which to render a love-song!
Mr U. has so far only accepted one of my efforts,
which begins—

> ' The leaf fell from the tree,
> The wind blew it away.
> I seek him who left me,
> Seek him night and day.'

You will see others, however, I hope, some day,
along with their airs for which L. B. has promised
to write accompaniments. Meantime, my studies
such as they are help to pass the time in a

place in which not one of the old familiar faces is to be seen.

By the way, an Indian official friend who is now in the employ of a Native State sent us last week a literal translation of some Indian verses, which should interest you more than my feeble translations. They are preceded by a note from him on their contents.

During the reign of Shah Alam II., when the officers of the East India Company were acquiring influence at the Court of Delhi, the Maharana of Udaipur asked his representative at the Imperial Court of Delhi to give him some characteristics of the British. His representative wrote the following verses in reply :—

'They have no kettle-drums with them, no standard,
No fine horses, no pack-ponies, no elephants, no heralds.
They do not pitch tents to live in, they do not put on fine clothes,
They travel during the night and are silent,
They listen to others, but are reticent themselves.
These Englishmen deny themselves nothing (*i.e.*, they eat beef
    and pork),
And are considering how to get possession of India.'

On receiving this reply the Maharana, who was accustomed to Indian pomp and ceremony, disbelieved his Vakil and asked him to furnish him with more accurate information. The Vakil then replied as follows :—

' Asafa Dowla is dead,
The Nizam is not sincerely loyal to the throne.
The days of the Peshwa are over,
Daulat Rao is a mere boy.
The mean backbiter (*i.e.*, a rival Maharajah) has proved a traitor
    to Delhi,
Now in his wisdom he gives his support to the Englishmen.
Oh Sun of the Hindus ! listen attentively.
These Englishmen will succeed in their plots.'

That was written in the middle of the eighteenth century, and has proved a pretty accurate prophecy.

DELHI, 1903.

DON'T be alarmed! I am *not* going to begin from
the very beginning and tell you all about the
Durbar; for by the time this reaches you, a fortnight hence, you must have read the multiform
accounts of special correspondents and have seen
dozens of pictures of the town of tents, the great
processions, the various events, and the *mise
ensemble* of the Great Durbar.

Everything was perfectly organised, with that
genius for big ideas and grasp of detail for which
our great Viceroy is already renowned in other
domains. No pictures or words, however, can give
you the 'feel' of it all: the crowds of thousands,
the geniality and spirit of goodwill that was
rampant; the living geography of the Empire
pourtrayed by the crowded divisions encircling
the Durbar area, which were filled by the Indian
and English notabilities of each different presidency,
province, and great native state.

The special events one can never forget at the
Durbar itself were the sight of the Imperial Cadet

Corps as they entered on their black chargers, seated on white leopard-skins, in their blue and silver uniforms, like a picture in some old fairy tale; the moment when thousands spontaneously rose in silence and many in tears, when the old Mutiny heroes slowly walked past with their tottering steps. And another memory will always remain with me too—the vision of Lady Curzon. I shall think of her always as I saw her when she passed in the royal procession, the trailing lilacs which fell from her drooping hat forming a background to her exquisite beauty. She seemed a part of the sunshine and to emanate joy.

I should like to live over it all again with you and tell you of many experiences. I had the honour of being presented to H.R.H. the Duchess of Connaught, who was very gracious and kind. Then came the State Ball, a gorgeous spectacle; with the queer sense of the transit of time, induced by the sight of our Royal neighbours at supper in the inner court of the Marble Palace, where the Great Moghuls had their throne. And there are homelier scenes to which I could take you — the Retainers' Review, at which east and west were united in helpless laughter over the Retainers' humorous antics, on horseback or on foot. Or our visit to the old pensioners' camp, luncheons with soldier friends in their mess-tents, dinners with different Lieutenant-Governors in their camps, and the tales I heard from one of our African heroes, who sat beside Botha at dinner one evening in London, when they discussed how they had managed to escape being caught, one by the other, on various occasions. But that must all wait till we meet next autumn, when I shall be less afraid of telling you piper's news.

THE BOWER, 1903.

DARLING JACK,—We have taken this house to
enjoy 'the peace that lies amongst the lonely
hills.' It is only five miles from Simla, so your
father can ride to and from his office in Simla
daily, while he has a huge shamiana in our
garden of roses, where he works in the early
morning.

In three months we shall start for home. You
know why I am glad to be away from the crowds
and distractions of Simla. Although death, as you
say, is not a sad thing but only the beginning of
a happier life, still, while we have human hearts,
we cannot help sometimes wishing we could only
all die together, and never be parted from those
we love best on earth, and just at such times we
feel nearest to those we miss most, when we are
quite alone.

We are not always alone, however, for some of
our friends come to see us from Simla and we
have one or two neighbours. I had tea with
Lady Curzon in her 'Retreat' yesterday after-

noon, which I greatly enjoyed. She is so vivid and beautiful, and so keenly interested in everything living or dead. Her two little girls have fallen in love with Rourki.

By the way I believe that I actually forgot to tell you about Rourki in my last letter. To begin then from the beginning. One evening nearly a fortnight ago your father came riding home, with the sais walking beside him carrying a baby-bear in his arms. Your father had bought him from a Thibetan he met in the hills, and he is the dearest, funniest, little brown thing you ever set eyes on, although I must confess I was not quite so enchanted with him at first as I am now. Rourki was such a wild little barbarian over his food, jumping into the soup-plate and scattering his bread and milk all over the floor with his impatient paws, rending the air with his greedy, guttural, terrifying yowls. A certain patient person, however, has already taught him company manners. I wish I could send you a photograph of the said person holding up one side of the plate while Rourki grunts his delight; or handing him the apricots he brings from Simla, which Rourki eats holus-bolus, stones and all.

You used to wonder how dogs, which had no soul, understood our language while Frenchmen and Japanese didn't, and I think you would be equally surprised at our baby-bear's cleverness, and how quickly he has made friends with us and does what he is told to do, which French and Japanese, and even Scotch schoolboys, don't always do!

He still does not like being shut up in a hut by himself when we send him to bed, and it rather goes to my heart when I hear him crying, exactly like a baby, for ever so long before going to sleep. It cannot be helped, however, for he would be too uncertain a companion in any one's room, and I am glad to say that he only cries for two or three minutes now.

Every one is devoted to Rourki and loves his quaint little ways. Some friends who live near us often beg us to send him to see them, especially if they have children staying with them, for he walks about on his hind-legs and plays with them so funnily, giving them soft pats with his paws while he stands before them. He was so tired after his romp with them the other day that he walked into dad's study on his return, lay down in a corner and went fast asleep.

'Pat,' the dog, and he snarled at one another for the first day or two, but now they are the best of friends, Rourki climbing on to the top of our rose-bushes and shaking the branches at Pat, while Pat jumps and barks and is quite beside himself with excitement. And, if you please, they both go out walking with us now, Rourki on his little hind-legs, except when he prefers to climb trees after squirrels, while Pat yelps from below at the monkeys, neither of them ever getting within yards of their prey!

The one bad habit that Rourki still has is climbing on to a table in the drawing-room, up-setting the flower-vases and then eating the roses. ' With all his faults we love him still,' and several people have asked us to give him to them when we go, as they love him too. I think we shall leave him with a young thing, who has never before been in India and who comes often to carry him off in her arms. The sad bit is that he is bound to go the way of his forebears sooner or later and bite somebody—and then? Promotion, I suppose, to the Lahore Zoological Gardens.

Well, no more about our pets on this side of Suez. You had better address your answer to this to ' Care of P. and O. Agent, Marseilles.' Rather a nice address, don't you think? After that no more letters to be written to your poor old father and mother for several months!

DEAR A., — Do you by any chance remember my writing a letter to you some time ago about Hinduism? It was written at your own request, just when one was feeling peculiarly shut out from the life of the people, and conscious of how little one knew of their point of view about anything, except so far as one could hope to find it in their literature, when that was confirmed by the daily ritual of their lives.

I think I may venture to say I know a little more of the people now, and although I still believe that all I wrote to you then was so far true, I realise now that it was only part of the truth. It is true, for instance, that the creed of the uneducated masses is a patchwork made up of samples of every form of superstition : the worship of stones, plants, tools, animals, ghosts, demons, dead heroes, tribal or Vedic gods and the inevitable Brahmin, with a new bit added at any moment by the latest variety in gods or doctrines. Also true that every bit in the patchwork must

be propitiated, just as a petition to the district
officer is sometimes preceded by a basket filled with
vegetables or rice.

True, too, that the typical Hindu is the victim
of hereditary fear, with the belief in transmigration as its culminating terror; that what he most
desires is to escape from life, from his feeble body,
his devastating climate, his precarious fate, and
his unpredictable re-births, and to cease to be,
through absorption in the Self, or the extinction
of Nirvana. He is in many respects the consequence of his history, his traditions, and his en-
vironment.

Yet all this is only partly true. Behind such
truth there is something infinitely more beautiful,
just as one has sometimes seen a vision of heavenly
skies behind lowering thunder-clouds and light-
ning-flashes. And the beautiful fact in the Hindu
background is the fruits of the Spirit of God in the
Hindu character.

As an administrator, the Englishman in India
exhibits an integrity, a whole-hearted devotion to
duty, a sympathy with the poor and distressed,
which has never been surpassed in the history of
nations. The Hindu caste-system finds no place,
alas! for a public spirit or the brotherhood of man.
Yet, broadly generalising, I should be inclined to
say that, taking the average type of both races,

and the functions they fulfil, the Englishman's character is largely moulded by the Ten Commandments, while the Hindu's gift is to exemplify the Beatitudes.

This is no doubt broadly generalising, but there is something to be said for the general impression conveyed by a race, or by an individual. A man might possibly scrutinise his own character at a confessional with more satisfaction, or less confidence than his public would accord him. Yet the general trend of his being, as it impresses others, is not a less certain test. It may be compared to his shadow, which is projected without his volition and visible to the mere passer-by.

When I think of the Hindus as a race, I am aware of a hundred contradictions. Their belief in Transmigration and their Pantheism show them good or evil spirits in everything, and lead them to worship stocks and stones. Yet the same creed saves them from the materialism which sees spirit in nothing. The Hindu thinks in terms of Eternity. Theoretically, the Self that is worshipped is without attributes. Yet if we are to judge a man's creed, not by what he professes, but by what he embodies in his life, we must believe that God, Who is not far from any one of us, has largely bestowed in His mercy the fruits of the Spirit

on many of his children in India because they
have loved them.

Far be it from me to ignore the whole truth.
Horrors are still perpetrated in the name of
religion in India, which could barely find a parallel
in the dark pages of the Inquisition. The crimes
that reach the magisterial courts are at least as
varied as those that confront the administrators
of the law elsewhere. Yet side by side with such
facts, those high notes of the spirit are touched
by a multitude; those notes which are not dictated
by law, by necessity, or even always by justice;
those high notes which are attuned to long-suffer-
ing, meekness, patience, gentleness, self - denial,
that sometimes spell failure in Time, but not in
Eternity; notes which the God - given Spirit in
man intuitively recognises and worships, as the
world bowed down before Gordon, dead at his
post.

It is easy to be convinced of the truth of one's
own intuitions, but not so easy to convey to others
the fugitive impressions on which they are built.
Let me, however, make the attempt.

Anyone could cite instances of 'man's inhumanity
to man,' born of the caste-system, and quote the
unhappy fate which has overtaken its victims,
when they have had enough courage on certain
occasions to break its chains. Yet within the

prescribed limitations of caste is not something to be said for an Empire which has no Poor Law, so certain is the charity of the poorest of the population to their own people, however remote the claims on their pity may be?

This self-denying, generous sympathy is not always merely extended to their own clan. I remember an instance of this, which came to one's notice in Simla. A poor young Hindu girl, the wife of a groom in our neighbour's establishment, had lost her husband, and with him her home, and all means of support. Her only relation was in a far-off corner of India. Poor creature! I heard her roaming the sides of the hill beneath us all night, uttering cries of despair and distress, like some wild creature robbed of her young. When I spoke to our head-servant about her next morning, I found that our own household, as well as her fellow-servants, had already collected quite a large sum of money to add to what her husband's employers had given her. Our old Hindu *chaprassi* was at that moment trying to soothe and comfort her, promising to see her off by the train, and with a father's tenderness trying to breathe some hope into her poor, broken heart.

This generous pity is not even confined to their own race, as one realised at the time of the South African War, when many of the country people held meetings to collect money for the widows and orphans of our soldiers, following the lead of some of our Indian regiments, — the Gurkhas specially stipulating that their contributions should be given to the widows and children of the Gordon Highlanders, their rivals in war, and their chums round the camp-fire at night.

Of the sympathy shown us in times of sickness and sorrow by those of our own household, most Memsahibs can speak with feeling. I can never forget an occasion on which it was given me by a stranger when one needed it most.

I was in a far-away bungalow, Jim and our host in camp, when the telegram came this summer which seemed to cut life in two. In the evening I sat in the verandah dreaming of those sheltering arms, wondering in what star of the blest was her home, alone with grief.

Hours passed,—then I was conscious that some one was near me, some one with feeble old steps, who was putting sticks on the drawing-room fire, blowing it up, slowly carrying a chair nearer it, then a light that was shaded, bringing with it all the sense of the sheltering care which might be bestowed by a kind, old nurse. Then the old steps came slowly out to the verandah, and stopped behind my chair, and a gentle, feeble, old voice said, ' Memsahib, may I say something ? ' ' Please say it.' 'It is God's Will.' 'Thank you.' That was all, but sometimes such things mean a great deal to us.

To give you one or two instances of how these people can 'love the highest when they see it.' Two Indian peasants came to see Jim one evening, to put a hard case before him. A neighbour had maliciously destroyed their well, on which the irrigation of their fields and their harvest depended. 'Now, what should we do, Sahib, to him?' they asked. Jim said, 'Suppose you forgive him?' They said they would think it over. They returned next morning, to tell him they had made up their mind to take his advice. To grasp what that resolve meant to them, you must realise that a good feud with a handy neighbour is a form of excitement which often becomes an heirloom in India.

Do you think it easy to forgive our enemies? I am afraid I should find it one of the hardest things in the world. Miss Sharp, a lady who has worked as a Missionary amongst the people of India all her life, told me of just such another triumph of the Spirit over the 'natural man,' which not many of us could hope to surpass.

A Mussulmani teacher in her school had been given a copy of the Bible by her son Ishmael. He belonged, his mother explained, to a club of young men who had not had much education, and who read together to increase their knowledge.   He said to her when he gave her the book, 'Mother, read this Injil.   You need not have any fear.   It is beautiful and good.'

So she read it with Miss Sharp.   One day as they read the words 'Love your enemies,' the woman stopped to say 'That is a command, Missie Bai, that cannot be taken as it stands.   It is quite impossible to obey it.   If you had an enemy you would understand.   It must be poetry, and poetry never means all it says.'   'But, Bibi, it is there as a positive command, is it not?'   'He could not mean it.   He must have wished us to remember that, as far as possible, we should make no enemies, and that we ought to be kind and loving to all. Why, Missie Bai, you need to have an enemy to understand.   I have an enemy and I know.   When Ishmael, who is twenty now, was a few days old his father died of cholera, very suddenly.   I had four children and nothing to live on.   His sister was rich and had no children.   It would have been natural had she offered to help me for a time.   Not that I wished her help.   Nobody has given me help yet—save God.

'What happened?   The body of my husband was not yet cold or carried away, when my sister-in-law came in, and before the mourners, and before my children, insulted me with words that no

respectable woman should hear. I pointed to the
door, and from that day have neither seen nor
heard of her. You know, Missie Bai, how careful
a young widow must be of her good name. Were
I to speak to that woman, my sons would cry out
upon me. It would be as if I acknowledged the
insult to be true.' Another hard case. Miss Sharp
only spoke of One who had suffered too. Next
morning she went to see her, and found her as
cheerful and brisk as usual. She began at once
in a matter-of-fact tone of voice:

'You remember our reading yesterday, Missie
Bai? How hard it was. After you had gone
away I tried to forget it. I cooked a special dinner
for the children. I read and I worked, but I could
get no rest. Then I lay down and covered my
head. But there was no rest for me. These words
came and wrote themselves on my heart. Each
word was so hard, 'Love your—that meant *my*
enemies,' and I thought of that dreadful day again
and I hated my enemy. My rest was gone. I rose
and put on my chaddar. I could not think very
much, but after a little I called Ishmael, and we
walked across the city in the darkness and I
knocked at my enemy's door. They had gone to
rest, but they rose and I crossed her threshold after
twenty years and we made peace.

This woman has never called herself a Christian,

but whom do you think she followed that dark night ?

There is something in the inner being of the best Hindus which makes them adore the personality of Christ. ' He is a Christian and like our old rulers, Edwardes, Chamberlain, Lawrence Sahib,' is—at least in our part of the Empire—the highest praise they bestow on any of our race. The mysticism which pervades their complex natures would illuminate for them the Fourth Gospel, and offers a response to the Sermon on the Mount.

Perhaps I may have failed to convey to you this impression. Yet if Goethe's words are true, ' *Dem Geiste bist du gleich den du verstehst*,' I for my part dare to add my faith to the belief of the old Brahmin sage in the Benares College, who said that if we are still in India a hundred years hence, his countrymen will be Christian. Yet that depends too on us, in more ways than one.

DEAR S.,—Jim has been appointed Secretary to the Government of India, in the Department of Revenue and Agriculture. This means that he has to deal with all questions affecting the interests and welfare of the agricultural population throughout India, which come up to the Viceroy in Council for orders, such as tenancy laws, systems of recording the rights in the land, principles of assessing land revenue, precautions against famine, methods of famine relief, grants of loans for land improvement or for the amelioration of agricultural distress, establishment of co-operative societies, agricultural research and education and experimental farms.

He has to read, study and advise on all such questions, not only bringing his own practical knowledge to bear on them, but the experience and opinions of many experts belonging both to India and other countries. He is now therefore tied to his office-table, no longer dealing directly with the people and their crops, but with files and reports, and his greatest difficulty is to find time to think!

Half of the year must be spent in Simla, the other half in Calcutta, where we now are. His day begins at seven in the morning, and from that hour till seven in the evening he works, with the sole intermission of an hour for breakfast and another for lunch. He has just to endure it, and so has his wife! Such is the history *tout entière* of many a civilian's life. It is something to be able to look after his creature comforts, and to be here to drive with him in the evening, to take his mind off those portentous files.

What a strange medley Calcutta contains! Such crowds of Bengalis as seem more than the sands of the sea in number; our Eurasian cousins; the business community; the various ecclesiastical establishments; the officials and lawyers; and, crowding the large Hotels, the strangers who come from the four quarters of the globe for the winter season. Dominating this cosmopolitan city stands Government House at the end of the long Maidan, where the statues stand of the greatest Governors of India. And who dare say that the spirit of the past has failed to survive in that gigantic building, which they rendered illustrious by their lives, and where their high ideals are still exemplified.

Calcutta, in which the business element largely

preponderates over the official, is a mental holiday. One lives so constantly in public in Simla, that the solitude of unknown crowds is a pleasant change. The streets filled with the tall grey offices of business men, the multitude of well-set-up shops, the sight of the river lined with ships of many countries, remind me so much of Glasgow, that if I heard the thud of the mighty hammers of the Clyde it would not seem wholly incongruous.

The business community speaks of Calcutta as if it were a living personality. 'Calcutta has a heart' is an oft-used phrase, the truth of which one can already endorse. Calcutta is genial and hospitable, and has some little social traditions which are all its own. Your host, for instance, meets you in the entrance-hall when you arrive to enjoy his 'burra khana,' and offering his arm conducts you up his palatial staircase to his capacious drawing-room.

On the following Sunday your husband pays his respects to his hostess, and within a week you follow his example alone. Sunday, after morning service, is the day and hour dedicated by the male population to calls. Four in a cab they arrive, the sun *topi* left in the cab, tall hats displayed for the nonce, and for the space of five minutes they remain, when their place is taken by another batch of callers, who often protest they have been impatiently waiting below in order to borrow the hats!

If you leave Calcutta by an evening train, how-ever late the hour may be, if a Calcutta *habituée* is one of the passengers, you will see the door of her carriage surrounded by a group of her kindly friends, men and women in full evening-dress, armed with magnificent bouquets and parting gifts.

No one is old in Calcutta; everybody is of the same age, and that is about twenty-five, and one is entertained by young creatures playing practical jokes on their friends (whose hair, purely by accident, is white) as if they had been only yesterday together at the same school.

I know no other town in India that has so much individuality or such different sides. Cal-cutta, for instance, possesses as many specimens of historical periods as those Eastern cities that are built in successive ages, one on the top of the other, only here the vestiges of the dead past remain side by side with the living.

Heading those ancient mementoes, in the church-yard of St John stands the mausoleum erected above the grave of Job Charnock, the famous merchant who built the first English factory in Calcutta, and the *beau cavalier* of an Indian widow, rescued by him from the funeral pyre, on whose grave, when she died in the course of nature, he sacrificed yearly a cock, according to rites he had by that time adopted.

Like their representatives of to-day, the old Merchant Princes of Calcutta lived both 'splendidly and pleasantly, devoting their days to business, their evenings to pleasure,' and if golf, paper-chases and cricket have taken the place of enjoying the air with their ladies in chaises or palanquins, and of fishing or fowling in budgerows, there is one form of sport which has never died out. The races which were annually held in old days are still perpetuated, with a cosmopolitan crowd of onlookers, and all the pageantry attending the Viceroy's arrival with his bodyguard in scarlet uniform, and the parade of the racehorses before the grand stand.

The stately Mansions of Garden Reach still exist, where the wealth and fashion of Calcutta lived in the days of Warren Hastings, when ladies addressed their husbands in the third person, and asked 'if Mr Phillips could falsely believe that his faithful Marion could ever neglect the cherished desires of her adored husband?' The stately Mansions however, like Marion's manner, are now out of vogue, and the well-to-do members of the community migrated northwards long ago, to the large-porticoed colonnaded white houses, built by an Italian architect in Chowringhee Road. There

Impey once lived, not far from the house which was eventually occupied by his maligner, Macaulay, whose residence is now imbedded in the popular Bengal Club.

Another monument of the past, a result of conditions inherited from the days of Job Charnock, survives in Kidderpore Orphanage. It is a gigantic edifice, like an early Victorian Government House. Aided by grants from the East India Company, it was bought from Mr Barwell to be a permanent home for the daughters of English officers and Indian mothers, when their fathers retired from the service, and left India for ever.

There the 'Orphans' were educated and there, within the memory of the present generation, balls were given once a fortnight, largely attended by lonely bachelors from up-country, who not unfrequently found amongst their buxom partners a wife.

I had tea one afternoon in Kidderpore House, with a dear Fife friend, and met the last batch of Orphans in her drawing-room; such quaint handsome old relics of the past they were.

There are no people in India whom I pity so much as some of the descendants of those mixed marriages, not the educated class, who make excellent clerks in government secretariats, find employment in the various railway or telegraph offices, or go into large commercial firms, where they prove capable shopmen or book-keepers. It is the incompetents whom I pity, the unfortunates who have fallen between two stools, and have neither inherited the thrift and resource of one side of the house nor the energy of the other.

Eurasians abound in Calcutta. A quest for some old dames, whom I had been asked to look up, led me into the queer overcrowded corners in which these poor people live. Their quarters were in some of the houses that had come down in the world. Rooms, which had originally been large and important, were now divided into minute spaces by thinly plastered partitions, half of the window belonging to one or other of the tenants. A painted imitation of a fireplace sometimes adorned the wall, and in one room curled paper-shavings of many hues hung over the painted grate. All the old ladies wore dressing-gowns, and everywhere the high-pitched chatter of their neighbours could be distinctly heard through the thin partitions.

What histories could be written of the hybrid habits, the misfortunes and vicissitudes of this luckless part of the community, who owe their existence to our presence in India! Of course there are splendid exceptions, but as a whole they are one of the most unfortunate races in the empire.

I can never forget the look on their upturned faces
on the last night of the year, when a good man
spoke to them.   It was so helpless, as if, with
their childish self-complacence in abeyance, they
acknowledged their inborn weakness and waited
for succour.   They have however at least one most
fortunate characteristic.   I have seldom met a
Eurasian who was what we call morbid.   Old,
decrepit, penniless, there was not one of their
race in St Mary's Home who was not ready at the
sound of a jig to totter to her feet, if only to hold
up her hands to the tune, and this light-heartedness must no doubt save them many a tear.

DEAREST A., — Did I ever tell you that Baron von Sternberg, whom you met when you were with us in Simla, was an intimate friend of the beautiful Uhlan person in blue and silver uniform, who was an inevitable feature in the front row of the old Opera House in Dresden on the nights on which Wagner's operas were performed?

Don't you see him again sitting bolt upright and motionless, his kind blue eyes following every movement of the adorable Prima Donna, and hear Madame Baumgarten's voluble, audible Schwärmerei poured into our all too receptive ears, and her tragic tales of a hopeless devotion baulked by a cruel and worldly parent, whose dying prayers had extorted a vow from our straight and motionless hero that he would resign all hope of ever uniting his fate with Tannhäuser's peerless Elizabeth, the Flying Dutchman's Senta, or any of the Wagnerian heroines that were represented for us by the beautiful Prima Donna, with her romantic

Uhlan in the foreground as the shadowy hero of all
the romance ?

Finally followed a letter to Scotland in Madame
Baumgarten's cramped spidery German handwriting
announcing his suicide. *Was für eine Geschichte*
it was, and half of it nonsense, according to
Baron von Sternberg, the worldly mother cut
out, the dying prayers and extorted vows, and
last of all the suicide, as his friend really died
of ptomaine poisoning, contracted at a dinner-
party at which Baron von Sternberg was one of
the guests.

I told him about our misadventure with Wagner's
sister, Frau Avenarius, when she was the first
guest to arrive at our little dance at Dresden, and
we had to tear down all the floral decorations with
which we meant to impress our German friends, as
the scent made her quite faint.

The idiosyncrasy apparently belongs to the family,
for whenever Wagner came to stay with the Baron's
people, either the flowers or he had to leave. He
was quite a child of the house, and used to wander
off to the woods by himself when the spirit moved
him, ' to hear melodies.'

Baron von Sternberg described with some humour
the crowds which assembled on the platform of the
Berlin Railway Station to welcome Wagner's return from his honeymoon with his bride, the late

Madame von Bülow, Herr von Bülow being himself amongst the rejoicing crowd. The philosophic
attitude of the despised ex-husband reminded me
somehow of J. G. C.'s running comment on her
mother's disapprovals at breakfast : 'And *yet* I
enjoy my eggs!'

Do you think such trifles hardly worth repeti-
tion ? I like them, because they bring home to
me that those immortals were really flesh and blood
like ourselves. I always thought of Napoleon as
a Pyramid or some kind of supernatural genie, till
I read Lord Rosebery's description of him sitting
in his house in St Helena, clothed in a pair of
pyjamas with a red bandana handkerchief tied
round his head. I realised then for the first time,
with a thrill of bewilderment, that he was a man !

The Baron has flitted to some bigger diplomatic
post, and we have other delightful representatives
of his Empire, always very pleasant additions to
our varied society. I love diplomats, their manners
are so beguiling, although the indiscretions which
lay bare dear human nature are distinctly conspicuous by their absence. Even when they seem
to present you with Blue Beard's keys, you may
be fairly certain that none of them would *really*
fit the only important lock !

We had an amusing discussion with a youthful
German secretary on the eve of his leaving Simla.

I challenged him to deny that Germany had secret
designs on our colonies as dumping-grounds for her
surplus population; that her admirals coveted some
of our coaling-stations and harbours; or that her
army and navy combined would enjoy having us
as their target.

Of course he denied every count in the challenge.
Germany, far from being over-populated and a prey
to land-hunger, had vast tracts of land within her
own boundaries, which were steadily being colonised
by his countrymen, who had found less favourable
conditions in other countries than the Fatherland
offered. Germany's war with us was commercial,
and she was perfectly satisfied with the result.

We could certainly understand his satisfaction
on this head, so far as it might be based on the
commercial supremacy of his countrymen in our
Indian bazaars, where the conquests might be
counted in thousands of thalers built up out of
farthing profits. Indian jewellery, Indian toys,
supplied by Germany, Indian pottery superseded
by German enamel ware, Indian brass by German
glass, clocks, watches, knives, ink-stands, scissors,
needles, matches, looking-glasses; oleographs of
gods of the Indian Pantheon hobnobbing on the
stalls with portraits of the German Kaiser and
Kaiserin.

Mein Vaterland, mein Vaterland,
This is the place for me,

might be inscribed in gold above the entrance to every bazaar.

Our discussion with the German Secretary was nothing to the affair with the Japanese Consul. Of all the reticent diplomats, by the way, the Japanese hold the palm. One of their most genial representatives, a gallant little major with a keen sense of humour, dined with us one evening alone, while the Russo-Japanese war was in its earliest stage.

You should have seen him and Jim on their knees on the drawing - room floor after dinner, with a Japanese map stretched out on the carpet and matches arranged to represent the positions of the different armies, arguing, if you please, as to what the next move should be !—the Japanese major illustrating his views by a parable of a big Russian knife threatening the life of a Japanese chicken, Jim moving the knife and the chicken to what he considered more telling positions. I closed the campaign by assuring the major that he might quite possibly conquer the Russians, but he need never hope to convince his host that he was beaten by any mortal man in an argument !

DEAR L.,—'How do we like Simla?' My dear child, how do you like Life? I suppose most people would answer the same questions in the same way, 'Sometimes very much. Sometimes not at all.' 'The world is too much with us late and soon' for a person who was born with Byron's love of thinking of his friends in solitude, and of solitude when he was with his friends.

The wicked fairy who presides at the birth of babies who are born tired, slips into their hands a caricature string, and on the day that she pulls it everything is exaggerated *en masse* and beyond recognition, beginning with our neighbours' innocent specialities. Rather high-pitched voices scream, rather low-pitched voices are inaudible, ordinary noses are lengthened till they positively seem to be trailing on the ground! Only solitary confinement has the power to break the spell.

This is the first evening we have had to ourselves for the last fortnight. It has poured every

day and all day for three weeks, not rain as you
know it, but 'the rains' as we hear them; as
rivers that spell landslips, and torrents that roar
down the roofs. Yet, thanks to the wicked fairy,
above their roar, above the sound of the sodden
splash of the rain from the pine-tree branches, I
hear nothing but rickshaws whirling past, their
bells tinkling and their runners shouting 'take
care' to the rickshaw men in front, all of them,
according to my imagination, carrying overwrought
humanity to their twenty-third or possibly fortieth
consecutive 'tamasha,' a ball, a play, a concert, or
more probably the inevitable 'burra khana,' with
which my mind is obsessed.

Which kind of dinner-party will it be? The
alphabetical sort, when all the 'A's' or 'B's' are
invited together? Or the Departmental dinner,
when the I.M.S. or the P.W.D. or the I.C.S.
are asked *en bloc?* How often will the word
'position' with a capital P be exchanged? We
are all so anxious in Simla to be in the right
position for our position, in the right place, and
talking to the right person at the right time, as
befits our position, whether our hearts are heavy
or our pockets are light, that I sometimes think
it would be a public benefit to burn its effigy,
and to induce Mr Stead to engage the shade of
Carlyle to deliver a funeral oration over its ashes,

and intimate where our real position just lies, as
vile wor-r-r-ms hovering betwixt heaven and heat!

I am afraid that the position of my tired pen
only points to the latitudes near the Equator
to - night, although perhaps it will veer when it
has had a good sleep. A friend once told me of
a letter she had received from a Scotch philosopher
on the eve of her marriage. He said he could not
hope she might have unintermittent happiness, for
that was not to be found upon earth, he only desired
she might be enabled to retain a due sense of proportion! This good advice is recalled by one's own
need of it, just at this moment. What has become
of the many original experiences we have had in
Simla, the diplomatic dinners, the dances by torch-
light under the pines, the musical fêtes on moonlit
lawns, the pageants of Viceregal Lodge, its pleasant
dinner-parties and brilliant balls? Where else have
we met so many interesting personalities, travellers,
diplomats, patriots of the desert, soldiers, men of
science, not to speak of dear women and winsome
girls, such crowds of people who are kind and good
as they have opportunity?

When I speak of Simla as a whole as shallow
and shadowless, and picture the afternoon as well
as the evening crowds of whirling rickshaws bearing their burdens to crowded drawing-rooms, where
every one, under the spell of a crowd, seems to

have their head slightly tilted over their shoulder, to be slightly *distrait* with their immediate neighbourhood, with 'dort wo du nicht bist ist das Glück' written upon their preoccupied features, —when I write as if this alone was typical of Simla, can I possibly have forgotten already that afternoon, hardly a year ago, when the Mall witnessed another sight?

Then the rickshaws moved so slowly along it in another direction, carrying such varied occupants. They were people of all classes, of every profession, sunburnt soldiers, pale - faced clerks, some poor woman with her child on her knee and a bunch of flowers in her hand, young people, old people, all silent, all sad, because they were all moving to a churchyard. It was large and full of the dead, but not large enough to hold the living—whom no onlooker that day could ever have described as shallow or shadowless.

For a dear woman was to be buried. No leader of fashion, if you like, she might be, but if sweetness, gentleness and unassuming goodness and kindness can make a face beautiful, then she had beauty. If we are not so much influenced by what people say to us as by what they make us say to ourselves, then no one could ever have met her without wishing they were even a little better than they had been. With a gentle humour all her own, and a kindly knowledge of human nature, like the sun in the heavens, she smiled on the evil as on the good.

'I asked her once " how she could have a certain notorious person to dine with her," but she only said "what am I that I should shut my door upon any poor soul upon earth!"' 'When I was a stranger to India she asked me to stay with her and be married from her house. I had never met her before, but she thought of everything, even of trifles I had forgotten myself, and was everything to me. She might have been my own mother. And it was not only for me she did such beautiful things. In the early morning of my wedding-day she drove three miles out of Peshawur, to lay some flowers on a soldier's grave, because his poor young widow would visit it that day for the first time.' 'She came to my cottage herself when my laddie died.'

These were the things that people said as they moved to the graveyard. 'She was a saint,' men said who had never spoken to one about 'saints' before, but who were as white and drawn as if she had been 'their own mother' too.

The sun was shining down on the Simla hills covered with deodars and rhododendrons, but the churchyard was black with mourners ; women who never showed anything but smiles to the world were silently weeping now; and when talkative Simla returned to the Mall, not a voice broke the silence of the long drive to our homes. Lady Elles was dead.

When I remember that day, I am tempted to burn my letter. But take it as a comment on the folly of turning too many nights into days. I suppose there are a few people in India, as elsewhere, who may be afflicted with what you once called 'swollen egos,' which makes them so sensitive to the slightest touch, that any contact with their neighbours affects them like a succession of blows. I think, however, most people would tell you that they have never known anything but kindness in India. I, for my part, can truly say that in all these years I have only had one unpleasant experience, and I have not the smallest recollection now of what the experience was! I only remember Jim's philosophic comment, when I told him about it, 'Nothing has happened, everything is exactly as it was a minute before it occurred, and you too are just the same. It does not matter.' '*What* does not matter?' 'Anything.'

And so to bed with 'Nothing matters' as the motif of sleep—and a happy uprising!

Dear L.,—We have greatly enjoyed seeing something of Sir Francis Younghusband, whom you of course know of, not only as our responsible British Commissioner in the Thibet Mission, but as 'Times' correspondent in the Chitral Expedition, as well as in South Africa at the time of the Jameson raid and its anti-climax, when Sir Francis' telegram of 4000 words gave us Krüger's future intentions, as communicated by himself.

I had wished to meet him ever since I had read his first book, 'The Heart of a Continent,' an account of a journey made when he was 23 and a young Lieutenant in the 1st Dragoon Guards, when he made his way to Manchuria, thence to Pekin, through the Gobi desert, Chinese Turkestan and over the Himalayas back to India.

During the perusal of the last part of that journey one went through every sensation of nightmare, while ascending the valley that leads to the Mustagh Pass, which had to be crossed. Sir Francis and his small party of followers found

308

themselves on the extremity of an immense glacier extending for miles, and blocked by cliffs of ice two or three hundred feet high, with caverns which reminded one of those 'caverns measureless to man' in Kubla Khan. They were now nearly 20,000 feet above sea-level. As they continued the ascent, the plot only deepened. Glaciers to right of them, glaciers to left of them, the ground quite impracticable for ponies, some of the men sent back to arrange their return journey.

Go on the rest of the party must, or retrace their footsteps for 150 miles, with only four days' supplies. At the top of the Pass a cliff to descend, almost sheer precipice, and although everything that foresight could obtain had been collected, neither ice-axes nor other mountaineering appliances were to be had, only some good strong ropes, a pick-axe, and for foot-gear some native boots of soft leather, which gave no grip on the ice. Down they let themselves, from any slight projection or rock, and what a relief it was to the reader when they reached level ground at last!

Speaking of the book and its writer one evening to his friend, Colonel Dunlop Smith, I heard a story from him which I must give you, to let you understand the stuff of which our Empire-builders are made.

Sir Francis Younghusband was still in his twenties, a Captain now in the King's Dragoon Guards and not yet appointed to the Indian Political Department. He had somehow heard rumours, which gave him reason to believe that Russians meant to pay a visit to neutral territory in the Pamirs.

Lord Lansdowne was then Viceroy of India, Sir Mortimer Durand Foreign Secretary. In the summer of 1890 Captain Younghusband was commissioned to travel round the whole of the Pamir region, which he forthwith did.

A year passed and then reports reached him, as reports do in the mysterious East, that a small party of Russians had entered the Pamirs and proclaimed them Russian territory. The report in this instance proved to be true, for in the course of his travels Captain Younghusband came upon an encampment of Cossacks, keeping guard over stores left by a party of Russians, who were meantime reconnoitring the neighbourhood. On their reappearance, with the Russian flag carried in front, they were invited to enjoy Captain Younghusband's hospitality in his tent, a civility returned by them the same evening.

Colonel Yonoff, who was in command, reappeared three nights later with thirty Cossacks, and the announcement that a despatch from his Govern-

ment instructed him to insist on Captain Younghusband removing himself from Russian territory.

Captain Younghusband disputed his right, and
asked what Colonel Yonoff would do if he refused
to make off. He said he would turn him off by
force. Captain Younghusband replied that he
would report the affair to his Government, and that
he would only go under protest, if Yonoff would
sign his maps, give him a letter and say in writing that he had been turned off the Pamirs ' by
order of the Czar.'

Yonoff gave him the letter, which also stipulated
that certain passes over the Pamirs, indicated by
him, were not to be used. Younghusband knew
of another, if perilous, pass, and agreed. Then,
these points settled, the two high contracting
parties had supper in Captain Younghusband's
tent.

The end of the incident was that thirteen days
later the British Ambassador at St Petersburg
had made a protest to the Russian Government;
subsequently the Russian Ambassador in London
apologised to Lord Salisbury for the illegal action
of Colonel Yonoff; and the Pamir Agreement
finally declared that the place claimed as Russian
territory was beyond the sphere of Russian influence.

Was not that a well-managed affair ?   Nothing
will ever convince me that good traditions are not
a valuable asset in life !

So much for his travels, and now for our talks
with Sir Francis, which we so greatly enjoyed,
although it is not easy to meet any one often in
the whirl of Simla engagements.   Now at a dance,
now at a dinner, on a walk round the hill, or again
on an evening when Mr and Mrs Denison Ross
discoursed enchanting music.

We heard little about his travels on these
occasions; only once, when something recalled the
visit you and I paid with H. H. C. to Freshwater,
and our walks and talks with the Poet Laureate,
when Sir Francis said that his pocket-companion,
on the eventful journey from Pekin to India,
contained his favourite extracts from Tennyson,
and that he gave it to Lady Tennyson after her
husband's death.

Another afternoon our talk was of one we shall
ever love, and I told him how strange it had
always seemed to me that he should have had
all the insight and the subtle intuitive power
which we associate with high - strung natures,
without being in the least highly strung himself :
of the bigness of his soul and heart and physique,
his joy in God, in life and in human nature, and

of how singularly unaware he was of his own goodness.

Sir Francis said that was the type of man he loved best. His experience had personally been that it was the fullest, healthiest natures that had the most wonderful spiritual insight, citing Walt Whitman, whose poetry he preferred to that of any living poet, adding that John Addington Symonds, of all people in the world, shared this opinion. Walt Whitman's attitude to life was so big, living amongst humble neighbours in the end, sharing their lives, giving them his best, quite natural, quite unconscious, and all the time writing his great poems.

Shall we ever understand, by the way, why certain things, music, art, poetry such as Walt Whitman's, or perhaps some human beings who feel it themselves, give us the sense of the Cosmos and the glory uniting the whole. We cannot live on those heights, such moments do not come at our bidding, but none who have ever had them can doubt their reality.

The great truths of science present this magnetic rod to those who can wield it. I could therefore well understand why Sir Francis felt that of all the people he met when he was lately in England, the man who impressed him most was Professor

J. J. Thomson.   For, when Sir Francis had been awarded the Honorary Degree of Doctor of Science at Cambridge, this great genius had shown him his model of the ultimate atom, composed of swift electrons whirling round a central point.

We all know that the last word has not yet been said about electricity, nor just how far it is the medium of thought and of the mysterious power which some people undoubtedly possess of divining the past happenings of other men's lives.   Personally I hope that such last words may never be uttered, for what would life be without mystery ?

DEAREST G., — Calcutta has the good fortune to possess a Bengali writer of plays, who is a very remarkable man. I met him by the merest chance in the course of a round of visits which I paid to Bengali ladies in their zenanas, a genial little Scotch lady, who is attached to the Scotch Mission College, having asked me to give prizes to the little Hindu girls who are taught in their own homes.

The general impression left on one's mind by our other visits was of whiteness and greenery, of spotless rooms, plants in flower, birds singing in their cages, glimpses of idol-chambers, with grotesque brass figures in a row on the planked floor, and benign hostesses of ample outline, who had something of the bovine mildness of the cows they worship in their own placid expression. It was pleasant to see the kindly relationship which exists between them and my cheerful little companion. There was always some history of the different members of the family, which had to be told by our hostess, and a present of fruit or flowers awaiting the family friend.

Miss S. was greatly disappointed that our host was not at home in the last house we visited, as she told me he was a most interesting man, and one of the best-known writers of plays in Bengal. We were taken to his private room, which was almost furnished with books. They lay on the table, sat on the chairs, and crowded the bookcases which lined the walls. There were books of travel, history, biography, poetry, philosophy, science, but above all numerous specimens of dramatic literature.

I was studying their varied titles when my little friend exclaimed, ' Ah, here he comes,' and I heard swift steps traversing the corridor, which ran round the central courtyard of the house. Even the steps would have arrested my attention, because an Indian's step is usually noiseless, as if he did not lift his foot from the ground. These were rapid, impetuous, resolute. Then our host entered, and I saw he was quite unlike any type of Indian I had ever met. He was tall and slight, with silvery, straight hair, which fell back from his lofty, narrow forehead to his neck. He had a hooked nose, a sensitive, mobile mouth, and piercing, dark eyes, intent and mournful in their expression. He might have been a lawyer-poet, if you can imagine such a conjunction of opposites, and he reminded me of some portrait of Molière or Racine, or of a dramatist belonging to that period.

I felt as if I had known him always, and as if we began as old friends. We sat down opposite to each other, and talked for an hour! Yet I can only remember bits of our conversation.

It began about his books : then it branched off to his plays. 'There are so few subjects with which I can deal,' he said, speaking very quickly and intensely. 'We are a conquered race. War I cannot deal with. You know our customs and our marriage laws. Love stories are out of the question. Sometimes I like to write a satire.' He threw back his head and his eyes blazed. 'I like to show up those creatures of my race, who go to England and forget their own traditions, and come back dressed like foreigners, monkeys, beef-eating rascals. I like to hold them up to ridicule, their clothes, their habits, and all their tomfoolery. But, best of all, I like to write about our religion. I adore Krishna :' and he bent forward and looked as if he were speaking to a disembodied spirit.

I asked him if he really adored him in all his aspects and incarnations, or adored the customs which had become a feature of his worship, and which could hardly be even discussed?

' These are human weaknesses, human mistakes.'

' Yet they came into his life, and are borrowed from that.'

' Still I flatter myself, Memsahib, I have the vanity to think, that our national gods——'

' Forgive me for interrupting you, but I would like to know if you really think we can be vain about God, and if you really believe that different nations can have different gods and that such things can be geographical?   May we not trust and believe that we have all one God and Father, who loves each one of His children?   Why should we not all love Him too?   What has nationality to do with that?'

Then I told him that the old Pundit in the Benares College had said that if the English Raj were here for a hundred years longer, the country would be Christian.

' If the English are here?   Memsahib, may I say something?   Do you know what we call your race?   We call you the Vaishyas, the merchant class.   You are interested in our fields and canals, in material improvements, but in us, in ourselves, in our homes, you are not interested.'

' But you must remember we promised after the Mutiny — and we have kept that promise — that we would never interfere with you in your personal life, or in your racial idiosyncrasies.   As long as you kept the law, we promised we would never interfere in your private life, within the four walls of your home.'

' I think, Memsahib, that promise has been carried too far.'

' Well, you and I cannot perhaps alter that. But tell me what you think of what the old Pundit predicted.'

Then he folded his hands, as we fold them in prayer, and said ' If you mean by it, not that we should forget our own history, our own race, not that we should dress like monkeys in the hope of becoming like Englishmen, but that we should worship Christ, that great Being about whom I cannot read without tears, then all I can say from my heart is Amen and Amen.'

Darling Mrs S.,—We have flitted to a house
which is nearer Jim's office than our last one
was. In every Hill Station we have so far been
successful in finding some home from which we
could look out on the Himalayas and beautiful
scenery. From our verandah at this moment we
see the near ranges of hills covered with crimson
rhododendrons and topped by gigantic pines, and
beyond these, far-away peaks crowned by ever-
lasting snows or wreathed in mist. At dawn or
sunset, by moonlight or in thunderstorms, they
are indescribably beautiful.

I am sure it is a mental rest for tired workers,
including their wives, to witness such beauty and
to be alone with Nature sometimes, and away
from the varied crowds in which one is too
often immersed. The owners of this house were
Mr and Mrs Everard Cotes, and if you wish to
know just how beautiful our garden is, you should
read her 'On the Other Side of the Latch,' and
learn how it grew.

From our morning-room, where we breakfast, we look out on our lilac-trees, an archway covered by masses of wistaria, and a flower-bed with rows of forget-me-nots, sweet peas, and wallflowers. When the time of roses has come, we shall see them everywhere, and the yellow China clusters, which will cover one side of the house, will tap on our window, and the air be full of the scent of deep crimson and yellow Gloire de Dijon roses.

I spend the forenoon in our red-matted verandah, where we have a writing-table and easy-chairs, and here too we have lunch on a little round table in a far corner. For thanks to our change of venue, Jim can come home for an hour in the middle of the day, and some of our special friends invite themselves sometimes too.

Komal, the cook, whom we inherited from A. and F. when they left India, and the Goanese butler, are two of those special treasures who are always to be relied on to be at their best! The butler especially is quite an old family friend, and tells me every morning what ' we ' require, and what has to be ordered, and keeps the men under him up to the mark. We never forget, by the way, to praise them when they so well deserve it, which I think heartens them up.

The old gardener is an absolute dear. He has learnt to arrange the flowers, which he calls his 'babas,' just as I like them to look, with ferns and mosses and wandering grasses which make them seem as if they were at home in the woods.

At the end of the second drawing-room, which is really the music-room, Mr Everard Cotes put some steps and stairs, which lead up to the window and are covered with pots of flowers in bloom, making such a pretty vista. Thanks also to our predecessors, who love to 'create' houses, the drawing-room is like a room in some old country-house, with latticed windows and a carved bookcase above the carved mantelpiece. In short, what with Lady Isabella's Chesterfield and your old bureau, the odds and ends of furniture, the pictures and the what-not that one has picked up in lucky hours, we feel already as if we had been established here for a century.

By the way, we dined with the great Lord Kitchener last evening, quite a small party, invited to meet his cousin and a Boer friend, a far-travelled person and sportsman, who fought in the South African war, and with whom S. C. and I foregathered last autumn on our voyage to India.

Lord Kitchener has carried his genius for organisation into Snowdon, which is transformed beyond recognition, the whole house replanned: a new hall, dining-room and library created, all of them filled with *objets d'art*, as our host has pre-eminently the collector's spirit which adds such a zest to life.

The hall to which we adjourned after dinner, to hear the Hungarian band discourse sweet music from the new gallery, has its panelled walls hung with trophies of war and the chase. There is a wonderfully cosmopolitan collection of rare old china in the drawing-room and a specially beautiful Japanese picture painted on silk, calculated to make any one break the tenth commandment.

Lord Kitchener has apparently the love of the soil inherited by man from his forefather Adam, for when we spoke of his new garden of Eden, beautified by terraces, scented by roses, and planted with fruit-trees, he told me he had transformed an island on the Nile, facing one of the cataracts, in just such a way. Some of us, haunted by thoughts of the morrow, extend our anxious fears into dreams of a useless old age. Who knows but that some day, years hence, when nodding over our newspaper in our arm-chair in front of the fire, we may read with surprise and envy that one of our conquering generals has followed the example of the warlike Roman Emperor, who in his old age resigned the cares of State and the charge of the Army to retire to a peaceful retreat in the Apennines, where he devoted the rest of his days to beautifying earth.

Darling G.,—Before this letter arrives you must have read every ghastly detail of the earthquake at Dharmsala in the columns of your daily paper. We thought of sending you a reassuring telegram, but came to the conclusion that the omission of our names from the list of the sufferers would be a sufficient guarantee of our safety.

As it happens, we were not even alarmed by the successive shocks, as we had not the faintest conception of their terrific force. What happened, as far as we were concerned, was that we woke up about 6.30, dimly conscious that the room was swaying. Then, when a large picture fell from the wall, I knew what the swaying sensation meant, and with the cry of 'An earthquake,' sprang into the middle of the room. But Jim, still drowsy, only said dreamily that our house was in the cleft of the hill, that it was lightly built, that there was no room above ours, his last sleepy murmur being that if he *was* to be taken, he could not imagine a pleasanter place for his last moments on earth than his bed. I was really no more alarmed than he was, and laughed as I saw him sleeping right through six successive, definite shocks!

And to think that only 500 yards away in the Cecil Hotel women were going through agonies of terror, one of them seeing her baby in its crib sliding suddenly before her eyes from her side of the room to the opposite wall, another carrying hers downstairs while the steps went up and down, as if they might hit her, she said, and some other woman losing her wits and screaming on end, as she has never ceased doing.

Such a contrast to our dear Mrs C., whose experiences were ghastly enough to shake any one's nerves, but whose sanity was preserved by her saving sense of humour. She is one of the people we have loved best in India from the hour we first met her in Rawal Pindi. She is like some French Marquise you might see on an ancient snuff-box, with her pink-and-white complexion and beautiful blue eyes, and her white hair which must surely be powdered for, notwithstanding her bountiful presence, she looks as young as her heart, and that too is large enough to have a corner in it for every person she meets. She is one of the very few who could echo our darling Mrs S.'s description of her own house as being ' like the ark, which both clean and unclean animals may enter '; and an eternal curiosity about everything that calls itself human has saved her, she says, from ever knowing what it was to be 'bored' in her life.

You can imagine how she is loved by us all. I always tell her that when I see a scarlet phalanx in a ball-room surrounding a sofa, and hear it emitting volleys of laughter like a succession of *feus de joie*, I know where the wittiest woman in Simla is to be found.

When the hour for our evening walk came then, on the eventful day of the earthquake, we set off to hear how things had fared with our friend in the Grand Hotel. Imagine our feelings when we saw the wing of the building in which she was quartered in ruins! We were told we should find Mrs C. in a far-off verandah, and there to be sure she was, holding a court surrounded by friends and wearing a large warm ulster supplied by the Hotel. When her entourage had made their adieux, we heard her laughing account of her string of adventures.

'I was lying in bed,' she said, 'when I saw the roof of my room coming down on me. I had hardly time to realise that I could never reach the door in time to escape from my fate, when I was engulfed by the roof, and went in my bed through the floor, fortunately feet foremost. Then I heard the voice of the Hotel Manager shouting my name,

in a tone that told me he believed he was addressing a corpse. I called out to him " I am not dead.
You must dig me out," which he did, and then
wrapped me up in a scarlet blanket. So attired,
I slid down a plank he had attached to the
window-sill and by which he had crept up to my
room.

'Hardly had I sat down on a chair when I saw
a man with a camera, preparing to take my
photograph, which I at once interdicted. Then a
postman held out a parcel to me, saying in his
staccato voice "Value-payable post, five rupees to
pay, please kindly sign and put date," and when
he was followed by a Frenchman whose first words
to me were "Mon dieu! hev a peppermint," and
who then proposed I should at once run away
from the earthquake, leave Simla and drive down
the hill with him in an ekka, there and then and
just as I was, in my red blanket, the mad in-
congruity of it all made me fear I might have
hysterics if I did not do something prosaic at
once.

'As my dressing-room and the staircase leading
to it were still intact, I went there to pack my
boxes, but was soon interrupted by the Hotel
people, who won't let us enter the house, they
are so afraid of another earthquake—so here we
have sat all day, receiving a succession of visitors.

I sent off a telegram to my General, by the way, just saying "I am all right." He had not then heard of the earthquake, so his first reply only was " Thanks, so am I," but a second has come since he heard the news, written in a more serious spirit.'

It occurred to us on our way home that the best gift we could send our friend and her daughter, in the General's absence, was a bottle of champagne, and next day she told us that, thanks to that tonic, her eyelids had come down, although her daughter could not close hers, having had the double horror of narrowly escaping the same fate in her flight from a collapsing room, and of looking in through a broken window on her mother's quarters in ruins, while a man standing beside her told her that she must be dead.

Mrs C.'s pluck and vitality stood her in good stead, and next afternoon saw her out again in her rickshaw, when, as she told us afterwards, she was much amused by the pleasantries of her friends. 'The first person to greet me,' she said, 'was Sir Louis Dane, who declared I must be an angel to fall without hurting myself.' When I repeated this to Mr Erle Richards who had joined us, his only comment was : 'Ah yes, and fallen angels are always so interesting !'

'Then I met the great Lord K. of K., who

wished to know what the owner of the Grand
Hotel had charged me? I asked "For what?"
"Why, I heard," he said, "that you had stepped
out of bed hastily, whereupon the floor gave
way beneath you at once and you suddenly
appeared in the room below." And this joke
he made me repeat to Lord Lamington and a whole
host of people at Sir Archie Hunter's dinner-party
that evening!'

Since that eventful day we have had constant
shocks of earthquakes, rumbling under our feet
at all hours, not exactly a *sauce piquante* calculated
to flavour existence, but we get more or less
accustomed to everything, even to dancing, with
the rumbles that reach us from Dharmsala as an
undercurrent to the beat of the waltz.

> Et on disait ' pauvre Constance,'
> Et on dansait jusqu'à jour
> Chez l'Ambassadeur de France.

By the way, I must tell you a story against
myself, which perhaps may amuse you, as the
characteristic *faux pas* of our friends sometimes
do. You know it is *de règle* for everybody in
Simla, at the beginning of every season, to write
their names in the Viceregal Lodge book. You
also know how sadly I share the family inability
to remember people's names, and still more their
official titles.

Before starting for Viceregal Lodge on this yearly quest I begged Jim to give me 'for reference,' as they say in State papers, the name of his official appointment in black and white. He said it was quite unnecessary, all that was needed being our address, as we have flitted this year to new quarters. Judge then of my feelings when I was confronted, on the steps of the Viceregal Lodge, by a lordly chaprassi in scarlet and gold, bearing a square white board on which was written, in large black letters, an intimation to the effect that gentlemen were especially requested to add their official title to their name and address.

What was I to do? To make any mistake upon such a sacred subject would be little short of the unpardonable sin. To beat a retreat would be cowardice. I looked round me in search of relief, but found no one to help me excepting one possible lady, whose air suggested a knowledge of India and the things that ought to be known. So summoning up my courage I informed her that I was Mrs James Wilson and would be so grateful if she would tell me, if she happened to know it, how my husband's official title should be correctly described?

'So you are Mrs Wilson?' she answered. 'I have heard about you from Mrs C., who told me to call on you. We have just settled down in Simla, in fact this is the first day I have been able to leave my boxes—all empty now—and I meant to call on you on my way home. No, I am afraid I can't help you about the official title, but I wonder if you could tell *me* how many m's there are in Commandant? My husband is a Commandant, and as I cannot spell anything, I cannot feel certain about the number of m's.' Neither could I, but I ventured to lay my stake upon two. Then, taking my courage and my pen in my hands, I took aim at the official title and actually hit it off! Can *you* give me now, I wonder, the address of a Home for Imbeciles?

CALCUTTA, 1905.

DARLING U.,—How does it fare with you in your
beautiful Peace Point, under the shadow of the
blue hills of Tasmania and in sight of the Southern
Sea? Send me one of those letters which you only
can write, with the charm that is *you* in their very
look. They always make me almost believe they
have lain in lavender!

Tell me what you have read and *musicirt*, and
how the 'cello behaves and the book-bindery, what
piece of old lace you are copying now, what are
the latest honours won by your boy at Oxford, and
last but not least, about all your dear people at
home. It is a roundabout way to hear of them,
but who cares how far news has travelled, if it
only arrives at last and is all that one hopes it
will be?

I have been thinking about you to-day, wishing
you had been with us when Mr Havell, the Keeper
of the Calcutta Art Gallery, was our guide and
showed us his beautiful collection of Indian pictures.
How you would have appreciated every point, every

subtle shade of their beauty! As it is, I can only attempt to convey some idea of them to you in an ignorant, amateur fashion. I did not even know that such Indian pictures existed till a week ago, when I saw a batch of them in a friend's drawing-room, one representing a group of men seated round a camp-fire, very well drawn and full of individuality and life, the firelight reflected on the trunks and branches of neighbouring trees, with a dark background and starlit sky. Another, two women seated on a white marble terrace, edged with flowers, the whole full of sunlight and the delicate sense of colour which one associates with Japanese art. Our host told us that we could see many more beautiful Indian pictures in the Museum than those he had had the good luck to pick up, and when Mr Havell, who is naturally an enthusiast for Indian art, offered himself as our guide in this new strange world of beauty, you can imagine how we appreciated our good fortune.

You must read the book upon Indian Art he is bringing out to realise how far India's influence on painting, sculpture, or architecture spread—to Northern Europe on one hand, through the Goths and Huns and their skilled craftsmen, and eastward to Siam, Ceylon, Java, Japan and China, where Buddhist missionaries carried their faith, and

Indian colonists, sculptors, and artists left their impress in undying monuments of their artistic genius.

There are beautiful specimens of the Persian school in the Calcutta Museum. Some of these painters found their way to the Court of that cosmopolitan genius Akbar, where they, along with Hindu and Mahomedan artists, became famous for their skill in drawing and painting portraits and illuminating legends and histories of contemporary life. The miniature portraits, with one of Saadi amongst them, were simply enchanting, reminding one constantly of the early Dutch and Flemish schools, and especially of Holbein. They found at least one appreciative contemporary European admirer in Rembrandt, whose home was at Amsterdam, then the head-quarters of the Dutch East India Company. Collecting Oriental wood-carvings and paintings was, as it happened, one of his hobbies, and some of his pen-and-ink sketches in the British Museum and the Louvre are copies of these Oriental miniatures.

I wish you could see their later portraits of Anglo-Indians of the Georgian period, 'his Margaret,' as they spoke of themselves in those days, and 'her Mr Phillips,' to the life, a realistic study in one case of 'her Mr Phillips' taking his ease

on a couch, smoking his hookah, with several
creature comforts, which are obsolete now, on the
ground beside him.

It is 'mystic, symbolic, transcendental' India,
however, that awakens one's greatest interest,
although, in its representations in sculpture or
painting, one has to forgive it some of its grotesque elements, which are the medium of its
expression.

Mr Havell is convinced that Hindu artists pur-
posely 'suppressed the details of the physical body
with the intention of suggesting the inner Self,
purified and exalted by communion with the
Universal Soul.'

This set one wondering why in so many countries
the attempt to represent the Infinite should so
often result in misrepresenting the Finite! Although a man's spirituality may transform his
being, why should it be supposed to deform his
anatomy? Since this does not occur in Nature,
why should it happen in Art? Surely it is better
to recognise the artist's limitations in this respect,
while bowing before his spiritual genius.

And yet it remains true that such spiritual
geniuses succeed in making us see the unseen,
which they saw with their 'inner eye.' The
mystical school of painting is what many of us
love best in every country, till we almost come

to love its quaint outlines too, because they have become associated in our minds with that spiritual insight which sees and hears what is neither seen nor heard through the mortal senses. One of the most beautiful pictures in the Museum is painted by a modern artist, Abanindro Nath Tagore, who belongs to this mystical school. It represents a male and female *Sidha*—spirits of the upper air, half-human, half-divine, who, with hands enlocked and bearing an instrument of music, are being borne by the winds on the clouds towards the Himalayas.

I long to possess some of these treasures, and Mr Havell has promised to send me one or two of the pictures that are offered to him by their owners to be bought for the Museum if they, when they arrive, should prove not quite perfect enough for his gallery. In fact I have one already, a curious Maeterlincky representation of a woman on a house-top, gazing up at the stars, and awakening one's fears that she may walk into space. You shall see some others I hope the next time we are at home together !

We are greatly enjoying our life in Calcutta, although greatly missing A. and F. S., who are now established at home. Jim is all day at the tread-mill of work in his office, but if he leaves it before it is dark we generally manage to do something interesting. We went, for instance, last night to a meeting of the Asiatic Society, when a Bengali, who had travelled in Thibet, explained how they elect a new Llama from amongst the Thibetan children, choosing the child who proves to their satisfaction that he has transmigrated from the Llama who has lately deceased. Curiously enough all Llamas used to die before they were eighteen years old. There is a problem for you to solve while you are lace-making!

By the way, when do you next go home to see your boys? Jim hopes he may be able to secure some leave next year and arrive in time for Jack's Christmas holidays. Could we not all meet in Switzerland?

Dear N.,—Why were you not with us last Thursday to take part in our 'Harvest Home,' and to dream that you heard old Mackenzie scraping his fiddle and saw M'Culloch cracking his fingers and emitting his wheezy, quavering 'hooch'? You should have been present to join in the fray, but as you were not, you must hear how it all came about.

The prologue to the play was that the Monsoon lasted for a peculiarly long spell this year, and was still with us when the date arrived which was fixed for the annual football tournament. The rain poured steadily day and night. The mountains were hidden by mist, the ground was a sea of mud. Everything was dreary and damp.

Our house overlooks Annandale, the cup in the hills in which gymkhanas, races and football tournaments are held. Down in the swampy hollow we could see the tents in which the football teams were housed, amongst them men belonging to several Highland regiments. Daily we pitied the lot of these men, with little to read and nothing to do, cooped up in their damp, crowded quarters.

One day it occurred to us that it would be a great pleasure to us, and also a pleasant change for the soldiers, if one or two of the Scotch teams came upon different afternoons to have tea with us. We consulted some of their officers, who happened to be old friends of our own, and they welcomed the suggestion.

So behold us seated round two tables in the dining - room last Tuesday, Jim presiding at one, and I at the other, with half - a - dozen ladies born, by good fortune, on the right side of the Border, to add by their presence to ' the gaiety of nations,' and ' the gallant Gordons ' in their element, very discursive, very punctilious, delightfully homely and frankly enjoying themselves.

The entertainment ended with an impromptu concert in the drawing-room, begun by our best soprano and continued by the men. ' I'll gie ye "the Auld Scotch sangs"' said one of them, fired by the music ; and swinging his kilt, as he marched to the piano, he sang the old plaintive air and the words I remember so well.

> Oh sing to me the auld Scotch sangs,
>   In the good auld Scottish tongue,
> The sangs my father loved to hear,
>   The sangs my mither sung,

As she sat beside my cradle,
  Or crooned me on her knee,
And I wadna sleep, she sang so sweet
  The auld Scotch sangs to me.

The people of India transmigrate onwards; we do it backwards sometimes. The soldier sang, yet it was not his voice I heard but that of another, whose voice has been silent for many a year, and the mist that came through the open window came from the hills of Nevermore and lay between me and the singer.

But to return to the present. There was a break in the clouds, although the sun had not yet dried the ground, when the football team of the 42nd followed their compatriots on Thursday to our second tamasha, which ended this time by the men dancing two sets of reels. If they fight half as well as they dance, I can only say that I would rather see any friend of ours as their host than their enemy!

A dear little curly-headed boy, whose father had been in the 42nd, was the hero of the hour. All the men worshipped him, and you should have seen them gravely marching down the avenue when they left us, with him at their head, and as gravely saluting him, when they handed him over to his nurse!

Speaking of dancing, I think I must tell you of a delightfully ambiguous compliment, paid me the other night at a ball. We have had a darling young friend, Mrs Dowding, staying with us, whose goodness, charm, and beauty have been appreciated by every being who has ever met her. I have so loved ' mothering' her, and having all her young friends about us. One of the nicest amongst them, a young A.D.C., joined us in the ball-room the other evening and, after securing some dances from her, asked me if I would sit out 'number three' with him. I said I should be delighted. Then, thinking of his short programme and many friends, I added ' But how about youth and beauty ? '

Imagine my amusement when he answered, ' I prefer you to *both*.' I turned to share my smiles with another resplendent being, only to be met by another magnificent bow and the assurance that he quite agreed with his friend. It reminded me so of Jack !

Dearest U.,—I have been living in the past with you all this morning, dreaming of those old days in Cannstadt, and of the hours I spent in my own particular nook in your sanctum, the look of it all, with flowers everywhere, books everywhere, and your pet pictures covering the walls. Most beautiful picture of all, I see darling A., as she sometimes stood in the doorway, looking in on us, a vision of sunshine and spring. I hear the tones of your haunting voice as you sang my favourite songs; or read, with a voice that was music too, your favourite poems and books that you wished me to know, weaning my thoughts from the dull and incommunicable grief, whose home was in the blood of one's veins.

I never think of you without a sense of the things which death cannot touch, and which are a part of the infinite beauty that overshadows our finite hour. That is why you are very near me to-day, for I have been reading something that is

342

so perfectly beautiful that I feel I must share it with you.

First, to tell you how the little book came into my hands. We have the good luck to have some of the *corps diplomatique* in Simla, and none of them are more delightful and socially contributive than the Consul General for Germany and his wife, Count and Countess Quadt-Wykradt-Isny. An ideal of beauty, refinement and charm, her life has been spent flitting from one continent to another, like some exquisite migratory bird, who builds her own sheltered nest wherever she settles, establishing an atmosphere of leisure and sense of peace such as one finds in the cool glades of summery woods.

What wandering polyglots some of our diplomats are! I remember the wife of a consul in Tangier telling me that she could never recollect in what particular language she had spoken to anybody, as to her they all seemed equally familiar. Her mother had belonged to one race, her father to another, her husband to a third—quite as complex as a descent from the tower of Babel, if one could apply such a simile to any member of the discreet diplomatic corps!

I could never imagine Countess Quadt possessing an indefinite memory about anything worth remembering, or any other indefiniteness, unless it be in her haunting charm; and wherever her wanderings carry her and Count Quadt—and I fear they will carry them soon from Simla,—they will bear with them still as their constant possession the love of their absent friends.

I found her sitting last Wednesday beneath a wide-spreading tree in her garden, reading a little book, with a yellow paper cover, which she held out as she came to meet me, saying 'I have finished it. It is exquisite. Would you like to read it too? It is "La dernière leçon de Léonard de Vinci à son Académie de Milan, in 1499."'

I opened the book and glanced through it at random, and these were the bits, scattered here and there, which I read:

'L'antiquité a rendu la beauté du corps d'une façon qui ne permet pas de mieux faire. Mais depuis qu'un homme est mort en Orient et que l'Occident le pleure chaque vendredi, une nouvelle beauté a paru avec la nouvelle vérité. Une âme a triomphé du monde par sa seule beauté.

'Ce qu'on dédaigne dans la réalité, qu'on le dédaigne aussi dans l'art. Je peux, à mon gré, représenter Isabelle d'Este ou une gardeuse d'oies, le duc Ludovic ou son palefrenier et cependant je ne le dois pas. Seules les figures suréminentes méritent l'honneur de l'art.

'Ne vous souciez pas de préciser l'expression.

L'énigme attire l'homme et le retient. Une bac-
chante, une nonne, toutes deux trop caractérisées,
n'excitent point l'imagination. Le spectateur
reconnaît tout de suite leur réalité et ne rêve point.
Il faut, au contraire, qu'il doute de sa compréhension
afin que son esprit surexcité abonde en commen-
taires. L'homme n'aime profondément que l'insai-
sissable et n'allume son désir qu'au choc de la
contradiction. Ceux qui cessent d'être dévots
deviennent superstitieux, voire magiciens, par
besoin d'inconnu, et le noble amour de la science
prend sa source dans cette tendance invincible de
notre nature vers l'inexplicable. L'amour de la
vérité, le plus noble mouvement de notre esprit,
cesserait aussitôt s'il parvenait à son but. La
recherche nous passione, elle exercise nos facultés,
augmente en nous la vie supérieure. Le bonheur
n'est qu'un motif d'activité et, si nous le trouvions,
il ne nous suffirait pas : nous irions à d'autres
recherches.'

So far did I read under the shade of the trees,
the rest until midnight last night. What a living
voice from the grave it is! Such an echo of our
own, so modern in spirit, and yet so much saner
than modernity, because one of the greatest
geniuses of all time had the courage to trust the
instincts of his soul. I know you cannot realise
its beauty as a whole from these fragmentary

extracts, but you shall have the little volume soon, as Countess Quadt has promised to procure some copies for me from her bookseller in Italy.

Meantime, one more page or so, which I know will appeal to you, for it is here he reveals the secret of the eternal enigma which no speculation can solve in his portraits. First, then, the methods of his art.

'Nous autres modernes nous ne pouvons inventer, après les anciens, que dans l'expression. Pour en découvrir la théorie, suivons la voie des sciences, l'expérience. Aux moments heureux, quand nous contemplons une magnifique campagne par un beau soleil ou que nous écoutons une suave musique, ou enfin qu'un être aimé nous tend la main, nous ne savons comment rendre notre joie : nous la disons indicible, inexprimable, ineffable, intraduisible. Eh bien ! je propose de dire l'indicible, d'exprimer l'inexprimable, de réaliser l'ineffable et de traduire l'intraduisible. Toutes ces choses sont bien au-delà des proportions : et leur peinture dépasse la représentation plastique, c'est une création spirituelle et qui attirera l'esprit. Ces figures donneront la même joie qu'un visage aimé. Mais le visage renouvelle sans cesse son accent et la figure peinte, non.

'La complexité de l'expression compensera dont la succession si variée des jeux de la physionomie.

En ce genre où je n'ai pas eu de précurseur, voici comme je procède. Je fais plusieurs dessins de la même tete, les uns très tendres, les autres ironiques, ici pleins de langueur et là tout à fait vifs ; et d'après ces versions du même texte, empruntant, d'ici et de là, une nuance, je compose un visage tellement énigmatique que chacun y voit ce qu'il veut, sans cependant se tromper tout à fait sur ce que j'y ai mis, puisque ma volonté était de tramer l'expression avec les fils les plus variés. Dans cet art la figure domine le spectateur par la puissance du regard, et inquiète son esprit par un effet, simultané d'accueil et de dédain, également reparti entre les yeux et les lèvres. Il y a une gloire plus grande à œuvrer en ce genre, parce que les mouvements de la pensée sont plus subtils.'

There you have the secrets of his magical art, which yet remain as mysterious as ever to all who would adventure to use them. The same hand, however, that essayed to reveal them adds, as he nears the end of his last lesson to his followers, his last secret, not unknown to many a soul that understands it, as he did :

' La partie s'efforce constamment de se réunir à son tout pour finir sa souffrance qui est son imperfection même. Comme le papillon vole vers la lumière, l'homme aspire à revenir à son point de départ. Son désir continuel se tend vers le printemps nouveau, et le nouvel été, et vers de nouveaux mois et vers d'autres années ; il trouve les choses désirées bien lentes à venir, sans songer qu'il désire ainsi sa propre mort. Ce mystérieux et fatidique désir est la quintessence, l'esprit des éléments enfermés dans l'âme et qui tendent sans cesse à quitter le corps et à retourner vers celui qui les a formés.'

Why is it that words such as these 'send a melancholy into all our days'? Is it because, as Wordsworth says about his star-gazers—

> 'When the soul a journey long has had
> And is returned into itself,
> It cannot but be sad?'

Send me a letter full of yourself and of your joy in the things that *are*, as well as in those that will be.

DARLING JACK,—Here we are back again after our lovely holiday. The voyage seemed shorter this time than it sometimes does. Taking them all together, fourteen voyages are now over, only five still before me—and then no more long good-byes to be said, first to one half of the family and then to the other at different ends of the world. Still how thankful we may be that we have not been separated for years.

We had such a cheery home-coming. The house had been dressed up to look its best, repainted and polished, with flowers everywhere, and our chairs drawn up by the drawing-room fireplace, the tea-table set, while Komal's best scones and his crispest toast were brought in by the smiling butler, before we had time to sit down.

There were letters of welcome awaiting us from so many friends. But there were two letters awaiting us, different from these, which did not add to our happiness. You remember K. S., who was always so kind to you when you were a child

349

in Shahpur? His sad life is over. He was so
lonely and wretched, we think he must have been
glad to die. He will not be lonely now.

How grieved you will be to hear that dear little
Miss M. is dead too. Such a faithful friend she
has been to us all! She used to spend Christmas
with us sometimes and was here, as you know,
during two or three summers, when I saw her at
intervals and had many a talk with her about old
happy times and her Jack.

I had often urged her to go home and have even
a short holiday, and gave her your message that
she must come to Winchester and let you look
after her, and do just what you wanted and asked
her to do, as usual. She laughed and then wiped
her kind, little eyes, but said she must fulfil her
duties to her present employers and work, too,
as long as she could, to lay up something against
her old age.

Then she had a very satisfactory situation which
she held for some years, and was overjoyed when
her people proposed she should go home with
them and stay for some time in Switzerland. Her
last letter to me was full of gratitude for this
chance of seeing her own people and of projects
for the visit to Switzerland, where she especially
looked forward to making a collection of wild-

flowers and to filling an album with sketches of them in their haunts.

Yesterday's letter told us she died on the voyage, after a short, sudden illness. We shall never forget her, dear faithful soul. What a pang this ending must be to her poor old mother, who so longed to see her again.

Do you remember our talk with the old porter at Winchester, who read us the epitaph on the boy of the many attainments who 'went to heaven instead of Oxford'? 'Not a poor exchange,' I said. The old man answered 'Yes, but there are human hearts and human hopes.' It is just that which makes me foolishly weep for our little Miss M., buried at sea, within reach of her home-coming. But she will weep no more.

Dearest M., — Safely arrived in Simla after a slightly adventurous journey. I reached Bombay on the morning of the 10th of May, and started at noon on my two days' journey. The only other occupant of the single long corridor-carriage was a nice little chaplain, bound for Rawal Pindi. On the following morning the Eurasian waiter came to tell me that there was no more food nor ice in the restaurant-car and that the car itself, with its meagre supply of boiling-hot soda-water, would be cut off that evening at Delhi.

Fortunately I had replenished my luncheon-basket in Bombay. My only regret was that the kind chaplain sturdily refused to abandon his own box of biscuits and chocolate, and share supplies. He reminded me of the vicissitudes of food upon all Indian journeys, and advised me to husband my stores. So we went on half rations.

There was always an absorbing panacea, however, for the paucity of food. With 'Stainer's

Harmony' and a manuscript book spread out on my knee, I settled down to write exercises, and 'untwisting all the chains that tie the hidden soul of harmony,' the hours flew happily past.

We sped into the Punjaub in the afternoon, and here we noticed, at each railway station we passed, little batches of Indians who roused our idle curiosity. Why were they there in groups? Why did they seem to wish to catch a glimpse of us as we passed? What was the meaning of a certain excitement in their general air?

At Delhi the crowd was greater, the excitement more evident. At first we were too intent upon ordering dinner and having it brought to our carriage to ask what it meant.

Dinner over, we wandered along the corridor. At one end of it was the mail van, filled with bags of letters and Indian postmen; at the other, through the open door, we saw quite a number of engine-drivers but never a European amongst them.

Our Eurasian waiter was awaiting his tip. 'What was the meaning of this crowd?' I asked him. 'It was the day the Mutiny broke out, fifty years ago,' he replied, with his vague and indefinite smile. 'Was it usual to have only Indian engine-drivers on a mail train?' 'No, Memsahib, but all Eurasians had gone to their homes, to protect their wives and families, because of the riots in Lahore.   But it was all right, Memsahib, because the ringleaders had been caught.'

All this was practically Greek and Latin to me. I had read about the riots in Lahore and Rawal Pindi in the Bombay newspaper.   I knew they had followed on the conviction of a newspaper editor.   I remembered he had tried to rouse disaffection in the Indian Army.   But what had all this to do with the Indian Mutiny ?

Every newspaper was sold out.   Jim had written to say he would meet me at Umballa, where I had to change trains at midnight.   So I must wait for his explanations of this vague situation.   Alas, at Umballa only a red-coated chaprassi brought me a letter which said he had been ordered to draft an immediate despatch, which made it quite impossible for him to leave Simla.   I had not a pleasant hour in the dark, for it was now past midnight, my little chaplain had gone on to Rawal Pindi, and I was both cold and hungry. However, 'good times, bad times, all times pass over,' and next afternoon found me at last in the old beloved surroundings ; and then I heard all that had happened.

Do you remember my telling you of a visit we paid to a wide-spreading tract of country which we had known in Shahpur days as a desert and saw transformed into the home of a million peasants? A serpent had entered that Garden of Eden and threatened Adam and Eve with eviction, with the most woful results and a hubbub which has barely subsided.

A sea-serpent it was, who had no doubt seen from afar the coasts of Russia, Japan and China, and then told what he saw there to the great rivers of India, who transmitted his message to some of the worshippers who came to bathe in their depths.

In plain English, a certain section of the people of India, influenced by the birth of the Duma in Russia, by the re-awakening in China and Japan, by the victories of the Japanese troops in their struggle with Russia, and by the success of the democratic party in our own latest political campaign, were fired by a desire to try issues with us and put in a claim for Home Rule.

Young Demos in India realised however that one answer to his demands would probably be that he only represented an infinitesimal fraction of the total population in India, and that the masses were content with the present régime. A number of the leaders of his party in the Punjaub, chiefly consisting of professors and students, newspaper editors and lawyers, acting in concert with their kind in Bengal and elsewhere, accordingly set to work to persuade the people of England that discontent was not local but general, and that all was not well in the Empire.

To make a long story short and leave out the subsidiary skirmishes, they laid siege to the colonies and cannonaded them with a Bill, a harmless if rather badly-constructed missile, which had been in view for some time. In the hands of the enemy it assumed deadly proportions, and was held up as a weapon destined to destroy every dream the poor peasant had cherished that his land and the fruit of his labours would remain in his family, even if he had no sons of his own.

It took a certain amount of time and effort to lodge this bomb-shell in the ignorant peasant's brain. But our fellow-subjects had learnt some of our western methods. Newspapers read in the colonies were fired with inflammatory paragraphs. Poets were enlisted to make ballads. One of these, with a refrain ' Oh Jat, defend your honour,' was set to a popular air. It caught on, and was nearly as popular as their old song of twenty-six stanzas in praise of the Sahib who had founded the colony.

Pamphlets about the Bill and its tragic forebodings were scattered here, there and everywhere in the villages, which had once been the colonists' home, and in the localities from which the old pensioners came. They were shot too into the colonies with the rapidity of a Maxim gun, or, to use a more homely simile, with the masterly activity displayed by the promoters of Eno's Fruit Salts, Pear's Soap, or Beecham's Pills.

When the peasant went to the post-office for his letters he was given one of those leaflets. When he got into the train, another. When he met the patwari he heard from him of a third. Post-cards invited the luckless creature to attend a meeting where he would hear of something to his disadvantage. And the only thing that he never heard was that the Bill was framed for the future disposal of unoccupied land, and did not affect the rights of any existing tenants.

When one heard of these clever webs, I can't say how I felt for the victims. One had seen them so pleased with themselves and their luck, and to think of them robbed of their joy in their treasured belongings! I pictured them clay in the potter's hands at each of these meetings, for I have never known a race who are so affected by eloquence. We once attended a meeting of the National Congress when it was held in Lahore, and I have not forgotten the spectacle we saw when a speech was working up to its climax. Thousands of people, with their eyes shut, swayed backwards and forwards like pendulums under the spell of the rhythm.

However, I might have consoled myself by remembering that the audience upon that occasion were not Jats.   Not every one was swayed by the Lyallpur oratory.   Some of the peasants, with thicker hides and sturdier nerves, had the courage to deny some of the most startling statements.

To pass on to the climax.   A mass meeting was arranged for at Lyallpur, to come off at the same time as the annual horse-fair.   I saw some photographs which had been taken of the orators. They were standing upon tables, so that their voices might reach the crowds who sat on the roof of the Agricultural Hall, swarmed on the staircase, and covered part of the neighbouring ground.   They did not however cover it all ; thousands preferred their annual sports, held on the same ground, over which their Colonization Officer presided as usual.   So one could see the two crowds in close juxtaposition, barely apart.

The majority of the people listened to the speakers, who poured out all that was left in the vials of their wrath on the Bill.   They listened and swayed, they caught fire and flamed, and when the end came and they were asked if the Bill must be fought tooth and nail and resisted, thousands of arms were held up in assent.

This was the end indeed of the orations and orators, for, after that meeting, their most eloquent leaders were sent to quarters where silence is usual. The excitement had lasted four months. Soon it blew partially over. The colonists came to hear what the Colonization Officer had to say to restore their faith and remove apprehension. The Mahomedans had always suspected the movement. By the end of April they seceded *en bloc*, and the other peasants followed by slow degrees.

There were flies in the ointment, no doubt; still the land, to be sure, was theirs and their children's, and was ready for harvest. So off to their fields they went and stood by their work, as their ancestors had done before them, even when alien armies roamed past in sight of their labours.

But what of the fighters, who had tried to enlist the peasants' services in their mixed ranks? What of the advanced party in the Punjaub and their political aims and ambitions? We know from whom they had caught their inspiration. But the question remains, Are they right in their premises? Will they lead to their hoped - for conclusions?

Imitations are seldom successful when the circumstances are diametrically different. In Japan the people are of one race and religion. They are a people, not peoples disunited by caste, by multiplied creeds, by factions, feuds and racial hatreds. They are not possessed by a frenzy to get at each other's throats.

The Japs are, moreover, educated. In India 90 per cent of the population are unable to read and write, and even amongst those who have passed through our schools and colleges too large a proportion with all their ability just fail to have common-sense, and with all their quick brains are yet not clever enough to grasp that not even an advanced political party can bind together so many conflicting elements, or wise enough to have re-alised amongst their many ideals the one ideal of honesty of purpose between man and man, which alone can be the foundation of a sound and efficient government.

One's hopes for the future of India rest on patriots of a very different type, patriots whom to know is to love. Great men who, because they are true to their own high ideals, can appeal to their countrymen to follow their lead and look to their inner equipment. Men who have worked not for mere political power nor for lucrative posts, but for the spread of sound education amongst the ignorant masses; for the elevation of the status of women, for the abolition of cruel and degrading customs, for the social improvement and good of their country.

If more power is to be given to Indians, it should be entrusted to the men who have been faithful over a few things, who have been slowly and surely trained in the service of the State and are fit to be trusted with authority over their fellows. It is they who most intimately know their country's needs and the remedies they demand. Good luck to them and their efforts.

Well, I have wandered far indeed from the history of my trivial experiences on my journey from Bombay and the signs of excitement we saw on the Delhi platform. But the story of all that gave rise to that was a long one to tell. It is not finished yet. May we live to rejoice over its end.

Darling Jack,—So you wish me to tell you a story, do you—just like old days? But what kind of a story is it to be? It can't be 'about something we have been seeing ourselves,' as you put it, for Simla, dear boy, is just like a bigger Murree, and you know we did not see many extraordinary things there, although we heard sometimes about them from men who had travelled far and wide in strange places.

So if I am to tell you a story now, it can only be one I have heard. I *have*, as it happens, been seeing strange and wonderful things through another man's eyes—great deserts where rain never falls, lakes wander and disappear, where no one has heard the footfall of man for centuries, although his steps may still be seen in the sand. Deserts in which, if you lose your landmarks, you may lose your way and perhaps your life. For the sands of the deserts continually shift and change the whole landscape in that great cradle of winds.

Can you guess where some one has carried us

far away, on some sheets of thin paper? Nowhere
else than to Central Asia, that strange, mysterious
country, the stage upon which Mongols, Turks,
Greeks, Indo - Scythians, Huns, Persians, once
played their part, to pass onwards, leaving traces
of their dead civilisations in marvellous works of
art, in buried temples, tombs, ruined watch-towers,
fortified walls, while the builders have gone for ever
themselves.

The wind is the only despot who has held his
own, and has done as he pleased through the ages.
He has done as he list and, obeying his will, lakes
have wandered, nations migrated, and empires have
disappeared. But the covering sand has followed on
the flying wings of the wind, and protected all she
took under her care. In wastes which have known
but scanty rainfall for the last two thousand years,
the sand keeps her buried treasures.

If we have seen much that the sands have held,
like a brooding mother-bird, under her care, it has
been, as I said, through another's eyes. For, from
those far-away deserts there came this week a long
letter from Dr Stein, which we have read and re-
read, going over with him the thousands of miles
he has travelled with his caravan and his Indian
assistants.

You saw Dr Stein years ago in Shahpur, when
he had come to India from his own home in Hun-

gary to prepare himself for his great task of exploring these desolate regions in Central Asia, by studying for nearly eleven years archæology, history, languages, geography, before he set out on his first and now on his second journey.

Imagine the things he discovered! What would we have thought when we played at 'adventures' in camp, and dug in the sands, if our spades had hit on a dwelling with beautiful wood-carving in it, and a large central hall, with piles of wooden tablets besides, on which letters were written in an Indian language more than a thousand years old, all their string fastenings unopened, their seals perfectly fresh, and representing Heracles with his club and lion skin, Eros and Pallas?

And how about finding in other houses underground weaving instruments, chairs, a boot-last, a large tray, a mouse-trap, a small heap of corn still in sheaves, and near that the mummified bodies of two little mice! Or if we had come, on our walks, upon sacred caves carved in the precipitous cliffs, with hundreds of grottos large and small, honeycombing in irregular tiers the sombre rock-faces, and had found that almost all of them had on their plastered walls a profusion of beautiful and more or less well-preserved frescoes, besides exquisite paintings on silk, banners with pictures of Buddha and of his worshippers in monastic dresses. Or

if we had hit on a Buddhist shrine with half-length
figures of beautifully winged angels in fresco, and
youthful figures representing the varied pleasures
of life.

That was what this great explorer Dr Stein told
us about in his letter, adding that thirty cases filled
with art-treasures had been handed over to him by
the old Buddhist priest in the sacred caves, who
attached little value to those beautiful pictures.
Do you wonder if we have thought and spoken
about little else since we read his account of his
wanderings?

You must read his book some day for yourself.
A celebrated actress, Fanny Kemble, said in her
recollections of her girlhood that when her mother
was feeling dull she always changed the furniture
of the drawing-room. Some of us would like to
change the furniture of our mind. It is then one
enjoys books of travel. They give us so many
new conceptions of the world, as if we were
shown new stars in the firmament.

Our spirits rise too when we see what man can
do without. These travellers take all that comes
in the long day's journey like men. Now in a
sandy desert where no water is, now plodding perhaps through snow with a cold wind blowing, again
upon solitary mountain-peaks or amongst barren
boulders, cold, wet and weary after a long day's

march, but never accepting defeat, rejoicing rather in the growing enjoyment of health, the exercise of every faculty and the conquest of difficulties.

> ' Beacons of hope ye appear!
> Languor is not in your heart,
> Weakness is not in your word,
> Weariness not on your brow.'

Such are the men who are heroes. Yes, we shall read a book some day, you and I, that will tell us of great achievements, and what is still better, we shall go and see for ourselves in the British Museum those ancient art-treasures which have been hidden for hundreds of years in the forsaken temples and caves, or under the sands of the desert of Central Asia.

CAMP, 1907.

DEAR G.,—It seems strangely familiar to waken
again to the coo of the doves and the parrots'
shriek, and to fall asleep as of old to the croon
of the Persian wheels that are worked through
the night by the patient peasants, to slake the
thirst of their fields.

Jim has exchanged his post as Secretary to the
Government of India for that of Financial Commissioner of the Punjaub. The tents and all the
paraphernalia needed to equip them for a continuous life under canvas for six months of the
year have been collected. The household, including
the Bengali cook and the Goanese butler, have
elected to follow our fortunes, and for the winters
that remain of Jim's service we shall remain under
the old conditions, until we leave India in less
than two years.

Before we turn our backs on the East, however,
Jim has promised that I shall see some of the
Native States, notably Rajputana, the land of my
dreams. Then Home and the boy !

Yet not even that thought can deaden the sense of tragedy that goes with us where we go and remains in the background of all that happens.

Sir Denzil Ibbetson, Jim's oldest friend in India, a man of most brilliant ability, one of the few who in spite of his strenuous life has forsaken none of his earliest ideals, his love of science, literature, art: a ruler of men, with a home where all who needed sympathy or cherishing were welcomed by him and his dear human-hearted wife; this man, who so lately became head of his Province, is struck down by a mortal malady and now faces the steady approach of death.

Great till the end, he stands with his hand on the helm steering right onwards, the pilot who soon must go under, although the ship will go on to the port.

Only a year ago, when he looked forward to governing his old Province, he wrote to Jim asking him, if he ever contemplated leaving his present post, to consider whether he would be willing to work immediately under him as Financial Commissioner of the Punjaub, as he would be glad for his part to have him. Jim was fired by the suggestion and rejoiced in the prospect of going, as he put it, ' back to the Punjaub, back to the land, back to the Ibbetsons.' Now all the colour seems gone from the landscape, although it appeals to him more than ever to stand by his chief in his need.

Human nature is so complex that it at no time seems impossible to enjoy things on the surface, with an undercurrent of sadness, and I try to hope that this merciful faculty may remain with our heroic friend to the close.

Dearest P.,—I have been submerged for the last two hours by the cares attending what a newspaper lately described as 'the sacred duty of entertaining.' An easy duty when the fates are propitious, but not when you have a collapsing dinner-party on your hands, as I have to-day.

Two couples who were coming this evening have been *commandirt* to Viceregal Lodge, the husband of another couple is down with fever and his wife does *not* propose to stay at home to nurse him, while a fourth lady asks if she may bring her young sister, who has arrived in Simla a day sooner than she was expected, and whom she does not like to leave alone at home on her first evening in Simla. So I have been writing notes to all our particular cronies in turn, to ask if they could come to our rescue, and have only now found two disengaged.

This leaves one so little time for mail letters that I can only tell you that your old friend Sven Hedin is in Simla—we met him last week at Mrs

370

H.'s at lunch—replete with health, sunburnt and portly, emanating vitality, a creature of jovial laughter, bubbling over with talk and high spirits, a true *guter Kerl*, giving his best to all-comers.

He was fresh from Thibet and his march, mostly on foot, over the Himalayas, and had to wait in a bungalow in the hills till clothes arrived from Simla to replace his Thibetan garb. What a memory the man has! He was ready and able to spin off the name height and breadth of every camel in his various caravans, and the vocabulary of all the strange folks he had met in his wanderings.

He displayed this marvellous gift still further when, at the conclusion of a very interesting account of his travels given by him last evening at Viceregal Lodge, which began at 9.30 and ended at midnight, he proceeded to give us the names of each one of the Trans-Himalayan peaks which had never been known before.

Indians, as I have learnt in my pursuit of the ins and outs of their intricate system of music, like to take hard labour by instalments. So I was not surprised to hear one of them, who was sitting behind us, very audibly yawn at this juncture. When his neighbour very audibly nudged him, his self-vindication, 'His Excellency the Viceroy has yawned,' might have been heard by the Hall!

One has to change one's mental focus in India as frequently as if one were in a modern Art Gallery, when a picture, a minute mosaic of colours scintillating like a cinematograph, may have as its neighbour a shadowy landscape after the manner of Corot.

Fresh from the peaks of the Himalayas, I was summoned by Jim to be introduced to 'one of the wisest men in India,' as he put it, Mr Malabari, a name which we already knew and revered. A Parsi by birth, a poet, an author, a journalist, pre-eminently a social reformer, he has done more than any other patriot in India to reform certain customs such as child-marriage and the restrictions imposed upon widows, which have blighted many a life.

We felt it to be a great privilege to meet him at last. He came to see us yesterday, and I was particularly interested to hear that one of the points that most impressed him on his visits to England was the power English mothers possessed to command the obedience of even their grown-up sons: a power which he said Indian mothers did not wield, although one had always imagined that it was their pre-eminent gift.

Yet no one can be held a greater authority on home life in India, nor has anybody served its best interests with more faithful devotion than this gentle old patriot, whom to know is to love.

CAMP, 1908.

WE have now been three weeks in camp, making
our way by slow degrees from Rawal Pindi, so full
of happy memories, to Shahpur, our old home.
Mr A., the nephew of one of Mr Jowett's oldest
friends, and to give you his full official title, the
Senior Secretary to the Financial Commissioner,
has been with us for the last three weeks, and
has driven me in the early morning in his motor
car from one 'halt' to another. I sat in the
back seat of the car, was forbidden to speak to
the man at the wheel, and in luxurious ease
enjoyed the varied landscape.

Such enchanting drives they have been, through
every kind of scenery. In some places the country
was a chaos of bare rocks, seamed with precipitous
ravines, shaped at times like forts and castles,
reminding one of Saxon Switzerland. At other
points of our drive there were stretches of moor-
land, with solitary tarns like eyes reflecting the
blue depths of heaven. Cultivated and wooded

plains led up to the far - distant Himalayas, glorified by the soft hues of morning.

Peasants were ploughing fields, which were to bear next harvest's wheat, with the peasant's patient air of resignation stamped on their bent frames, which Millet has immortalised. Little, fragile, innocent trees stood at regular distances from each other, like those which form the background to Perugino's Saints. There were the blue distances with dark - outlined trees which Turner loves, and beyond all, the far-off faint-blue hills. Don't you think one sometimes finds that while Art reminds us of Nature, Nature sometimes also reminds us of Art? And not only that. If it is only beautiful enough, we are flooded by a sense of all beauty, we hear the beat of rapturous poetry, the lonely notes of truth, the highest notes of goodness struck in the white heat of love. It is as if when one only of these notes is sounded, 'a bolt is shot back somewhere in the breast,' and we hear the other notes of the chord — the far-off music of the spheres.

But I am wandering far away from my drives and their varied beauties, the gnarled rocks, the bosky shades, the pools with reeds and water-lilies and the distant hills. Wandering still further away from history, and the memories which may sleep amongst these lonely scenes, for we were in the very heart of battlefields. It was along this tract of country — now smiling like the patient souls that can survive earth's tragedies and smile—it was along this tract that the successive hordes of invaders came to loot and disappear, or to conquer and remain. Beneath the shadows of these hills how many of those wild armies have returned from their inroads with sufficient plunder to make their tents upon the barren steppes of Central Asia glitter with their gains! Those gnarled rocks have echoed to the cries of wretched women and their children, carried off as prisoners to be sold as slaves, their fathers, husbands, sons and brothers slain. It was on the other side of the broad - flowing Jhelum that Alexander the Great met and defeated mighty Porus, two thousand and two hundred years ago, before he sailed away homeward down the Indus with his cohorts, who would fight no longer. All its conquerors have entered India over mountains, all save one or two, who could claim to be younger branches of the great Aryan race, certain Portuguese, Dutch, French, and British merchants who have entered India over sea.

Yet the British too had battlefields in the Punjaub. Only sixty years have passed since, with the battle of Gujrat, we held the Land of the Five Rivers, only fifty years have gone since we recaptured Delhi, and then, for the first time in her history, the whole continent of India acknowledged one sovereign only, our beloved Queen.

Those days have been brought before us by a long talk we had with an old man, who lived near Gujrat when it was taken. We met him as we were starting on our evening walk, the last of a long string of Indian visitors, who had flowed through Jim's office-tent throughout a day of overwork. He looked such an old dear, however, in his long embroidered coat and spotless muslins, and had so much of that pathetic appeal for sympathy in his eyes which frail old people have, that we asked him to return with us to our drawing-room tent, and there we sat listening to his lengthy old-age monologue.

It was a homely tale he told, his fingers held out to emphasise its points, delivered in old-fashioned Punjaub dialect with some of the grim realism in its phrases of our native Doric, the oriental imagery and eloquence of another class conspicuous by their absence. It was pervaded by the charm of his own personality, which cannot, I fear, be conveyed to you or translated by mere words.

Its first interest for us, however, lay in the picture which it gave one of those bygone days, with the little details, still remembered by this old man, of his youth.

'I was living, when I was eleven years old,' he said, 'with my father and my grandfather. There was a tower not far away where my grandfather "Dada" lived in his young days for safety against robbers. The Hindu Chibs who lived in Deva on the hill were robbers. They came down on villages, sometimes even on Gujrat, and carried off everything they could lay their hands on. Mahomed Yar and his men at Dilawarpur fought with them and beat them; and his men sat on their skulls in the evening, when they smoked their hookahs. But their brothers came again. Maharaja Ranjit Singh burnt their village, but they built another, and they came again.

'Robbers, armed Sikhs, and strong men came in bands in those days to fight for everything they could lay their hands on, whether grain, jewels, cattle, beds or clothes. Those who could, built themselves towers from which they could shoot at them. Sometimes they shot at other towers in their neighbourhood (I remember nine of them) for fear of their neighbours too. Even the peasants wore arms when they ploughed, sowed, or took in their grain.

'Misar Rup Lal, who was one of the best governors under Maharaja Ranjit Singh, once came to see my grandfather, and I heard him tell my grandfather how difficult he used to find it to terrorise the robbers, until he one day caught them red-handed, when he cut their bodies into quarters, and stuck the bits on the gates of Hoshiarpur town, and that frightened the others away.

'The Maharaja used to take a third, or a fourth, and sometimes a half of the wheat, sugar, cotton, or millet that was harvested. But Misar Rup Lal said he found it quicker to count the number of sugar-cane presses that were in use in each village, and charge the village a hundred rupees for each of them.

'Sometimes there was nothing to take. For five harvests once there was no rain, and so no crops were sown. I was a child then, but Dada said that by God's mercy they could always give me milk, for we had buffaloes and goats, and money enough to buy grain at seven pounds for the rupee. But those who could not, died and their bodies were thrown into wells unburied. Mothers threw their children into the rivers, others went, while they had strength, to Peshawar and Kashmir. All who had not shared with those that had. That was the great famine. But Ranjit Singh, when there was no famine, used to take a third or a fourth.

' Ranjit Singh was fairly just, but he could neither read nor write, and all that happened did not reach his ears. One of my uncles had not enough money to pay the Sikh Governor of his part of the country all that he asked. So he was tied on the back of a camel, carried to the Sikh fort, and put in prison.

' Our old family Brahmin went to the fort to do what he could to help him. The forts were towns with high walls round them, built for defence. An old lady lived in the fort, whose ancestors had ruled the country before the Sikhs. My family had done her family a service in the past. Our Brahmin went to salaam to her and petitioned her to intercede for my uncle with Maharaja Ranjit Singh. So she interceded for him and he was released.

' In another tower, the priest knew a shopkeeper who had put his savings into a pair of famous gold bracelets, which he always wore and talked about to everybody, so that their fame spread, and the Governor of that fort heard of them too. The Governor had a case brought before him. A man accused the shopkeeper of using false weights or bad flour, I do not know which it was, but no one believed it. The Governor, who was judge as well as collector of revenues, sentenced him as guilty, fined him the gold bracelets and wore them himself.

'The shopkeeper, who had treasured his gold bracelets as if they were his sons, went off his head when he had to part with them, and wandered about the country mad, till one day when he was bathing in the river Jhelum, a robber struck him on the head with a thick stick, and cracked his skull; with the strange effect that the man recovered his senses. He then went to Maharaja Ranjit Singh and laid his complaints before him, when the Maharaja himself ordered the unjust Governor to restore his bracelets.

'Ranjit Singh had a general, an Italian soldier, called Avitabile, who was a severe governor. One day he had condemned a highway robber to be hanged. The man said "Before I die I have only one wish, and that is to see my mother." She came, and the man, with his hands tied behind his back, bent forward as if to whisper to her, and bit her on the neck. Avitabile said to him "You brute, she is your mother." The robber answered "I bit her because it is owing to her I am here. When I was a child, she told me to steal the neighbours' chickens, then she told me to steal their sheep, then to break into their house, and then to take to the road. She is to blame for it all." The mother said "It is true." Avitabile said "Let the robber go, and hang the mother." So the mother was hanged.

'I was with my Guru one day. He taught me the Persian language, for I wished to get a place as clerk to a governor, and to be able to write his orders in Persian. We were reading Saadi's "Garden of Roses" that day, when I heard a sound like people pounding rice. It made the house shake. The Guru said "It is not rice-pounding, it is big guns." We went up on the roof of the house and saw much smoke. It was from the cannons drawn up near Gujrat. The English were firing on the Sikhs. The sound began at eight in the morning and stopped at noon. Next morning I went with my father to Gujrat to see if any of our friends had been hurt. But we found them all safe because Gough sahib had said "The town is not to be looted!" He said, "The people in the town have nothing to do with the Sikhs," so the shops had not been touched, nor the men, nor even the women and children.

'I saw a great many sepoys lying dead in the bed of the river. A man came into the town next day, who told me he had seen naked sepoys running along the road. They were naked, because the people in the fields had robbed them of their clothes.

'It was on the road one day, in the year that the sepoys from Bengal and the East had mutinied, that I saw Nuckolsain. He was in a mail-cart

passing through Gujrat on his way to Delhi, followed by his column. They could get no bullocks,
for they were all taken already to carry other
soldiers' clothes, food and powder. So many English soldiers followed him in carts, drawn by men
taken from the villages. I never saw Nuckolsain
again, but when I was in the office at Peshawar, in
charge of the records of trials which Nuckolsain
had judged, I remember seeing one, which had
specimens of the hair that women had torn out of
each other's heads, pinned in as evidence. And I
heard a story in Peshawar about how he had
treated one of the followers of Amir Dost Mahomed.
This man had been insolent to Nuckolsain when he
was in Kabul, and when he came down in the train
of the Amir, when the Amir was on his way to
meet John Lawrence, Nuckolsain knew his face
again, and when the man did not salaam to him, he
put him in jail, and would not let him out, even
when the Amir asked him, until he had had him
caned. Nuckolsain feared no man, and was a great
Bahadur.

'When Colonel Paske sahib was Deputy Commissioner in Gujrat, I was his clerk and went with
him to the battlefield of Chillianwala, to settle
where the monument was to be put up to the
English soldiers who were killed there. The
villagers showed him a place where they said the

English soldiers had been buried. The villagers dug till we saw some bits of red uniform and brass buttons and some fair hair. So the monument was put up there.

'That was fifty years ago, the year we heard a soldier read by beat of drum in Gujrat bazaar something to tell us Queen Victoria was our Rani. I am an old man now. I have served Sarkar for fifty-two years, and Sarkar has been very good to me. My only boy serves Sarkar now too, and I hope Your Highness will see to it that he too has some promotion. I have brought some grapes and some melons, and my last request is, that the Mem Sahib will honour me by taking them from an old man.'

I willingly did so, and gave him a small keepsake, a little brass tray we had bought in Nuremberg, on an off-day of the Baireuth festival, with the old town embossed on its surface. It was all I could find in our tent, and he gazed at it with a puzzled air : but I hope he took it for what it was worth, for it was meant as a sign of affection.

DEAR P.,—I must confess to being in love with the Colonies, and it is partly for a very foolish reason, and because they remind me of something I had quite forgotten—a dream I used to make up for myself, so long ago that I think I had hardly escaped from the mild guardianship of our nursery-governess.

I remember when I was a child being greatly impressed by an old-fashioned story-book I read which was called 'The Cottagers of Glenburnie.' All that I recollect now of its contents is that it gave the history of a village in which all the houses were tumble-down, all of them had wide puddles in front of their doors and all of them had tumble-down inhabitants. Somehow all of these inhabitants were eventually transformed into model villagers and lived happily ever afterwards.

This story for some reason so possessed my youthful imagination that it became the inspiration of a constant waking-dream. It transpired, so I loved to believe, that I was after all a foundling, the

child of just such parents in just such another
village as Glenburnie, and that I was claimed by
them and restored to my real home, when I was
fourteen.

Arrived at home at last, I found that my father
was a drunkard, my mother a slut.   But what
could be expected in such comfortless surroundings,
and what might not happen if they were only
changed?   There was a capable young carpenter in
the village, and with his silent but invaluable help,
with the discovery too of a lumber-room behind the
kitchen, which had every bit of broken furniture
that the heart of woman could desire, absolute
wonders were effected, and my parents became in
consequence the most striking embodiments of
content and smiling smugness that the world had
ever seen.

Whether I ought to marry the young carpenter
for all he had done for the furniture, I could never
quite determine.   That bit was always left un-
finished, and my dream began from the very
beginning, and was thought out again.

And now behold I was in the new Glenburnie of
my dreams and to complete the contrast I had, as
it happened, visited Glenburnie as it used to be
just before we entered the kingdom of the Colonies.
Alas it was the very first village I had visited in
India twenty years ago.   But what had become of

all the women's ornaments and pretty clothes? The Indian official who was with me said they had worn them the last time he was there. A crowd of villagers had met me at the entrance of the village. Where were the signs of the prosperity that should have followed on their autumn crop? They were crying out to me that they were dying of hunger, oppressed by taxation, bereft of the pity and mercy of their government, they were clamouring for alms! Alas for the dramatic powers of an excitable people. The Tahsildar at my elbow sternly said it was not true. Did not the canal irrigate their fields, was not the government tax on their crops less than a fourth of their profits, was not their land worth ten times its former value? They should blush for their deceit in posing to the Memsahib as fakirs and beggars! I chaffed them gently for their unique welcome, the men on the outskirts of the hubbub smiled, and I left them, pondering on the problems of our rule and on the dust of Indian villages.

My first visit to the new Glenburnie was on my first drive in the Colonies, when the chaprassi stopped the tonga with a note from Jim, who thought I might possibly like to visit a village of Indian Christians, of whom there were three thousand settled in the Colonies, chiefly members of the American Presbyterian Church. This little fraction of them were on our old friend Mr B.'s property. What another world it was, with its wide spaces and firm broad roads shaded by trees, and radiating from its central square. In the middle was the well, and round it the little shops, the grain merchant's conspicuous amongst them, the usual display of foreign baubles in the others.

I had not time to visit all the spacious courtyards with their well-fed cattle and busy occupants, and to tell the truth, I had not too much energy after my long bumpy drive; but I went to see the gentle pastor's wife in her roomy house, well aired by windows, innocent of glass but crossed by bars of wood. I saw his little prophet's chamber too, where he says his prayers, with the family Bible on the table and his business books on a small shelf, for he is the manager of Mr B.'s property.

I also saw the church, which I am thankful to say is built according to their own unborrowed ideas. There are neither seats nor pulpit in it, the women sit on one part of the floor of the room, the men in another, and here their pastor speaks to them every Sunday, prays for them and for himself, and they sing hymns to their own native airs with words written by their poets.

A conviction is spreading in different branches of the Christian Church in India that the Indian

Church should be the outcome of racial temperament, and should develop from within, and along
its own lines; and so, I cannot help thinking, St
Paul also would have felt.

The essential spirit, the love, the sense of union,
the desire for service, may be a common possession :
but East and West do not give expression to such
states of being in the same way nor with the same
ritual. Perhaps, who knows? the spirit of peace
and goodwill may come again as a message from
East to West, and a spirit of tolerance for different
temperaments, different interpretations and different
points of view be extended by the various bodies
of the Western Christian Churches to each other,
as it is extended by them to the Eastern. It is
certainly a consummation devoutly to be wished.

To return to the Colonies and the Indian Christians in the village. Every man, woman and
child I met shook hands with me, as if a common
bond must make us friends. Poor souls, I daresay
they have their failings like their neighbours, their
struggles to be better are but young. Generally
speaking, with all due recognition of manifold
exceptions, truth and honesty are not the most
transparent virtues of the Indian race, and I daresay some of these Indian Christians need time and
God's support to make them theirs.

But if they fail sometimes, why not have some

pity for their failures? People have a great deal of charity to spare for the wicked nowadays. I sometimes wish they would extend it to the good. If any one has ever known what it is to try to eradicate hereditary failings, whatever they may be, from his own obstinate blood, he at least will have a corner in his heart for others who are in the same plight.

The pastor asked me if I would like to hear his people sing a hymn, and they all sat down on the ground and sang one in their unself-conscious way, and I doubt not it was heard by One who was the Light of Love and Pity and the friend of publicans and sinners.

Then followed a visit a few days afterwards to such a large village built on the same pattern and filled with old Sikh pensioners, manly great big men with divided curly beards, who stood to attention and were all on the *qui vive* to show off their new quarters and their many rooms and well-fed cattle. The head of the village was full of an old soldier's reminiscences of his Colonel Sahibs and Major Sahibs and his Colonel Sahib's fair-haired boy, who used to receive him when he was Subahdar, dressed up as a little officer of the Guides, with the regulation sash and turban and a miniature sword and gun, and then go through his drill for the Subahdar's approval. And Memsahib had to stop the tonga as she drove away, to look at the old photograph he had hurriedly got out of his new wooden box and see his group of the said officers, with the Subahdar himself in the corner, in his uniform like the rest.

I think, however, I liked the Junglis' village best of all and the Junglis, the old nomads of the desert. There was something in their bluntness, something in their hearty laugh and in their obstreperous pride in their new possessions—for they had never owned a house before—which reminded me of a sturdy Scot become garrulous in his old age.

There was nothing hidden which they were not anxious to reveal. What a round fat sleepy baby was awakened from its sleep in the big sheet hung from the branches of two trees in the wide courtyard. Such a baby as never was, such an Indian baby as I had never seen before in India, every curve of its little naked body as round as it could be. Grandpapa laughed as if he was its mother. It was the cow that did it, every cow was well fed now; just look at all the cattle, such a herd, and all their own.

This was the new Glenburnie indeed in all its glory. I must come into the house, not one-roomed, oh dear no, his daughter and her husband had a room, his sons had each a room, and all the menfolk of his family eat together every evening, on the stone platform underneath the trees, both especially built and planted for the purpose, and it was there that they afterwards smoked their hookahs. I must look at the earthenware pots, piled one above the other in rows from the floor to the roof. The jewels were in them, one in that jar, one in the other, scattered up and down so that robbers could not tell in which jar they might be, and indeed his wife forgot herself once where she had put her ear-rings, and was in a fine state, thinking they were stolen. They could not be stolen all the same, for what a crash there would be if any robber tried to move a jar with all those others piled above it!

One wall of the room was far too like that of a curiosity - shop for the perfect peace of mind of a certain lover of quaint old beauties, who might not dream of striking a bargain with the owner. There were steel pots on nails, with glittering brass knobs and long handles, like old-fashioned bed - warmers. There were great big beautifully shaped brass kettles, quaint cupboards with zinc ornamental clasps and pretty carvings, dear old wooden chests all filled with grain, and painted beds and stools ready against a daughter's marriage.

No wonder the old headman laughed with pride

in his house, he who had only known a tattered
tent in the jungles in the old days of the Bar.
If I could only wait and see all the other houses,
he said, but alas, there was no time, only enough
to wander round the big central courtyard of this
quarter of the four-quartered village, each quarter
like a village in itself, but only one of many in
this new Jungly settlement.

It is well to weep with those that weep, but
for tired hearts there is a welcome pleasure in
the chance of rejoicing with the fortunate, and
the pleasure of these old Junglis, with their pride
and satisfaction in their plenty and to spare, was
like the robin's song in winter or after storms,
the patient cuckoo's note of spring.

The Colony seems to have created a frankness
in those peasants which I never knew elsewhere;
perhaps it may only be engendered by the prosperity of altered circumstance as one might find
it, say in Canada, amongst lucky working men.
I noticed this particularly in a village to which
I went alone, or rather with only a chaprassi and
an Indian official. The inhabitants had come from
two overcrowded districts in the Punjaub. They
gave me a frankly humorous description of their
groundless fears before they left their old surroundings. Fears of the Jungly robbers of the
Bar, fears of this and that, fears of they knew

not what, all made them leave their wives at home.

The Sahib was not pleased to find they were alone on his first visit. Men who had no wives or children as pledges of their intentions to remain were not satisfactory settlers. It had been stipulated they should come. So, after this remonstrance, they induced one wife to come, and when the Sahib next visited them, behold, he saw a woman with her sheet over her head churning at the front-door. When the Sahib went on to the next house, she could always run out quickly by the back-door to that one also, and behold, she was sitting at the second front-door again with her sheet over her head, and this time she was busy with her spinning-wheel!

However, they soon got tired of their empty houses. Their food was not cooked rightly, their clothes were not mended, the butter was not churned, the wife was not there to make their *chapattis* or bring them to the twenty-seven acres. The wife was indispensable apparently, even in her lowly niche in India. So wife and children came, and all was well at last in Glenburnie!

DEAR E.,—After endless experiments and many fruitless quests, I have come to the conclusion that the only place on earth in which peace and rest can really be found is in an Indian railway carriage, reserved for any couple taught by the tread-mill of hard work to appreciate silent isolation. To start one evening and know that there in solitary confinement you will be at least for twenty-four hours, where no posts, no callers, no duties can disturb you : to sleepily remember that in the next carriage you have three silent, deft attendants, who will pack, unpack, waken, feed you, undertake in short each manual duty that should be yours in sterner circumstances ; what more could even the tiredest bit of tired humanity in this twentieth century desire ?

To realise moreover, joy of joys, that a mysterious unknown country lies before you, not to be studied, administered or reformed, but only to be enjoyed, that in short, you are On the Road, this surely is pure and unadulterated bliss !

' Let the blow fall soon or late,
  Let what will be o'er me;
  Give the face of earth around,
  And the road before me.
  Wealth I seek not, hope nor love,
  Nor a friend to know me;
  All I ask, the heaven above
  And the road below me.'

Part of the charm of being On the Road is, I
think, that for a vagrant spell one's spirit of irre-
sponsibility is transferred to all one sees. The
figures who pass are to us only bits of the landscape, they have no cares and duties; for us they
are only parts of a vast diorama, going on its
diurnal round with the great globe. When the
dawn wakens, every living creature seems to wake
to music; sorrow is unknown. When the night
comes, not a single human heart is breaking in
the little villages we dimly see as the day ends,
where lights are twinkling like the stars of earth,
emblems of the peace and rest we know ourselves.
When we leave the Road, life as it is waits for us
again. Meanwhile we are careless wanderers, seeing
all things through rose - coloured spectacles and
intent on joy.

During the last fortnight we have spent seven
days and nights in the train or steamer, and have
visited in that time eight lovely places in our
several pauses, beginning with Jeypore, Udaipur,
Chitore and Ajmire in Rajputana, then Bombay,

Madras, Colombo and Nuwara Eliya, and have enjoyed them all. All are beautiful, but Rajputana is the most beautiful of all.

If you wish to know its inner history read Tod, the Sir Walter Scott of Rajputana, and return with him as your guide to feudal times, to the age of chivalry and its code of honour, to the realms of romance. Read Rudyard Kipling and his 'Letters of Marque,' and learn what he thinks of the Rajputs. They were a wonderful people. No note in the scale of life was unknown to those demi-gods, who claimed no other than the sun, moon or fire as their progenitor, for centuries disdaining to intermarry even with their royal neighbours.

Theirs was the grand manner which translates the commonplace of daily intercourse into poetry; theirs the virility which can endure hardness and conquer the impossible; theirs the indifference to death which inspired their women to lead forlorn hopes as lightly as they might foot some country-dance, or to make *en masse* the great *Johur* when the men, rather than surrender, killed wives and children first, then rushed themselves upon the spears of their enemies.

With all their strength, their self-respect and pride, the race had that rare temperament to which the losing cause appeals. Artists to the finger - tips, lovers of beauty, their palaces like marble monuments to the pride of life, they were content to follow their hero if need be, and share his fallen fortunes to the point of poverty and privation, their service beautified by the old setting of reverence and devotion.

In a land which proverbially worships the rising sun, to possess as they did the unswerving faithfulness of Tom Moore's sunflower, which 'turns on her god when he sets the same look which she turned when he rose,' that alone would endear them to me. Small thanks to us Celts, with our melancholy temperament, born as we are with our heads turned backwards, always gazing at a dead past, seldom great successes ourselves — except in Highland regiments — small thanks to us if we have a soft corner in our hearts for failure. Our imagination is tuned to understand how it must feel from inside to be on board a ship which must eventually go down.

The Rajputs were of a different build. They were dominant, virile, bent on conquest, so their reverence for their compeers fallen on evil days was all the more adorable. Of course they had *les défauts de ses vertus* and were by no means paragons. The notes of their scale formed discords too, and histories of rapine, treachery, murder and revenge are written big over every inch of the country. The forts which crown the hill - tops, the stone bastions on their sides, bear witness to long centuries of feuds, when brother fought against brother, clan against clan, and battle began and ended their lives.

See them now, bristling with the fiery pride of Lucifer, doomed or gifted with a memory that never dies, every man of them carrying a matchlock or dagger, as his forebears did before him, and judge what they were like when they could do what they pleased. The British Government has stopped their feuds, but who can alter racial temperament ? Who, at its best, would ever wish to change it here ?

For me there is an intangible magic in Rajputana unlike anything I have known elsewhere. How can I describe it ? Have you ever felt the power which a great actor has to remind you of all the good-byes in the world when he says the single word farewell ? Rajputana has something like that inexplicable gift. It awakens memories of far-off elemental things known dumbly by us all, while ghostly melodies of triumphs won through death seem to fill the air.

To descend however to the concrete, let me tell you about Jeypore, our first halt. Jeypore is dominated by the genius of a dead king called Jey Singh, who was the contemporary of Aurungzebe the Moghul Emperor of Delhi, and of James the First of England, and a much greater genius than either of them. He was a soldier and a diplomat. He built this city, with its palaces and gardens and its pride of life. He was a man of letters who collected a magnificent library, and most remarkable of all, considering his race, he was a man of science and an accurate astronomer.

Side by side with his great palaces is a large walled-in enclosure, where there stand great structures, ninety feet high, like mathematical diagrams in stone. Here in solitude he studied the heavenly bodies and worked out problems long ago, which are verified by modern science.

From the multifarious observatory we went to the broad central street of the city and saw what he had accomplished there. The town is shaped like a cross and every house in it is like a palace of pink stone, with trellised lace-work in stone against the blue sky. The central street was filled with colour and busy men and graceful alert women dressed in every hue, the women with a step in walking which would not have been amiss in a measure. Elephants in splendid trappings swayed with clumsy dignity, their mahouts astride their bulky necks. Little lacquered carts jingled past; naked children chased each other in the sunlight; branded bulls chose their favourite eatables from various shops with the portly dignity of Brahmins ; and solitary worshippers disappeared beneath the archways of dark temples to salaam to Juggernaut.

Suddenly we came upon another memory of Jey Singh. At the head of the street are six cages built to hold tigers, and there they are where he planned they should be, six ferocious beasts of prey. Did he wish to remind humanity of the other side of existence, so near they are to the semblance of life and beauty, their hungry growls heard as an undercurrent to chatter and laughter, their restless paces in their narrow cages like the throbs of passing Time, or the hurrying march of Destiny ?

As I gazed into the cruel eyes of the most ferocious tiger, their horrid glare recalled for an instant so vividly all the madness, discord and cruelty that life contains, that I was petrified with horror. Our Hindu friend, with the intuition of his race, said gently behind me, 'Every creature God has made has its own place in His world,' to which I irrelevantly replied, 'that after all the law of reciprocity ran through all creation, and that the half of sentient life devoured or was devoured by the other.' Poor man, it was his turn to recoil in horror ! For a Hindu fondly imagines that he is true to his creed, and that he

eats no living creature, forgetting that they are
in the very air he breathes!

After our visit to the tigers' den we went home,
as the heat had grown oppressive, but in the cool
evening we drove with our kind guides to Amber,
the palace and city which Jey Singh deserted
to build this town, shaped like a great amethyst-
coloured cross in the shadow of fort-crowned hills.
The road to Amber is hedged with sprawling cactus
and skirted by tall villas with the faded ochre colouring and narrow red-tiled roofs which one associates with Spain. Their high-walled gardens hold
formal groves of oranges and citrons, and are entered
by stone gateways surmounted by umbrella domes.
The yogis, smeared with ashes, dehumanized by
bhang, who crouched beside half-ruined tombs on
the bare hills; the crocodiles which sprawled and
blinked their leering eyes on the muddy edges
of the Man Sagar Lake; the parrots screaming
from the tops of mulberry trees ; peacocks with
their gorgeous tails spread in the sun, made up
the features of a landscape which would have been
a fit setting for those weird Oriental tales, in
which animate and inanimate nature are inter-
changeable, and nothing is pre-eminently normal.

Then we left the screaming parrots and the
strutting peacocks to their empty busyness, and
entering a silent valley saw before us the dead

city of Amber and the deserted Palace looking
down on the ruined town and up to the Fort of
Jaigurh, although too desolate now to need protection or to fear attack.

There she is in her snow-white beauty with the
same air of eternal silence which broods amongst
the peaks of Granada, and the deserted Palace of
the Moors. Once upon a time these lonely hill-
tops echoed to the sound of tramping feet, when
the soldiery of Rajputana, headed by their chiefs
and led by their Rajahs, marched out to war.
Once upon a time these Halls of Victory were
filled by courtiers who sat in Council, intrigued
and flattered, braved and dared, and played their
virile parts in the great game of life.

It was in those little narrow marble rooms, where
the white walls glitter with many-hued mosaics,
and long-dead secrets haunt the air, that the
Queens of Jeypore sat in their zenana twilight
and heard the coo of the dove and the splash of
fountains and listened to the eunuchs' gossip of
the Court. On the flat roof of this Palace they
slept beneath the stars or, with the first note of
battle, streamed out as Goddesses of War.

'Where are the snows of yester year?' The
Courts of Honour, the Halls of Pleasure are silent
and empty, and from the battlements you look
down upon the ruined town, in the hollow of the

Pass, and on the gaunt skeletons of old houses with their dark empty windows, like gaping sightless eyes.

A solitary conch called stray passers - by to worship. Was it a priest of Shiv, the God of Destruction, who blew the hideous blasts? Their harsh echoes died away, and silence fell again, that silence which one seems to hear, the silence of empty habitations, more melancholy than that of graveyards where the living never stirred and blustered, struggled or despaired.

No Wagner opera was ever fuller than this enchanted land is of *motifs* striking on the inner ear, mystical, recurrent, melancholy or triumphant. But what would become of our poor souls and bodies if it were not for the intervals we are given at Baireuth? The greater the enjoyment, the sooner comes the moment when you feel ' Ich kann nicht mehr.' We had only a few hours left for Jeypore next day before starting for Udaipur, so after we had seen the beautiful Museum and the School of Art, and all the wonderful things which Sir Swinton Jacob has initiated in Jeypore, I felt the moment had come for the frivolous joys of shopping. Off I set, with our Mahomedan friend as guide, to buy any pretty things I could find for those dear ones who have spelt Home for us and our boy, through all our years of wanderings.

The difficulty was to settle what would be most acceptable. How well I can sympathise with the old lady you told me about, who set off round the world last year to escape the pains and indecisions of choosing Christmas presents! Perhaps the best criterion is to get for others what one would distinctly prefer to keep for oneself!

On this occasion I was quite pleased with the result of my quest. Our Mahomedan friend had several beautiful old shields and swords which some high-born old ladies, fallen on evil days and widowhood, were compelled to sell. Add to these some dear, time-worn, dark enamel charms, with unintelligible signs which ward off bad luck, lapis-lazuli necklaces, an enamelled dove found in the ruins of an old palace in Ispahan, some pretty brass-work and gold and silver ribbons, and you can imagine my comparative peace of mind at the end of my wanderings in the town. What I could never resign to any friend were three old Indian pictures, especially one of them, a long narrow roll with an illuminated border, displaying in the centre a procession of Mahomedan noblemen on horseback, accompanying the last Moghul Emperor to his coronation in Delhi.

I hope the old man who sold it to me was not mistaken when he asserted that the Custodian of the Museum could find no room for it on his

crowded walls, as one felt it ought to be there.
A picture of a Moghul Coronation painted at Delhi,
however, would probably be more appreciated there
than here.   I have sent it to you in its own quaint
tin box, because 'We almost fear to have that
which we fear to lose.'   So keep it for me as the
apple of your eye!

DEAR G.,—We are now at Udaipur and on the edge of a desert, which begins far away in the North-west of Africa, where I knew it first.

How often have I sat, as the sun was setting, at a certain window in Tangier and waited till the moon shed its pale splendour over wastes of colourless grey sand. They stretch bereft of vegetation, void of life, across the Continent of Africa, through Arabia, Persia, Sind, till they end here in Rajputana, where I sit and think of them again.

The sea, as big and vast as they, has known storms and shipwrecks, but in the desert all is still. To appreciate the length, breadth, depth of this great silence, one must first have known many people, and heard the history of many human hearts. Then to be in a desert, to hear no sound, to see nothing but endless, lifeless sand, is to know when waking the peace of dreamless sleep.

From the Nirvana of the Desert, however, life

calls one soon again, life, dear life, with all its
ups and downs, its happiness and pain. It is
characteristic of the contrasts that are found in
India, beginning with its history, where slaves
have founded dynasties and kings become fakirs,
that here on the confines of the desert we are
closely surrounded by scenery as full of sunshine
and beauty as that of the Italian Lakes, — the
Italian Lakes moreover in the days of feudalism
and pageantry, when the Duke of Milan was
rowed across Lake Lugano in his many-oared barge,
no braver sight, I am certain, than what we saw
this morning from behind the trellised windows
of an Island Palace, when the Maharana of Mewar
swept past in his barge on his way to visit an
old Temple on the further shore.

Picture him again at evening, riding out at
the head of his nobles, leaving behind him the
marvel of his white marble Palaces, and having
as the foreground of his cavalcade low-lying land
where trees like willows grow and droop in shallow waters, and are the homes of kingfishers,
storks, and strange varieties of long-necked cor-
morants who shadow the lotus-strewn marshes of
the lake. Can't you imagine how old-world it
looked? Where do you think too they were
riding? To another Palace, to which tame boars

come galloping in flocks at evening, when a bugle calls them to be fed !

The animals in Rajputana are so endearing, the great big patient elephants which crowd the Maharana's courtyards, with their babies tethered to some marble pillar near them, the antelopes and deer that fear no friendly Hindu's hand and treat the world as their playground. Even the birds, including the pet Totas as they call their parrots, who croak in Hindustani dialect, seem tamer here than elsewhere, and as much at home with humanity as if they were still in the Garden of Eden. Only the Maharana's kennel, where every specimen of the canine breed is displayed, spoke of tigers who have felt their fangs, and of battues which from all accounts spell wholesale destruction.

Our most memorable experience in Udaipur, however, came at the end of the day. We had said good-bye to the State Official whose services, along with the use of his guest-house, H.H. the Maharana had graciously placed at our disposal. We had strayed by ourselves through streets where the town-houses of noblemen and statesmen jostle with those of artisans, as they used to do in the old streets of Edinburgh in the days of the Stuarts. We had had a chat with an old dame who came hobbling out of her garden to give us some flowers, singing a quaint song of welcome in a quavering treble, and we had looked at her grandson's lesson-books, printed in Sanskrit character. We were finally wandering round the great Temple of Vishnu when we were accosted by one of the hereditary priests, with whom we entered into a conversation which ended by an invitation from him to sit in the precincts of the Temple, view the service and hear the Temple music, which he proposed to begin at once for our benefit.

So behold us perched on a platform in front of the Griffon Garuda, facing the Temple of Vishnu, and fully appreciating an opportunity which is seldom offered to our countrymen of being with the people in such a moment of their lives.

Alas, it was a moment which only served to accentuate the points on which we could not meet. This Temple of Vishnu, a tall dark narrowing edifice, is externally divided into numberless tiers profusely covered with carved friezes of animals, and the naked and repulsive figures of men and women, gods and goddesses. The discordant blare of the temple trumpets, the vociferous clang of the bells, were tuned to the discord in form of those repulsive crowds. The air was heavy with the smell of incense. Far in the recesses of the temple we could dimly see the representation of Vishnu, who according to the Vedas in three steps strides through heaven as the sun, and in the Puranas has become the great preserving power and second member of their triad. In this temple he was displayed in the form of a large black idol, dressed in short scarlet skirt and bodice, with white slits of eyes in a flat countenance.

The worshippers came flocking to his shrine in crowds, women carrying their babies, girls with flowers, boys who kissed the stone steps of the staircase, an old man who ran up them with arms outstretched, crying 'Joy and glory.' The crowd chattered to each other, sometimes sang, sometimes sat on the staircase to finish what they had to say to one another, and then made way for new arrivals.

Through it all the trumpets blared, the bells jangled, and the outlines of the idol in the temple, the crowded animals and obstreperous humanity on the frieze grew dimmer with the dying sun. The sun sank and we too went our way, sad yet happy to remember that God who knows our frames remembers we are dust, and knows too, better than we do, where in the worst as in the best of us, the wisest or most ignorant, the gold lies hidden in the dross.

CHAKRAMDAS, 1909.

DARLING JACK, — Here we are at Chakramdas. Our tents are pitched in green fields, the sun shining through clouds and lighting up the branches of the wide - spreading trees, making pathways of light down their glades, and vivid patches on their brown stems and on the grass. There is a glimpse of hazy blue hills beyond. The birds are singing, crows croaking, and my fingers are benumbed with cold.

Do you remember Chakramdas, and the day that the kite swooped down and carried off the leg of mutton from the dish that Akbar was carrying to the table under the tree, where we were having our lunch? Or the walk through the wood, which we took every evening to see Puffing Billy at the railway station? Or the whipping you had when we found you had disposed of nearly the whole contents of a bottle of *pomade divine?*

Nurse A. had just said to me, ' I think, ma'am, he has done everything now that a child ought

not to do.' I said, 'No, Nurse, he has not yet
swallowed a boot - button,' and then we were
alarmed at your silence, and traced you to a corner
of the passage !

We dined yesterday in the house where you
were born, just seventeen years ago, and saw the
church where you were christened and Aunt A.
was married, and the churchyard where good, kind
Dr M. lies buried.

We gave an entertainment to all our friends,
the squires and the people of the neighbourhood,
on the polo-ground, where we used to play golf.
I wished that a certain Winchester 'man' could
have been there to help to dispose of some of
the cakes, sweetmeats, oranges and apples, and
bottles of lemonade that came by the morning train
from Lahore, and to enjoy the dash of the polo-
players and tent-peggers, the shouts of the crowd,
who watched their favourite games, ending up with
the tug-of-war. It is our last *tamasha* in India.
It is sad to say good-bye to so many old Shahpur
friends, beginning with Malik Umar Hayat and
his dear household. But there is distinct consolation in knowing that my twentieth voyage
will be my last, and that all three of us will now
be in one country and have but one home.

Everybody has been so kind to us. You know
that your father resigned his post in the Govern-

ment of India, because he preferred being amongst the people he loved to writing all day and every day at a desk in an office. He decided to ' go down the ladder,' as people call it, for it meant less pay and a lower grade in the service. But he went 'down,' after all, to the people, and what a welcome he had! Everywhere we went in the Punjaub we found the peasants and squires had made gardens round our tents and planted them with flowers, and put up archways of welcome.

Your father is what is called ' Financial Commissioner of the Punjaub' now. Every morning he rides through a number of villages and talks to the people about their land and their crops, their various interests and troubles. Every day he sits in his office-tent under the trees, decides cases between landlords and tenants, deals with great irrigation schemes, hears the desires and complaints of the villagers, and does his best to remedy any just grievances they may have and advance their welfare.

Hindu and Mahomedan gentlemen dine with us sometimes, and we dine with them. I have often been greatly touched by what they have told me about the influence your father has had on their lives. One of the Shahpur squires said to me, ' I was under the Court of Wards when I was a boy, and remembering all that it did for

me, I have sent my boys to be educated at the
Chiefs' College in Lahore to gain a wider view
of their duties. When I grew up, it was he who
influenced me to become an Honorary Magistrate
in my own neighbourhood, and when he told me
I should work for my country in wider fields, I
went to Afghanistan as Agent and stayed there,
far from my home, for three years.'

An Indian official, who knew we were leaving
India and came to bid us good-bye, said to me
that 'the lessons in honesty, industry, and conscientious discharge of his duties, which he had
learnt in his early days from his kind and sympa-
thetic master and guide, would ever remain in
his heart of hearts, and that with the help of
God he would follow them to the last moment
of his life.'

Dear boy, what greater happiness can life ever
give us than just to know we have been able
to help some other human being like that ? Not
even the Star, which the Viceroy pinned on his
breast in Calcutta, gave me such pleasure as what
these kind people said, and what our friends wrote
when they heard he had been given that honour.
And amongst all those letters, so many from our
old friends in the British and Indian Regiments,
and the different Indian Services, so many from
old friends at home, there was a bundle I have

kept for you. It is made up of letters from
people in poverty and in distress, from poor
unhappy Eurasians, from the maimed and suffering, who know the dark side of the street, for
their love for him and their memory of what
Wordsworth called ' the best part in a good
man's life, his little unremembered acts of love,'
is what I prize most.

I was so glad he had returned to his place
amongst the homely, rough - hewn peasants, and
those who perhaps needed a friend. And do you
know what I read on one of the first arches of
welcome? These words from my father's hymn :
' Trust in God and do the right' ; and when I went
to the boys' and girls' schools, as I have always
enjoyed doing, I found that hymn was in all their
primers, and that the boys knew it by heart.

A Mahomedan Squire is also translating his
' Gold Thread' for the children, and a Hindu
Civilian has given it to his daughter too, to translate. How little he thought when he wrote that
story, so long ago, for his own children amongst
the hills of Moffat, that it would be read some day
by the children of India, the land of his dreams
and prayers.

So trust in God, dear boy, and follow the ' Gold
Thread,' even when it leads you up to the lions
that are after all chained. For I think of some-

thing else he wrote too : ' The evil that men do lives after them, but I do not believe the good is oft interred with their bones. It rises from their graves and walks the earth until the Resurrection morning.'

THE END.

Ibbotson   368

Malaban   372